"Simply and honestly said, there is ROI on every page. This is one guide I won't be lending. It stays right on my desk. I only wish *By the Seat of Your Pants* was available twenty years ago, because, for a serial entrepreneur like me, having this one, insightful, incisive, energizing business blueprint could have saved my life—and butt—a thousand times over. The School of Hard Knocks is highly overrated!"

—Vickie Abrahamson, Cofounder and EVP,
Cultural Analysis, Iconoculture, Inc.

"*By the Seat of Your Pants* shows a business can be run with enlightenment as well as efficiency. This terrific book is brimming with brilliant strategies for achieving both."

—Ken Blanchard, co-author of *The One Minute Manager*®
and *Customer Mania!*

"*By the Seat of Your Pants* is packed with road-tested tips and real-world success strategies you can start using today."

—Mary Brainerd, President/CEO HealthPartners

"Tom's highly readable style simply and methodically presents leading-edge techniques, great checklists, and profound wisdom for maximum workplace effectiveness. I know of no better way to leverage your time than reading and implementing this compendium of Tom's wisdom. The best business management guide on the market. It should be required reading at every business school in the country."

—Rinaldo S. Brutoco, President, World Business Academy

"Having a special appreciation for entrepreneurs, I've watched and cheered on Tom Gegax for years. Here's a man who grew a company from zero to $200 million in a quarter of a century, built a solid team of people dedicated to each others' success, eventually sold his company to a global corporation, then shared his good fortune with the team that created it. Now he shares his no-nonsense secrets for success in a no-nonsense management guide."

—Marilyn Carlson Nelson,
Chair and CEO, Carlson Companies

"I've never seen a more gifted tactician than Gegax. *By the Seat of Your Pants* provides business leaders academically sound concepts packaged in actionable steps that Gegax has proven in the crucible of high-stakes business. It should be required reading for all MBA programs."

—Terry Childers, Gatton Endowed Chair in Interactive Marketing, University of Kentucky

"Tom Gegax has written the essential guide for business leaders wanting higher profits and lower stress."

—Deepak Chopra, author, *Book of Secrets: Unlocking the Hidden Dimensions of Your Life*

"*By the Seat of Your Pants* is a hard-hitting, highly relevant business success guide. My advice: get your hands on it before your competitors do!"

—Michael Coles, President & CEO, Caribou Coffee

"This guide is essential reading for all students of free enterprise. It's real, practical, and pragmatic. Tom Gegax is a mentor for all of us to follow."

—Joel Conner, President, Luigino's, Inc. (makers of Michelina's and Budget Gourmet) and member of the executive committee of the board of directors of Students in Free Enterprise

"*By the Seat of Your Pants: The No-Nonsense Business Management Guide* is true to its name. It's a guide—a practical, useful, insightful management guide."

> —Kenneth E. Goodpaster, Koch Endowed Chair in Business Ethics, College of Business, University of St. Thomas

"I've been investing in start-ups and mid-sized companies for many years. Never have I found a guide for growing companies more complete than *By the Seat*. I bought copies for the leaders of every organization in my portfolio as well as my own staff."

> —Esperanza Guerrero-Anderson, President & CEO, Milestone Growth Fund

"*By the Seat of Your Pants* provides business insights and management secrets critical for success in any business environment. Every entrepreneur and corporate manager needs to read this guide and share its valuable lessons with others."

> —Joel Hyatt, Cofounder, Hyatt Legal Services; Lecturer in Entrepreneurship, Stanford Graduate School of Business; CEO, INdTV Holdings

"Everything you need and nothing you don't. *By the Seat of Your Pants* is a must-have for anyone with P&L or management responsibility."

> —Irwin L. Jacobs, Chairman, Jacobs Industries

"*By the Seat of Your Pants* is the best one-stop shop for running first-class organizations I have seen. The depth and breadth of Tom Gegax's personal management acumen brings great value to entrepreneurs and seasoned business execs."

> —Harvey Mackay, author of *Swim With the Sharks Without Being Eaten Alive*

"The most practical advice is always given by someone who practices what they teach. Tom Gegax has mastered the art of business, and his writing is a true, practical manual to be guided by."

—Horst Rechelbacher, Founder of Aveda Corporation, Intelligent Nutrients, and Horst M. Rechelbacher Foundation

"*By the Seat of Your Pants* is one of the most potent management guides I've read, jam-packed with the essentials for successfully managing a business and leading people."

—Alfred Schwan, Chairman, The Schwan Food Company

"Gegax's warm-hearted and tough-minded approach in *By the Seat of Your Pants* yields healthy profits for entrepreneurs and corporate managers alike."

—Glen Taylor, Chairman, Taylor Corporation;
Owner, Minnesota Timberwolves

"*By the Seat of Your Pants* is as complete as the best business management textbook and as accessible and entertaining as a newsmagazine. A lot of books talk about what needs to be done to run excellent organizations. This guide tells you *how* to do it."

—Paul Wilkens, Ph.D., Adjunct Professor of Management,
Florida State University

BY THE SEAT
OF YOUR PANTS
THE NO-NONSENSE BUSINESS
MANAGEMENT GUIDE

TOM GEGAX
with PHIL BOLSTA

Minneapolis, Minnesota

ISBN-13: 978-1-931945-16-5
ISBN-10: 1-931945-16-0

Library of Congress Catalog Number: 2004106495

Printed in the United States of America

09 08 07 06 05   6 5 4 3 2

Minneapolis,
Minnesota

Expert Publishing, Inc.
14314 Thrush Street NW,
Minneapolis, MN 55304-3330
1-877-755-4966
www.expertpublishinginc.com

This book is dedicated to my father, Bill, who as I write this is battling valiantly to overcome a horrendous stroke. He's modeled many of the characteristics of an enlightened executive throughout his life, a fact that took me years to fully appreciate. He gave me—and taught me how to use—my first planner when I was fresh out of college. His kindness, his compassion with people from all walks of life, and his willingness to be of service to others have inspired me to be a better businessman and a better human being. He often said as I was growing up, "Son, the most important word in the English language is 'empathy.' Always treat your employees right." Though he endured devastating losses—he lost his father at a young age and witnessed the deaths of many of his buddies in World War II—his love for God, country, and his fellow citizens never wavered. Dad, this one's for you.

CONTENTS

VI.   HELL-BENT AND HUNGRY

X. BONUS SECTION: WEATHERING WORST CASE SCENARIOS

FOREWORD

By Richard Schulze
Founder and Chairman, Best Buy

I met Tom Gegax at an Entrepreneur of the Year awards ceremony in 1994. I had been aware of Tom and of Tires Plus' success. Before leaving that evening, Tom invited me to lunch. A couple weeks later, we met at one of my favorite restaurants. During the meal, he asked if I would mentor him. It wouldn't be much of a time commitment, he promised. We would get together for lunch every few months (after all, I had to eat anyway, he said) and he'd ask me questions. I was impressed with his earnestness, so, after thinking about it for a few days, I agreed.

Sure enough, Tom was thoroughly prepared for each lunch. He squeezed every ounce of value out of our time together. He came to every meeting with a carefully thought-through list of questions and a real determination to thoroughly understand every issue. He would keep asking questions until everything was clear. Here was a man who was not going to rest on his laurels. He was tireless in his pursuit of knowledge, and genuine in his attempt to learn from all who had achieved business success. Tom's hunger for insight into business management was insatiable. He frequently brought me members of his management team to engage in our dialogue to share the learnings and double-check the facts.

That determination paid off. In a competitive industry dominated by multinational firms, Tom and Tires Plus out-executed their much larger rivals. He and his team turned Tires Plus into an important industry force with a unique culture, outstanding service, and a commanding market share.

Tom is a consummate team player, dedicated to what I value most in a leader—respect and consideration for everyone in the organization. He knows you win with motivated people supported by efficient business practices. That creates a culture of caring, accountability, and continuous process improvement.

Tom's business management guide has all the good stuff and none of the fluff. Let it guide your every step and the decisions of those throughout your organization. Then you, too, can find yourself on the road to undreamed of business success.

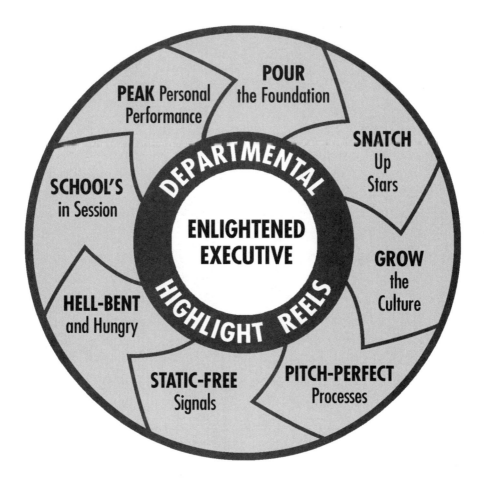

THE SYNERGY CIRCLE

PREFACE

Outsiders started sniffing around for the secret of our success after revenues climbed to $200 million from $40 million in just eight years. From the "brain pickers" who wanted to buy me lunch to the guy who playfully rubbed his shoulder against mine at a reception and said, "Rub some of that magic on me," everyone hoped I could reduce it to one miracle-making word—like the tipsy executive in *The Graduate* who pulls aside young Dustin Hoffman and advises simply, "Plastics." Actually, the secret to how we thrived while competing against the world's largest corporations *can* be reduced to a single word—synergy.

We didn't take our rocket ride until we hit on just the right blend of organizational ingredients. Our meaningful mission guided savvy people in a caring, accountable culture, one supported by efficient processes and clear communication. We added in the right mix of inspiration and incentives, educational enrichment, and encouragement to grow through self-mastery strategies. We also mixed in success secrets from seven key departments. This synergistic, no-nonsense business management system is what produced the record EBITDA (earnings before interest, taxes, depreciation, and amortization) that fueled our ride.

The title of this guide, *By the Seat of Your Pants*, conjures up a frantic, disorganized business leader who's overmatched by today's hyper-speed business world. Back in the early days of flying, the phrase was used to describe how pilots could guide their planes without complex navigation and control systems. They felt the plane react to every nudge of the stick. Take a guess at what the largest point of contact is between pilot and plane. Yep, pilots received most of their feedback through their trousers. "Flying by the seat of your pants" came to mean that, instead of acting *proactively*, you were operating *reactively* by constantly changing course in response to feedback. In other words, you were figuring things out on the fly instead of creating and executing a solid flight plan. Apply that style of management to the business world and most leaders will tell you they've experienced the fear and anxiety it produces. This guide's title names the pain, and its pages offer the cure.

Don't get me wrong; a big part of running a business comes down to gut feelings and reactions to daily challenges. Keep relying on your intuition—you wouldn't have gotten this far without it. Careful, though. Overreliance on instinct can lead to corner-cutting—why waste time with planning and analysis when you can shoot from the hip? Well, because one hiccup and you can shoot yourself in the foot. Sure, a seat-of-the-pants approach may get the job done in an entrepreneurial start-up—for a little while. But the brushfires start flaring up as business increases. As the flames lick your elbows, denial kicks in; you can't face the possibility that your instincts can't save your neck just one more time.

That's where this guide comes in. Sustainable success—in business or aeronautics—requires a healthy blend of intuitive skills and efficient processes. Barreling along without a comprehensive, top-notch business management system can lead to sloppy execution, sinking morale, and missed numbers (or runways). Don't put it off. Stress short-circuits intuitive wiring, and your talent for making mid-course corrections won't pull you out of a nosedive. There's no getting around it—flying by the seat of your pants is a recipe for stressful days and sleepless nights. What's at stake? For entrepreneurs it could mean living on savings or handing over control to outsiders. Seat-of-the-pants managers without ownership stand to get pigeonholed, demoted, or sacked. I hate to see good people with good ideas lose their dreams. That's why I wrote this guide.

A lot of these ideas led to my greatest business victories. I also learned more than my share through boneheaded moves and stinging defeats. I'd like to think I made those mistakes so you don't have to. Don't wait for a crisis, like I did, to sound the alarm. Let this guide be your wake-up call. If I had read it at the beginning of my career (heck, at any point in my career) my blunderbuss days would've ended a lot earlier.

If anything on these pages looks familiar, don't skip past it. Instead, ask yourself, *Am I doing that? If so, am I doing it well? If not, why not?* Sometimes it's the lessons we've already mastered that trip us up. I'm reminded of Cameron Tague. In 2000, Tague attempted to scale the sheer, one-thousand-foot Diamond Face on Longs Peak in Colorado. The expert climber didn't bother roping up on an easy traverse along the Big Wall's wide, sloping ledge, where five-year-olds and a six-piece band had safely climbed. You can guess what happened. Tague's mind apparently wandered, he pulled on a loose rock, and plunged eight hundred feet to his death. In business, we walk the cliff's edge every day—and none of us can afford to get careless.

WHY THIS GUIDE DELIVERS A RICH ROI

It's packed with proven, practical tips and savvy success strategies.

I'm not proposing drawing-board theories that should work. These are practices that do work. I've been there, grown that, from five vantage points. I was an executive at one of the world's largest corporations, a start-up entrepreneur, and a CEO directing sixteen hundred employees. Now, I consult businesses, nonprofits, and politicians. I also serve on numerous boards, including the Center for Ethical Business Cultures. As my first company's majority owner, I had the freedom to experiment in my workplace laboratory, studying the science—and art—of business management. By reading this guide, you'll learn everything I learned during the day-to-day mess of meeting sales and profit projections, making payroll, and facing the consequences of every decision.

The proof is in the puddin'—I ultimately turned a $60,000 loan cosigned by my parents into a $200 million business that a multinational corporation gobbled up.

It charts a new course.

Hard-nosed accountability and efficiency (profits first) and an enlightened approach (people first) are combined in a practical package that honors both. Best as I can tell, this is the only business guide to strike that balance. It's the leaders who are both tough-minded and warm-hearted that wind up with happy people producing healthy profits.

It's the whole enchilada.

Many business books focus on just a few engines that propel a business—how to get started, how to hire, how to sell, how to motivate. They're important, yes. But it's difficult to lift off the runway without understanding how all facets of a business are linked together. The first eight sections of this guide connect those dots. A ninth, Departmental Highlight Reels, leverages those linkages with killer tips that help you manage every function of your company. And a bonus section, Weathering Worst Case Scenarios, offers guidance for toughing out inevitable business crises.

It's a step-by-step desk reference.

Keep this guide on your desk. No matter what challenge arises, a quick scan of the table of contents will take you where you need to go. Job candidate coming in? Flip to the hiring section and follow along. Ideas slipping through the cracks? You want the section on efficient systems. Sales slacking? Grab a yellow highlighter and make a beeline for the Sales chapter. No matter what page you land on, you'll find street-smart tips to help you

- increase your brand equity;
- boost your market share;

- strengthen your supply chain;
- inspire employees to delight customers;
- cut costs and improve your bottom line;
- manage the finance function and lender relationships;
- protect your business interests;
- harvest outside advice;
- compress your success cycle;
- establish the foundation for value creation;
- find, hire, and keep the best people;
- create an energized, ethical culture;
- build good teams;
- deal with dysfunctional behavior;
- design and execute strategic and operational plans;
- run meetings that staffers anticipate;
- manage airtight processes;
- ensure ideas are well executed;
- form lasting stakeholder relationships;
- receive and deliver clear information;
- optimize employee performance;
- develop strong leaders;
- raise your game—and everyone else's.

How to Navigate This Guide

People often ask, "What's the first step I should take?" It's hard to say. A circle has no beginning or end. Ideally, you'd start by pouring the foundation of mission, vision, and values. You'd then snatch up stars, grow the culture, implement pitch-perfect processes, and communicate via static-free signals. You'd also coach your people to be hell-bent and hungry, teach them that school's always in session, and help them achieve peak personal performance. All the while, you'd be studying and applying my departmental killer tips.

There's only one problem—you live in the real world. Business, and life, are messy. So, where to begin? Start by identifying the source of your most acute pain—what's keeping you up at night?—and jump right in. Morale tanking? Ineffective communication may be the culprit. And when your people emotionally check out, that also undermines your processes and sabotages your mission, vision, and values. Or, start with a department—supply management's failure to negotiate better purchasing deals impairs marketing's ability to promote competitive offerings. That depresses sales, which leaves your best salespeople vulnerable to poachers from more profitable companies. Click. Here's your light-bulb moment—every element in the Synergy Circle is linked to every other element. If any aspect of your business wobbles, the other dominos start toppling. Ah, but when everything is running efficiently? That's when the magic happens.

How to achieve organizational harmony? It becomes clearer as you morph into an enlightened executive. It starts with polishing your leadership skills, brushing up on departmental know-how, and studying self-mastery strategies. Hint: reach first for low-hanging fruit—it's important to chalk up early wins. Some shifts only require simple tweaks in thinking. Others take more dedication and planning. Get your team involved. Brainstorm solutions you can all call your own. As relationships are repaired and strengthened, as people feel respected and valued, change occurs. The synergy snowball keeps rolling, picking up steam, until you see no beginning and no end. Just results.

The Synergy Circle system works for your company no matter how long you've been in business or what stage of development you're in. The business world has two constants—change and speed. And it has one variable—your ability to keep up. Enlightened executives do more than keep up; they lead the way. If you've read this far, you're already making progress. May your journey be enjoyable and profitable. I'd be honored to be a part of it.

—Tom Gegax

tom.gegax@gegax.com
www.gegax.com

Minneapolis, Minnesota

ACKNOWLEDGMENTS

I am deeply indebted to the thousands of teammates who helped me develop a company we could all be proud of. Their willingness to listen, to learn, and to share their thoughts and insights contributed significantly to the development of my leadership methods. I learned just as much from them as they learned from me. Special thanks to Don Gullett and Larry Brandt, my fellow owners and principal shareholders.

Thanks to my life partner, Mary Wescott, for her steadfast support and encouragement in whatever I do.

Thanks to my executive assistant, Edie Sandmeier, whose coordination skills and overall assistance keep things moving forward and on the right track. And to Jason Goldberg, director of Gegax Management Systems, whose bold ideas helped determine the book's architecture and marketing strategy.

Words seem wholly inadequate to express my eternal thanks to my co-writer, Phil Bolsta. There are few business writers who can write with authority and authenticity about both business and personal enlightenment. He interviewed me for an article seven years ago; when we met, I knew he was the right person to help me turn my leadership system into a complete resource guide. His vibrant style makes reading about business principles more entertaining than I thought possible. From day one, we enjoyed a harmonious and effective partnership.

Thanks also goes to T. Trent Gegax, a ten-year *Newsweek* magazine vet, who provided masterful, ongoing mentorship and priceless, chapter-by-chapter editing. As the Michael Jordan of our team, he not only led us to a world-class title, he made all of us that much better in the process.

To my mother, Lib, for a lifetime of unconditional love. And to son Chris who, like his brother, Trent, continues to alert me to my blind spots through candid, caring feedback. And to my two new daughters-in-law, Samara Minkin and Heidi Gegax, who have already heightened my awareness in many important areas of life.

I'll always be indebted to my business mentors: Dick Schulze, Curt Carlson, Carl Pohlad, Dean Bachelor, Tom Macintosh, and John Berg.

Numerous friends, colleagues, and industry experts sacrificed substantial chunks of time to offer comments on and refinements to the manuscript, or to help in other important ways. Their expertise and insight helped elevate the material you are about to read. My thanks to Matthew Abbott, Scott Bakken, Doug Barber, Romaine Bechir, John Berg, Anil Bhatnager, Bruce Birkeland, Alexis Bloomstrand, Rinaldo Brutoco, Jim Bundick, Terry Childers, Larry Dennison, Neil Dolinsky, Sherri Engstrand, Mari Fellrath, Kirsten Finstad, Brian Freeman, Pam Gegax, Vivian Glyck, Joe Goldberg, Don Hays, Bill Hibbs, Marcia Hines, Andrew Humphrey, Ron James, Ryan Kanne, Elizabeth Kautz, Tom Kieffer, Ed Klemz, Gregg Kloke, Mike Koenigs, Ann Krzmarzick, Tom Kuhn, Bea LaMonica, Charles Lukens, Dave Mona, Craig and Patricia Neal, Greg Nemec, Gregg Newmark, Ken Noyes, Donald O'Connor, Richard Perkins, Sr., Tom Porter, Gayle S. Rose, Barry Rubin, Gigi Bechir Rudd, Nancy Sabin, Larry Sandman, Mark Sathe, Alfred Schwan, Jay Scruton, Mike Sime, Darrell Skramstad, Sandy Stein, Skip Thaler, Jeff Thull, Kathy Tunheim, Ken Volker, David Wagner, Bob Wahlstedt, and Tom Zosel.

Special thanks to my reviewer all-stars, who soared above and beyond the call of duty: Vickie Abrahamson, Carl Baldassarre, Dave Cleveland, Allen Fahden, Shelly Fling, Andrea Luhtanen, Tom Macintosh, Jay Novak, Bink Semmer, and Sven Wehrwein.

A big thank you to former colleagues who contributed integral remembrances and stories: George Argodale, Jim Bemis, Darrel Blomberg, Brad Burley, Mel Donnelly, Tom DuPont, Don

Gullett, Eric and Gwen Heimer, John Hyduke, Chris Koepsell, John R. Leach, Mark Lessin, Gabe Lopez, Scott McPhee, Jim Pascale, Eric Randa, Wayne Shimer, Chris Speake, Trent Stoner, Dorie Thrall, Joe Thul, Dave Urspringer, Steve Varner, Dave Wilhelmi, and Jim Wolf.

Thanks to Arielle Ford and Brian Hilliard for suggesting the title and helping me directionally; to Jack Caravela, Jay Monroe, and Harry and Sharron Stockhausen for their creative contributions; to Tita Gillespie, Mel Vork, and Mary McCarty for their editing prowess; and to Earnie Larsen, Brenda Schaeffer, and Barbara J. Winter for their inspiring self-mastery contributions.

Finally, immense gratitude goes to my Higher Power, the constant companion who's gifted me with an abundance of ideas and the drive to keep moving them forward.

AN INSIDER'S VIEW

By Jim Pascale

Former Vice President of Franchise Operations, Tires Plus

We were getting ready to expand into Denver. We had already entered into a number of store property development agreements, and Tom's cofounder, Don Gullett, had invested eighteen months in learning the Denver market and working its commercial realtors. But we had also recently expanded in other states and those stores were adversely affecting our net income. So I spoke up in an executive team meeting. "I don't think we're ready to do this," I said. "Look at the cash flow and the cash draw in all these new markets. They haven't matured yet. Going forward with Denver would stretch us too thin."

Most everyone around the table disagreed, strongly, and insisted that Denver move ahead. I remember looking down the table at Tom. I could see him thinking. After a minute or two, he said, "No, Jim's right. We need to take a harder look at the numbers." Tom asked Jim Bemis, our CFO, if the facts about our new stores matched what I'd said. Bemis nodded. So, Tom pressed pause on Colorado until our other new markets started maturing. (A year later, we hit Denver.)

That was a very important moment. It further raised my respect for Tom. The message was: *Speak up, even if you're the lone voice of dissent. Your input is valued.* It showed me that when I said something it could make a difference. It could even change the course of our company.

Tom hadn't always been so open to opposing views. He and Don had started the company from scratch, and Tom had been used to giving the orders. But as the company grew, he realized that if he insisted on making all the calls he would turn into a human bottleneck. So he began encouraging his team to be assertive, to take initiative, and to share opinions, especially if they differed from his own. I watched him transition from saying, "Listen, this is how we're going to do this," to, "What do you guys think?" It was a significant change that took some getting used to.

I'll never forget an executive team meeting back in the midst of Tom's transition. It was the late 1980s. He had just returned from a seminar on corporate culture. Tom was especially concerned about something he'd learned and wanted to discuss it. He looked around. "I don't think I've surrounded myself with yes-men," he said, "have I?" "No, Tom," everyone said. "Not at all." He thought for a moment. "But sometimes," he said, "to be honest, I think we do get some yes-men behavior around here." Without a trace of irony, everyone said, "Oh, yes, Tom. Yes we do." I was laughing so hard at the end of the table that Don had to poke me.

What Tom learned as he matured as a leader is that there's a fine line between hiring yes-men and hiring loyal order takers who are willing to speak up when something needs to be said. Tom straddled that line and saw successes and failures on both sides. It reminds me of Stonewall Jackson, the Civil War general who took great pride in being the best order taker in the Confederate Army. When a superior gave Jackson an order, he followed it and he completed it. There was no dissension, no questioning. In his writings, Jackson felt there was great value in surrounding yourself with good order takers because problems arose when people were argumentative and didn't believe in the mission.

I'm also reminded of the Thunderbirds, the U.S. Air Force flying stunt team. In 1982, four members of the team were practicing loop formations in Nevada when the lead plane suffered mechanical failure and the other three pilots followed it right into the ground. When I read that, I thought, you know, blindly following the leader may be required for the good of the cause. But if he's headed straight into the ground, you had better trust your instincts and correct course before it's too late. That's what I think Tom was looking for in our culture—people willing to follow the mission yet unafraid to speak up. It's a significant issue for entrepreneurs who start small and grow so large that they have to transfer a big chunk of decision-making responsibility to others.

Above all, Tom valued education and self-development. He was always flying out of town for conferences, and he always shared what he learned with his team. Continuous education dominated the culture to such a degree that managers had to do forty hours of education in order to be eligible for annual bonuses. Today, as vice president of franchising for a nationwide franchising company, I'm constantly doing sales and management training for franchisees from across the country. Yet, I barely have to prepare. I just go in with a list of bullet points—customer service, sales, interpersonal dynamics, coaching—and re-present what Tom taught. Without fail, a line of people awaits me at the end of the day to thank me for all the incredible tips. Yet, it's just information that I absorbed during my years at Tires Plus.

A few months ago, I conducted regional education seminars in six major cities. The hundreds of franchisees who attended rated them the best business workshops they'd ever taken. They appreciated the real-world techniques for ramping up operational and people skills. They had never had that kind of education before. I was especially struck by one comment from the feedback forms. "You're a godsend!" a franchisee wrote. "You're the best thing that ever happened to this organization." It boggled my mind that somebody wrote those words. I just laughed. Anyone who came out of Tires Plus could have done what I did and looked great doing it.

Now you can, too.

NOTE TO READERS

In the interest of fairness, both male and female pronouns are used throughout this guide. Perhaps someday a suitable alternative for "he or she" will be accepted into the language. Until then, alternating "him" and "her" strikes me as the best option.

EUREKA!

MY BOSS JUST DOESN'T GET IT

Taking Inventory, Just in Time

Somebody blurts out those six words every time I give a talk. It's clear that employees are fed up, run-down, and exasperated from working for seat-of-the-pants leaders. Desperate, they ask, "How can I get my boss to understand this stuff?" The bad news is, there's a long list of stuff to get. The good news is, it's really not that difficult to get it. The even better news is, you're about to learn how to master it in bite-size chunks.

Chances are you think you already know this stuff. I was cocksure I did, until 1989, when the one-two punch of divorce and cancer sent me reeling against the ropes, and a cash-crisis uppercut left me sprawled on the canvas. Not only was I clueless that I was unenlightened, I didn't have a clue that I didn't have a clue. Even if you're smarter than I was, you're way too time crunched to hunt through hundreds of books, tapes, and seminars for the nutrient-rich intel you need. No problem. These pages are packed with the real-world know-how and street-smart success secrets I accumulated while growing a start-up into a $200 million company in a fiercely competitive industry. In the four years since I sold my business, I've applied the same strategies in my consulting work with remarkably consistent results.

These principles will boost your EQ (enlightenment quotient) whether you just launched your career or are already king of the hill. They're applicable whether your home base is a Fortune 500 executive suite, an entrepreneurial start-up, a manufacturing plant, a retail store, or a political or nonprofit organization. What does "enlightened" mean? Here's how Daniel Webster defines it:

1. freed from ignorance and misinformation;

2. based on full comprehension of the problems involved.

Bingo. Clarity of mind and clarity of vision. Scarce commodities that will make you infinitely more valuable and transform you into a CEO—chief enlightenment officer. If Webster were still calling the shots, I'm confident he'd green-light my definition of enlightened executive: *A tough-minded, warm-hearted, systems-disciplined leader who inspires people to actively embody the organization's mission, vision, and values.*

WHAT'S THE DIFFERENCE?

Are your shoes charred from stomping out brushfires? Do you have nightmares about UFOs (unreachable financial objectives)? Do all-star interviewees turn into duds? Do meetings cause more problems than they solve? Is your office a ghost town at 5:02 p.m.? If these symptoms are familiar, you may be a seat-of-the-pantser. The polar opposite is an enlightened executive who's calm, confident, and in control. Here's how to distinguish the two:

Seat-of-the-Pantser	Enlightened Executive
Every encounter is driven by his self-centered agenda.	He knows "it's all about me" is only where things begin—he must take care of himself (intellectually, physically, emotionally, spiritually) before he can help employees fulfill their potential.

Seat-of-the-Pantser	Enlightened Executive
She operates with no strategic plan, or one that projects too far into the future. Either way, she's constantly putting out fires.	She recognizes that the high-speed marketplace demands a flexible strategy. She knows how to break down a strategic plan into operating plans, and then parcel off the right assignments to the right people.
He cuts corners whenever possible, in shortsighted pursuit of a better bottom line.	The high road is the only road. He knows shortcuts can become "longcuts" because they often have to be undone or redone.
She micromanages, oblivious to the toll it takes on employees' creativity and motivation.	She knows the level of supervision required for each team member and knows when to step out of the way to let talented, motivated employees sprint for the goal line.
He's ready to unload on any employee who offers constructive criticism.	He solicits ideas for improvement—for his performance and the company's—through formal and informal channels. He recognizes it's the people in the trenches who have their fingers on the consumer's pulse.

Seat-of-the-Pantser	Enlightened Executive
She treats employees as if the only reason they're taking up air on the planet is to do her bidding.	Her attitude toward employees is, *How can I help them grow and succeed?* rather than, *How can I use them to get what I want?*
He passes on the best and brightest potential hires in favor of mediocrity—out of fear that someday, somehow, someone toiling under his command will outshine him.	He knows hiring the best candidate possible for every position will elevate everyone's performance.
A daydreamer, she's often oblivious to what's going on around her. She views details as distractions.	Her cat-like sense of awareness leads to more empathetic relationships, constant quality upgrades, and creation and protection of competitive advantages.

The pages that follow give seat-of-the-pantsers the tools they need to evolve into enlightened executives.

LIVING BY THE SEAT OF MY PANTS

My Journey from Clueless to Cashing In

I had sold my company. The papers were signed. But the payment was two weeks overdue. I stared at the ceiling much of the night wondering how a "guarantee" to buy Tires Plus, my regional chain of 150 retail stores, had eroded into a "maybe." Tomorrow—tomorrow!—Bridgestone/Firestone had promised, it would wire the cash by 10:00 a.m. to seal the deal.

Tension in the office the next morning was thick enough to clobber with a tire iron. My CFO, Jim Bemis, called the bank a few minutes past ten. No wire. He checked again after lunch. Nope. Finally, at three in the afternoon, Jim stepped into my office with a crooked grin. My cofounder, Don Gullett, and I held our breath. Four words sweeter than cotton candy danced on Jim's lips: "It's in the bank." That was all he said. It was all he had to say. A whoop and a holler later, we were high-fiving and hugging anything that moved.

Bridgestone/Firestone's stutter stepping had sent me hurtling down the high-stress highway without any brakes. I didn't understand the holdup—until a week after the sale. That's when Bridgestone/Firestone issued a tire recall that made banner headlines around the globe; it threatened to implode the entire corporation and strip the luster off its trusted name. I figure our deal had been on life support. I'm sure the only thing that saved it from flatlining was a hefty down payment and signed purchase agreement.

Don and I enjoyed divvying up the spoils. Tires Plus teammates pocketed $10 million in stock options and loyalty bonuses.

Houses were remodeled, college plans were made. One teammate and his wife used their windfall to bounce back from a disastrous side enterprise that had plunged them into debt.

After cashing out, I dove headfirst into consulting, writing, and speaking. Of course, fiscal fitness is a hollow victory without the physical fitness to enjoy it. Today, at fifty-eight, according to my doctors at the Mayo Clinic, I have the heart of a thirty-year-old. I'm also blessed with the love of my family, friends, and Mary Wescott, an indispensable source of inspiration and strength.

THE REARVIEW MIRROR

Spinning the odometer back thirty-nine years slides you into the front seat of a life speeding out of control. I was a nineteen-year-old sophomore at Indiana University, stone-cold broke with a pregnant new bride. Each morning I woke up to the crash of car-metal wrapping around the tree of my life.

I struggled to hold back the fear and despair welling up inside, but everything boiled over one hot summer afternoon in 1966. My '59 Chevy was a sauna on wheels. When I close my eyes I can still see the slow-motion film loop of my bathing suit-clad buddies speeding by and waving on their way to the beach. Choking back sobs in my sweat-soaked janitor uniform, I veered off the next exit to get to the Ford Motor Company factory for my three-to-midnight shift.

The next ten years were a blur—rushing from college classes to the factory, changing into my janitor uniform at stoplights; delivering school newspapers; peddling insurance to fellow students; at twenty-one, an HR job at Shell Oil in Chicago; transferring to fieldwork; another son at twenty-four. At twenty-nine, dreaming big, sharing my idea with Don, a sales guy working for me. Thumbs down at nine banks, approval at number ten. The birth of Tires Plus.

Fast-forward nine years to 1985. I was about to earn my second Bachelor's degree—courtesy of turnaround consultant Dean Bachelor. Expansionitis had Tires Plus gushing red ink. Dean was hired to stop the bleeding. After exhaustive due diligence, he sat me down, looked me dead in the eye, and said, "Tom, the biggest problem in your company is you."

His words hit my heart like a jackhammer. I fought off a wave of panic as Dean rattled off my transgressions and shortcomings. Our debt-to-equity ratio was four to five times higher than our bank's comfort range; I was aggressive and insensitive with employees; I hadn't analyzed our fixed and variable costs to arrive at a break-even point, a critical calculation that should be at the heart of every major business decision.

My head was spinning. I had to collect myself, swallow hard, and acknowledge that my company was growing faster than I was. Of course, I was a baby CEO (all of thirty-eight) but that mattered squat. I had to toss my ego out the window, roll up my sleeves, and get to work.

Ratcheting up my business and people skills bought me another four years. But I still wasn't there. By 1989, Tires Plus had more than doubled—again—and in the midst of all those heady numbers life snuck up and smacked me down with a triple trauma. In the course of six months, my doctor diagnosed me with cancer, my twenty-three-year marriage disintegrated, and my CFO told me the company till was a million bucks short and our credit line was exhausted.

Boom. Overnight, three critical pillars—health, family, career—seemed to be turning to dust. And damned if that entire time I hadn't thought I was Mr. Got-It-Covered. Now, zombie-like, I came in to work, locked my office door, set my phone to Do Not Disturb, and spent hours curled up on the couch. Those were the good days. It was months before I could face myself in the mirror and begin taking responsibility for righting everything that had gone so disastrously wrong.

INNER YEARNINGS, HIGHER EARNINGS

Looking back, I see with equal parts amusement and horror that I had been flying by the seat of my pants. I was running as fast as I could but always seemed to be a step behind. I hadn't yet acquired high-caliber communication and relationship-building skills. I hadn't yet implemented essential business management disciplines like strategic planning and budgetary protocols. I wasn't following skill-training and task-follow-up methodologies. And I was a mediocre leader because I was blissfully unaware of a basic universal law—life is like a card table. The four legs of healthy intellect, psyche, body, and spirit are required for a well-balanced life. Ignore one leg and the table wobbles. Disregard two or three, like I did, and it can't help but collapse.

It was time to work and live in a more balanced, disciplined way. I morphed into a knowledge junkie, devouring books, tapes, and seminars on business management and personal growth. For a know-it-all, I was amazed at how little I knew. I sought out the best and the brightest business mentors (Curt Carlson of Carlson Companies, Carl Pohlad of the Minnesota Twins, Dick Schulze of Best Buy). Funny, but I had always prided myself on my knack for recognizing flaws in others. Now, I turned the interrogation kliegs on myself and stared into them, unblinking, as I stripped away layers of denial, defensiveness, and doubt. It was painful but exhilarating work.

One by one, I started connecting the dots. Improving my mental clarity and emotional health helped me spot and deal with unhealthy behavior in others. I was more caring, which inspired employees and family members to be more committed. My new systems-disciplined mindset led to greater efficiencies, smarter decisions, and peace of mind. The more I profited on a personal level, the more my company profited. Revenues began doubling every three years, reaching $200 million by 1999. Profits performed even better. I had learned the first lesson in

Enlightened Leadership 101—establish effective protocols that hold people accountable. Then, if you focus on the well-being of your employees and customers—as well as your own—success will naturally follow.

The lantern is lit. The path awaits. Let's get going.

I.
POUR THE FOUNDATION

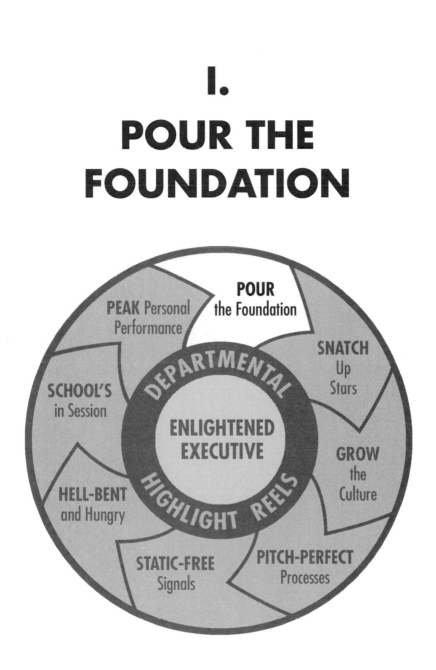

PART I

MISSION CRITICAL

A Precision-Guided Mission Statement Is a Must

Picture a general addressing his nervous troops on the eve of a decisive battle. He implores them to fight fiercely for the honor of everything and everyone they hold dear. He stresses that the safety of their loved ones rests on how courageously they perform on the midnight battlefield. Then the general strides over to a second group of soldiers and orders them to conquer the enemy or die trying. The objective, he thunders, is to earn him that elusive fifth star and secure a heftier pension. It's a safe bet the first group of soldiers will hit the battlefield with a steely resolve to give their all. It's just as certain the second bunch would rather smash rocks in the hot sun than put their leader's objectives ahead of their own self-interest.

The do-or-die spirit of an army unit is the essence of what an enlightened executive must instill in the men and women under his command. That lofty goal is attainable, but only if the answers to three fundamental questions are clearly articulated, strategically disseminated, and consistently reinforced:

1. Why does the organization exist?
2. Where is it going?
3. How does it need to act to get there?

The answers to these questions must be precisely expressed—in a mission statement, vision statement, and statement of operating values—and held with conviction throughout the culture. "Conviction" is the operative word. If a company's mission, vision, and values aren't genuinely believed and championed by top management, they're just words on paper. Ah, but when conviction is convincing, the organization rises above the sum of its parts and produces inspired employees. Until it clicked into place at my company, I never would've believed how much passion and creative energy could be unleashed when mission, vision, and values are moving in sync. The change is palpable. It's also contagious. That's where I got the title for this section. When you hit your mission statement, vision statement, and statement of operating values, you're symbolically and literally "Pouring the Foundation."

The next chapter zeroes in on the first body of business' holy trinity, The Mission Statement. Sure, it's Business 101—something most companies have in place. But is it working? In seat-of-the-pants outfits it's often just slapped together, a generic, white-bread substitute devoid of motivational nutrients. Or, tons of time have been invested only to produce something too generic to be memorable or too complicated to remember. Even if a mission statement jumps those hurdles, it often hasn't been integrated effectively into the culture. Take a look at your mission statement. Is it on the front or back burner of people's minds? Does it drive your company's culture and inspire employees? Or, is it trotted out like a what-were-they-thinking wedding gift that only sees the light of day when the in-laws visit?

A mission statement is fundamentally immutable. Carve it in granite and display it behind unbreakable glass. Market forces, business strategies, and senior management may shift, but a good company's core purpose is timeless. Through boom and bust, 3M's mission will always be, *"To solve unsolved problems innovatively."* Likewise, even when aggressive competition impacts Sony's marketing tactics, its mission remains, *"To experience the joy of advancing and applying technology for the benefit of the public."* These missions don't reference profits or shareholder value. Their purpose is to inspire people to throw themselves into work they love and make a difference in the world.

The power of a well-stated mission lies in its unifying effect. Like a maestro, it directs everyone to play the same song at the right tempo and in the right key. Without a codified mission—or when a mission statement gathers dust like a gold-plated plaque in some long-forgotten storeroom—exuberance and gusto give way to inertia and apathy.

ONE

MISSION IN MOTION

Embodying Your Mission Statement

"To help restore people to full life."

That's the essence of Minneapolis-based Medtronic's six-part, 171-word mission. It's also the mantra Ann Krzmarzick heard in each of the eight interviews she endured to become a communications specialist at the world-renowned medical technology company. It was a test of sorts. If Medtronic's mission didn't resonate, the human resources manager told her, she should look elsewhere for employment. Ann smiled and nodded. It was a catchy sound bite but she figured it would have about as much impact as a bumper sticker on her day-to-day duties.

She figured wrong. Ann quickly discovered that those seven words were the beating heart of Medtronic's corporate body. "I didn't realize," she said, "that the light of that mission would shine so brightly on the everyday work in communications, given that we're fairly removed from direct patient care." The mission was consistently—almost reverently—referenced in every meeting and memo. It informed every decision at every level. It even reached all the way to the annual holiday party, where six bona fide patients share their stories of heartache, hope, and renewal. There's never a dry eye in the house. Surveys reveal that nearly every one of Medtronic's twenty-six thousand employees knows the company's mission statement and how it applies to their job. They're inspired because they know their work makes a big difference in people's lives. Is it any wonder that Medtronic always appears on *Fortune* magazine's list of "100 Best Companies to Work For"?

At Tires Plus, we expressed the guiding principle of our company's existence through our thirteen-word mission: *"Deliver caring, world-class service to our guests, our community, and to each other."* A noble sense of purpose was essential for attracting quality employees. Most people consider working in the tire business only a little more appealing than getting a root canal. The industry is often thought of as dirty, unprofessional, and sometimes even dishonest. So why would people come work for us? Not to sell tires, but to improve the lives of customers, employees, and the world at large. After all, it's people, not tires, that make the world go round.

I served as a walking advertisement for our mission statement, as illustrated by this story offered up by my cofounder, Don Gullett. Don, whose development department was in charge of remodeling and upgrading our stores, chartered a small, four-seat aircraft one day so he, a contractor, a real estate agent, and I could visit all four of our stores in and near North Dakota. We landed in Fargo first and rented a car. "As we were driving into the parking lot of our store there," recalled Don, "Tom jumped out while the car was still rolling, ran over, and started talking to two people. The three of us just looked at each other, wondering what he was doing."

I had spotted the couple coming out of the store and had sensed by their expressions that they weren't happy. I asked if there was a problem. (There shouldn't have been because a big part of our mission was empowering store employees to resolve customer complaints.) I found out what they were upset about, got them to walk back inside, got it resolved, and turned them into happy customers. "It would have been very easy for someone in Tom's position to have remained in the car until we had finished parking," noted Don. "But by the time we had gotten out of the car and into the store, those people would have driven off. So Tom jumped out and went out of his way to introduce himself and correct the situation. I'm sure he left a lasting impression on that store's personnel, not to mention those customers."

Our corporate commandment—"Thou shalt be caring"—was like a global positioning satellite that helped our people navigate the choppy waters of day-to-day decision making. More importantly, it helped managers identify and capitalize on "coachable moments"—instances when an employee's actions conflicted with our mission. For instance, our follow-up system required us to contact customers not more than forty-eight hours after providing a price quote. On a regular systems-review visit to a suburban Minneapolis store, I checked the phone log and saw that a teammate was skipping the follow-up call. Turns out he hadn't been properly trained and wasn't sure how to do it. So I spent some time teaching him the ropes via the Confucius Checklist (chapter 41). When it was time for him to make an actual call, I listened in.

The woman he called told him she had opted to buy new tires from Firestone. "Oh, that's too bad," he said, "you really missed out." After he hung up, I said, "Wow, you basically told her she made a bad decision. How do you think that made her feel? Do you remember what our mission is?" He stammered, "To give caring, world-class service to our guests?" I asked if that phone call was consistent with the mission. He acknowledged it wasn't. "If somebody tells us their needs were taken care of," I said, "our reply should be, 'I'm glad you got what you needed. Your car is safer and will handle better now and that's what's most important. Next time you're in the market, we'd love to have another opportunity to serve you.'" I stressed that alienating a potential customer today means we're also slamming the door shut on future sales. But that's not why people should be treated with respect. When you genuinely care about their well-being, without regard to expectations and outcomes, the goodwill generated benefits everyone.

We upheld our mission statement's integrity just as vigilantly for our "internal customers." If an employee treated a colleague rudely, I challenged him. I wanted amends made and behavior corrected immediately. "How would you feel if somebody treated you that way?" I'd ask. "How would you react?" I'd remind the offender in no uncertain terms that our mission called for everyone in the company to deliver caring service to each other, and that caring about and being of service to others was what we were all about.

RETOOLING YOUR MISSION

Is your company's mission in mothballs? Two words: huge opportunity. Reigniting your mission can set off sparks that fire up the whole team. Stir things up at the next executive team meeting. Ask if anyone can state the mission from memory, or at least its essence. If they can't, chances are no one can. And that means your mission registers a big fat zero on the inspiration scale.

Looks like it's time for an update. First, convene a brainstorming session with top brass. The leaders (hopefully) have an innate sense of the company's purpose. (Hint: a management consultant can smooth the process if her focus is fixed on facilitating; the question of purpose requires an insider's insight.) How to begin? Start by describing your offering. Ask, "Why is that important?" Challenge what the group comes up with, asking again and again, "How does that help our customer?" Go deeper still until you finally punch through the brick wall of logic and tap into people's hearts. After five or six iterations—the whole thing could take two or three sessions—odds are you'll nail the essence of why you're in business.

Now, it's tweak time. Create opportunities for every employee to pitch in. Reach out to resident wordsmiths and deep thinkers by posting drafts of the mission wherever people will see it—elevators, bathrooms, paycheck envelopes. Send it out in an e-mail blast. Call a company-wide meeting. Tell people how to submit their ideas. Getting everyone involved—and assuring them that all suggestions will be valued—builds trust and teamwork. Before you know it, a well-scrubbed mission statement will be hanging on your office wall.

SOWING SEEDS

Your responsibility as CEO (chief enlightenment officer) is to champion the company's mission until it guides every member of your team like the North Star. A leader breathes life into a mission statement by consistently modeling it. Only then can it evolve into a force that shapes employee behavior. It's like Johnny Appleseed, only with words, sowing seeds that take root in minds, hearts, and souls. Feature your mission everywhere but in employees' dreams— in orientation seminars, employee manuals, visual reminders, promotional materials, staff meetings, performance reviews, one-on-one coaching sessions, special functions, and ceremonies.

To promote awareness of your mission:

- ✔ Use it as a **litmus test** in one-on-one and group meetings—"Is this in sync with our mission?"

- ✔ Ask people to **commit it to memory**. At team meetings, randomly call on someone to recite it. Reward a correct answer with a gift certificate.

- ✔ Hold an annual **team meeting** to make everyone aware of the company's mission and how it meshes with their daily routine.

- ✔ Hold an **essay contest** with a topic like, How our mission helped me make an important decision. Or, How our mission inspires me to give my best. Or, simply, What our mission means to me. Post the entries on your intranet or bulletin board and award a prize to everyone who enters.

- ✔ Start a "Mission Mentions" section in the **company newsletter** to officially recognize employees for embodying the mission through words and deeds. At smaller shops, low-tech bulletin boards work just as well as high-speed e-letters.

✔ Post a **suggestion box** and solicit comments about how the company can follow through on its mission.

✔ **Encourage employees to speak up** if they run into circumstances that clash with the mission. Make multiple reporting channels available.

PART II

DARE TO DREAM

Turning Vision into Reality

You've just received an advance copy of *Business Week*. Emphasis here is on the word "advance"—the cover date is ten years in the future. To your delight, the cover story features your company. Before you riffle through the pages, pause for a moment. What would you like that article to say about your company—its image, its culture, its values, its accomplishments?

What can you do today to turn those hoped-for headlines into scrapbook clippings? Championing your mission statement was a good start. Now that everyone's on board the mission train, how do you keep them on track without derailing into complacency or chaos? And how can they pick up a head of steam while they're at it? Hitch up the engine to the ol' Double-V—vision and values. Unlike your mission, which states your firm's purpose, a vision statement asserts where your company is headed. And a statement of operating values spells out the personal traits required to achieve your mission and vision.

The synergy of mission, vision, and values can unleash a torrent of opportunities for excitement, enrichment, and enlightenment. Don't have all three pieces—mission, vision, and values—in place? Be a catalyst of creative energy until your efforts take hold and begin to crest. Pieces in place but not breaking through the surface of awareness? Get them rolling until every employee can catch the wave.

Hurry, surf's up!

TWO

THE VISION THING

Composing Your Vision Statement

Think of your vision statement as a list of dreams committed to paper. It's a collection of shooting stars that inspire people to reach for the heavens. I not only shared our vision with new hires, I reinforced it every quarter at regular team meetings. I never missed an opportunity to plug it. Our people worked harder when they were excited about where we were headed. More importantly, they'd give blood when they understood how our arrival would affect them personally.

I saw the fire in their eyes when I'd single one of them out and say, "Joe, how old are you going to be in ten years? Forty, huh? Well, if we grow 15 percent every year for ten years and turn our vision into reality, how will our built-in compensation performance incentives affect your salary? And what kind of opportunities for advancement do you see yourself having in a $1.7 billion company? With your help, and the help of everyone in this room, we can make it happen."

People crave a clear sense of purpose (mission) but they also love to be on a winning team (vision). Show them the way by painting idealistic, yet reachable, targets. Help them plug into the high-voltage current of your company's vision, and the results will be electrifying. Here's the six-part vision statement we came up with at Tires Plus:

1. Become a national player with $1.7 billion in revenues and eleven hundred stores by 2010.

2. Become the marquee tire company in the U.S.

3. Become the No. 1 or No. 2 market-share leader in every market we serve while creating a fair return for our efforts.

4. Serve guests so well that 99 percent recommend us to family and friends.

5. Develop the strengths of a big company while maintaining the agility of a small one.

6. Provide a nurturing and healthy environment that establishes us among the most desirable companies to work for in the U.S.

Unlike a mission statement, you can tinker with a vision statement. How? At the close of each year, determine whether your objectives need to be modified in light of unexpected events. But don't tarnish them with the rust of lower expectations unless you've got a compelling reason.

Need to update your vision statement? Follow the steps you took to retool your mission (chapter 1), keeping in mind two distinctions:

"Bold" and "fearless" are the operative words. Shoot for the moon, like JFK in a 1961 speech to Congress: "I believe that this nation should commit itself to achieving the goal before this decade is out of landing a man on the moon and returning him safely to the Earth."

Telescope out seven to ten years. Peering that far requires visionary thinking and a willingness to look beyond current capabilities and market conditions.

THREE

CHARACTER COUNTS

The Link Between Core Values and Higher Profits

If a scientist extracted your company's DNA and placed it under a microscope, the image she would see is your operating values. A statement of operating values is the cultural backbone of your organization. It's a list of valued traits and behaviors required of all employees. Your vision statement shows employees where you want to go. Your operating values spell out how to get there.

These core values should run so deep through your culture that the hurricane winds of markets, product offerings, and economic conditions can't uproot them. If you can imagine any circumstances that would force one of these values off the list, then it's not a core value and should never have been identified as one. Like your mission statement, these values—or success behaviors—must be championed and modeled by management. Otherwise, employees will shrug off an aggressive "Values We Value" campaign as just another disingenuous corporate initiative.

Articulating its values helps an organization avoid hiring and harboring people who don't measure up. For instance, if hiring managers scope out candidates based on attention to detail, world-class service skills, and innovative thinking, it's unlikely that a disorganized, lazy conformist seeking a rut to burrow into will sneak past the front gate. And those who do will soon either run for the door or be shown the door.

The ideal Tires Plus employee possessed six qualities. Scott McPhee, our retail operations veep, coined the acronym COPPSS to make these attributes easy to remember: Caring, Optimistic, Passionate, Persistent, Systems-disciplined, and Spirit-filled. We snapped up everyone we could who embodied these six keystone COPPSS:

1 **Caring.** Twenty-four years in my workplace laboratory convinced me there are two kinds of employees—those who are deflated and those who are energized by interactions with others. Granted, the distinction may initially be difficult to discern. Nineteen out of twenty job applicants will assure you they "love working with people." Yet, six months into the job, the self-proclaimed "people person" is bellowing, "These people are driving me nuts!" We sought out employees who loved to make someone's day. Every business, regardless of its offering, is in the business of helping people. And every employee, no matter how removed from customers and colleagues, contributes to the organization's CQ (caring quotient). The higher the CQ, the more harmony in the workplace. And that means happier, more productive employees.

Stress and losing ourselves in our work are just two of the factors that can push aside "the better angels of our nature." Several years ago I found myself hunched over my laptop on a flight from Minneapolis to San Diego. I was trying to nail a deadline under less than ideal conditions, made worse by the oaf in front of me who fully cranked his seat into my lap. Agitated over this guy boxing in my six-foot, two-inch frame, I sank my knees, already pressed into his seat, a little deeper to send a message. Forty-five minutes later, a woman in her eighties rose in front of me and used a walker to reach the restroom. I was horrified. I had zinged an elderly lady, of all people, with my knee-jerk reaction.

To this day I draw upon the image of that woman when I'm in a rush. It reminds me to always recognize the humanity of other people. This intent is beautifully expressed by the Sanskrit greeting *Namaste*: "The divine in me bows to the divine in you."

2 **Optimistic.** In the Optimism Olympics, Eddie Haskell wouldn't even be allowed in the stadium. At best, Eddie's oily brand of optimism on *Leave It to Beaver* was annoying ("Mrs. Cleaver, I know your dinner party is going to be a big success!"). So is the modern corporate equivalent ("That's an awesome report, Boss; it's going to double our revenues!"). At worst, it perpetuates dishonest behavior.

On the opposite end, overt negativism kills initiative and deadens spirit. It's also contagious. I've seen one employee with a rotten attitude seductively infect his colleagues until a black cloud hovered over an entire department. Grousing about co-workers is especially toxic. It sows dissension and doubt throughout your shop. Pessimism becomes self-fulfilling. Once your people lock themselves into it, they wind up spending more energy justifying their negativity than in searching for solutions.

Take the time I got steamed during a biannual operating plan review. Dan, one of our regional managers, had unilaterally reversed our formula of devoting 10 percent of a plan analysis to identifying obstacles and 90 percent on how to hurdle them. His presentation turned into one long excuse for why he hadn't met his profit goals. Typically, I'm gentle with underperformers, especially in front of their peers. But Dan wore my patience thin. I asked him point-blank why he hadn't told us about his problems earlier so they could've been solved by now. He mumbled something about not being able to get people's attention. It was clear he still didn't get it. A few months later we had to "free up his future." Not caring on our part? Not excising a cancerous attitude like that wouldn't have been caring to our team.

The healthy middle ground between mind-numbing positivism and gloomy negativity is a place I call authentic optimism. It welcomes thoughtful dissent, inspires the confidence to hurdle any obstacle, and reframes roadblocks as opportunities to get better. For instance: "Yeah, landing this account is a challenge. But if we study the offering our competitor submitted and put Sue on this, we can do it." As the placebo effect proves, optimism can create ideal outcomes. It's also a basic law of the office that people will scale the tallest filing cabinet to help cheerful colleagues succeed. Art Linkletter summed it up perfectly:

> *Things turn out best for the people who*
> *make the best of the way things turn out.*

Optimism poured out of our phones daily: "It's a great day at Tires Plus. This is Tom. How can I help you?" You should have heard the reaction when I first proposed that greeting. Groans all around. But I insisted, and soon it became second nature. Eventually, we became aware that a number of Fortune 500 companies had appropriated our greeting. I think that's great. The world needs all the optimism it can get.

On the other hand, does this attitude sound familiar: *The glass isn't just half empty, it's cracked down the middle and smudged with Chapstick.* Yeah? Here's hoping you can convince your people there's a more pleasant—and productive—way to look at the world. It ain't easy, that's for sure, especially if they've been counter-programmed since childhood. But help someone change their mindset and you change their life.

3 **Passionate.** Selling a new idea to colleagues is like a district attorney trying to persuade a jury to lock up the bad guy—conviction equals success. More precisely, success hinges on the *passion* of your convictions. In its purest form, passion is the combustible mixture of meaning and purpose. A passionate pitch is more likely to get a warm reception. But check yourself. Passion needn't be volcanic. Quiet, controlled passion also packs persuasion. Besides, erupting too often raises eyebrows. People are more apt to help someone who maintains an even keel and hollers "Man overboard!" only after a really loud splash.

A lack of passion is a deal-breaker whether you're introducing a new initiative, coaching an employee, or apologizing to a customer. Tone and body language speak louder than your words ever will. The B.S. Detector goes berserk when verbal and nonverbal cues don't jibe. With phony passion running rampant nowadays, don't be surprised if people put up their guard or search for ulterior motives when you express yourself more passionately. The cynicism will fade once they see you're consistent, or if somebody credible vouches for you. Dave Wilhelmi, our vice president of marketing, ran into skeptics all the time. "A lot of people thought Tom's passion was fake or somewhat calculated at first," said Dave, "but the more they got to know him, the more they saw it was real." Dave recalled a party we threw in 1998 to celebrate winning U.S. Tire Dealer of the Year. "Tom gave one of his typical heartfelt addresses, thanking all the people who were such a big part of our success," said Dave. In the hallway afterward, Dave ran into a new vendor-partner who asked whether Tom was always so passionate when he talked about the company. "It's as if you can feel everything he's saying," the guy said. "I just smiled," recalled Dave, "and said, 'What you see is what you get.'"

4 **Persistent.** Our first three tire stores were small converted service stations that also sold gasoline. With the late-70s energy crisis in full swing, my gasoline allocation was grossly inadequate and I struggled to meet payroll. So I wrote an appeal letter for more gas to the federal government—denied. I called the Department of Energy's midwest office in Chicago to request a meeting with Ray Fiene, the director—denied (I was told in no uncertain terms that Mr. Fiene was unavailable). Undaunted, I hopped a plane to Chicago and tried to sweet-talk his receptionist—denied again. Now, I had seen his picture once so I plopped down, scanned the lobby, and waited. A few hours later, there he was, hurrying past me on his way to the men's room—opportunity. I followed right behind him. There, at the urinal, I sidled up beside him, apologized for the intrusion and launched into my pitch. He shot me a look of disbelief. Then he laughed and zipped up. "Okay, kid," he said, "get into my office!" I did. He heard me out and upped my allocation. That's how my company survived its earliest, darkest days.

A persistence deficit will derail even the most talented professional. Murphy's Law—*Whatever can go wrong will go wrong*—will never be repealed. But that doesn't mean you can't hurdle or dodge Murphy through dogged persistence. When employees bounce off obstacles, educate and inspire them to find another route. Don't let them raise the white flag if what they're striving for is in line with the company's mission, vision, and values—and within budget. Calvin Coolidge's "Law of Persistence," dated though it may be, has had a place on my wall ever since I started my business:

Nothing in the world can take the place of persistence.
Talent will not; nothing is more common than unsuccessful men with talent.
Genius will not; unrewarded genius is almost a proverb.
Education will not; the world is full of educated derelicts.
Persistence and determination alone are omnipotent.

Right on, Calvin. It's unbelievable the number of people I've seen limp away after stumbling over a roadblock or two. Little did they know that success was waiting just around the bend.

5 **Systems-disciplined.** In my younger, ego-drenched days, I often challenged authority—professionally and privately—and relished every opportunity to beat the system. Hindsight is humbling. It's now clear that playing by the rules produces less chaos and honors others more.

Choosing to ignore even a minor procedure can be costly, a point I liked to dramatize at store manager meetings. I'd stand in front of the room and ask what a phone call from a potential customer was worth. I'd say, "When we don't do the things we're supposed to be doing when they call, you might as well do this." And I'd take a $100 bill out of my wallet and slowly rip it in half. "Tom's point," said Dave Urspringer, a manager whose Coon Rapids, Minnesota, store always excelled, "was that if a prospect called and you didn't use the approved script to determine their needs, and then ask to reserve the tires that filled those needs, you're losing a chance to help a guest and basically throwing $100 out the window because that's what an average sale was worth. That really made an impression."

Does this mean all rules should be slavishly obeyed? Of course not. Veering off onto the dirt shoulder and roaring past law-abiding traffic may be necessary in emergencies. Just keep an eye on your rearview mirror to make sure the dust you're kicking up doesn't cause a fender-bender or pileup. (For more on systems, see chapters 19–23.)

6 Spirit-filled. On a business trip to Paris in 1998, I had the honor of meeting François Michelin, then seventy-three years old and head of the company bearing his name. Impressed with his vitality, I asked how he stayed in such great shape. "Spirit!" he told me. "When translated into Greek, *pneu*, the French word for tire, means spirit. Air is to the tire as spirit is to the human body." He emphasized the point by giving me a big hug. *Wow*, I thought, *I hadn't realized I was in such a spirit-filled business.*

"Spirit-filled" evokes the image of pumping your tank full of air at a metaphysical service station. I believe spirit is an inherent part of who we are—something to be released rather than created. Spirit flows from seeking meaning and purpose in life. It does not mean espousing religious beliefs around the watercooler. It means having the courage to hold fast to your cherished values and be authentic. When you're connected to spirit, you're unconsciously modeling a better way to live and work.

This wisdom is implicit in "May the Force be with you," Obi-Wan Kenobi's benediction to Luke Skywalker in *Star Wars*. Call it what you will—spirit, God, the Force. It's the omnipresent intelligence that governs everything. Align yourself with it, with the pure intention of benefiting the world, and you'll emerge from the shadows of self-absorption into the sunshine of selfless service and synchronicity. Doors will open, obstacles will vanish, people will appear—meaningful coincidences that nudge you ever closer to your goals.

Connecting with spirit is a primal need. Mythologist Joseph Campbell spoke of our innate desire to "feel the rapture of being alive." I felt this euphoria of living more intensely the more I avoided spiritual tranquilizers—unhealthy food, booze, lack of exercise, denial, guilt, inappropriate anger. Russian philosopher P. D. Ouspensky explained that most of us move through life in a waking sleep that prevents us from tapping into our spirit. If that sounds familiar, stop hitting the snooze button. It's time to wake up.

KEY POINTS: **MISSION CRITICAL**

A Precision-Guided Mission Statement Is a Must

✔ **A well-crafted mission statement is the foundation of an enlightened organization.** Revisit your company's purpose for being and, if necessary, distill it into an inspiring new mission statement. Great things happen when people rally around a common goal.

✔ **Work in sync with the mission.** The mission is only as effective as its embodiment in the actions and attitudes of team leaders. Employ it as a polestar to correct and redirect employees. Otherwise, it's just one more empty piece of paper pushed by a corporate kingpin wanna-be.

✔ **Champion the mission at every turn.** A CEO (chief enlightenment officer) can make an enormous impact by promoting the company's mission. Look for creative ways to help it seep into your firm's culture. Invoke it at team meetings and in one-on-ones. It'll guarantee that daily decisions mesh with future plans.

Key Points: **DARE TO DREAM**

Turning Vision into Reality

✔ **Re-craft your vision statement with boldness and idealism.** Look at least seven to ten years out, well beyond organizational capabilities. Declare a destination, rally the troops, and the roadmap will begin to take shape.

✔ **Spell out your core operating values.** Defining "success behaviors" for employees weeds out the wrong people and keeps the right ones on track. Through the collective power of employees' actions, these fundamental principles will define the character of your firm.

✔ **Revisit your vision statement occasionally but preserve your core values.** Update your vision statement when goals are attained or market forces render it irrelevant. Operating values, however, are organizational DNA and off limits to tampering.

II.
SNATCH UP STARS

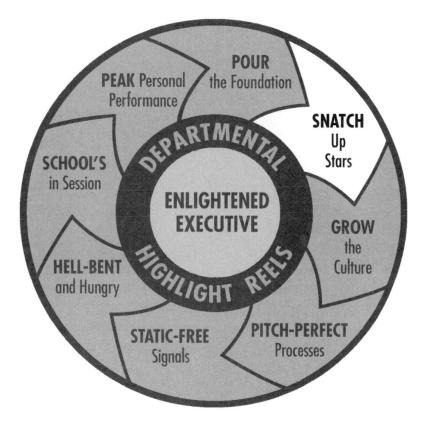

PART I

HUNTING THROUGH HAYSTACKS

Finding the Best People

With three words, Dick Schulze jolted me into a higher level of awareness and sent shock waves through my company. Dick, founder and chairman of the board of electronics giant Best Buy, was a mentor to me. Over lunch in 1994, I casually mentioned that I was working harder than I ever expected. He asked how long my management team had been together. "Twelve years," I told him proudly. He nodded and said, "There's your problem."

I was stunned. Dick was right. We were reaching many of our goals, but our rapid growth was noticeably outpacing the skills of some key execs. Back in my seat-of-the-pants days, I had masked my fears and insecurities by wielding an iron personality. I subconsciously hired submissive people in constant need of my unerring guidance. As I woke from the nightmare of thinking nobody else could do anything as well as I could, I realized my micromanaging had created a play-it-safe culture in which people did just enough to get by. I had begun backing off but was still conflicted about how to handle mediocre performers. Speeding back to the office, it hit me that my personal vow to be kind and caring could coexist—had to coexist!—with expecting outstanding results and holding people accountable.

One by one, over the following weeks, I challenged all twelve members of my executive team. Half responded beautifully by tirelessly upgrading their skills. Wayne Shimer remembered it as a sort of near-death experience. "Tom sat me down," recalled Wayne, "and said, 'Wayne, you're just not giving the team what it needs. If you can't make it work in the next ninety days, we'll have to make a change.' I said, 'Fine, I understand. I'll either make it happen or I'll be gone.' And I made it happen. That's the way Tom operated—tough, but not rough. I respected that."

The other six execs were unable or unwilling to raise their competency ceiling. Three were reassigned and three left the company. My executive team flowchart suddenly looked like Swiss cheese. It was nerve-racking to have so many key positions open, but I knew that filling each slot with exactly the right person called for patience. After all, only when the right people are in place can a company fulfill the promise of its mission, vision, and values.

FOUR

BEATING THE BUSHES

Talent Scouting

Tom Greenwade's Oldsmobile must have been caked with dust by the time he pulled up to the bleachers in Baxter Springs, Oklahoma. The baseball scout was there to bird-dog the third baseman for the Whiz Kids, a local semipro team. But it was the young shortstop who caught Greenwade's eye by belting two monstrous home runs into the river well past the fences. Since the phenom was only a high school sophomore, Greenwade vowed to return bearing a contract on the young slugger's graduation day. True to his word, two years later, Greenwade attended commencement ceremonies for the Commerce High School Class of '49. And that's how Mickey Mantle signed his first New York Yankees contract.

Business is a lot like baseball. Get the right talent and you can be a champion. It's unlikely, however, that a few tiny lines in a classified ad are going to reel in a big home run hitter. Finding the best people requires the diligence and resourcefulness of a top talent scout.

To attract and find top-notch talent:

Turn your workforce into an army of bounty hunters. Dangling a cash reward in front of employees is a good way to get their attention. Ninety days after a candidate was hired, we added a bonus of up to $500 to the referrer's paycheck. (We also gave finder's fees to suppliers and vendors.) Caveat: employees can be your best recruiters, or your worst. In an enlightened environment they'll deliver a steady stream of quality candidates. Unhappy employees, however, tend to bring in unhappy prospects.

Pluck prospects from your web of business partners.
When we needed a new CFO, the first thing I did was contact our
accounting firm. I asked the partner in charge of our account if he
knew anyone who might fit. He recommended a financial wizard
named Jim Bemis who had just resigned from a troubled company.
Snapping up Jim was critical to taking our company to the next
level. Word travels fast in professional circles so don't be shy about
mining business contacts for referrals.

Crank up your visibility. The real estate mantra "Location,
location, location" doesn't just apply to valuing land. It also helps
land valuable employees. Ask yourself, *Where are the people we
want to hire?* Hit those locations and start schmoozing. Join the
Chamber of Commerce. Attend all the business, community, and
charitable events you can. The next hand you shake may point
out your superstar.

Keep your radar on high alert. Wayne Shimer, who headed up
recruiting and retention, was in Omaha in 1998 to guide the opening of some new stores. Standing at an ATM machine, of all places,
he met a guy who was wearing a shirt, tie, and name tag. "I asked
him, 'How are you doing?'" recalled Wayne. "'I'm doing *great!*' he
said." Impressed, Wayne struck up a conversation and discovered
that the guy was bored with his sales job at a hat shop in the mall.
They exchanged cards and Wayne returned later to scout him out.
"The guy was fantastic," said Wayne. "I hired him on the spot and
he's still with the company today. And doing very well, thank you.
He went from earning in the mid-twenties at the hat store to the
mid-sixties today."

Keep your radar on because you bump into potential stars all
day long—the cheerful, efficient waitress who clearly enjoys working with people; the friendly clerk who makes you feel like you're
his favorite customer. When I saw a smile on someone's face and
a sparkle in his eyes, I told him he gave great service. "How long
have you worked here?" I'd ask, and follow up with a couple more:
"Do you like what you're doing?" and "Is there a good career path

for you here?" If the answer to the last two was yes, I'd thank him and be on my way. But nine times out of ten he'd say it was only a temporary job. I'd tell him I was always looking for good people like him. If he showed interest I handed him my card. I've hired dozens of people through such everyday encounters.

Be a quality magnet. Attracting quality employees is a lot easier when you're a quality employer. Talented people seek organizations with exceptional standards and sparkling reputations. To paraphrase the Center for Ethical Business Cultures, the most valuable employees want to contribute to their customers and to society, and to learn and grow themselves in the process. Effective and ethical leadership offers the opportunity to do so. In the ongoing war for talent, possessing an ethical advantage can be the hook that lands the best people.

Don't take no for an answer. When somebody was right for us, we didn't mess around. We took him to dinner, introduced him to the rest of the team, and did whatever it took to persuade him to sign on. One of my recruiting execs once said we should ding a candidate because he wasn't pursuing us vigorously enough. "Heck no!" I said. "The stars don't have to go hard after companies. We're the ones who need to pursue *them*." Some twenty years ago we were searching for a specialized sales rep. I knew Tom DuPont was the guy for the job by the end of our first interview. But he had just left a similar job at a competing firm and nursed doubts about staying in the business. Over two weeks, I bought him lunch, brought him back to the office, and called him three or four times. "Tom just kept coming at me and coming at me until I finally relented," recalled DuPont. "He kept telling me, 'You've got to join the team!' He was very persistent. That really made me feel great because it's always nice to feel wanted." DuPont took the job and stayed with us for ten years until he left to start his own company. Moral of the story? Don't let the good ones get away. Pursue them relentlessly. They can't see the other side of the mountain like you can.

Explore the jungles of guerrilla recruiting. Recall bank robber Willie Sutton's famous line? Asked why he robbed banks, he quipped, "Because that's where the money is." Apply Willie's logic to the office—an obvious place to find people with the skills you're looking for is on your competitors' payrolls. As a fast-growing company with an insatiable appetite for talent, we sometimes marched right into a competitor's store and told the staff we just wanted to say hello to our neighbors. Oh, and by the way, we'd say, we're always looking for help. Did we mention our $500 referral fee? Invariably, we heard one of three responses: (1) "Don't let the door hit you on the way out," (2) "Five hundred bucks? Sure, I'll keep my eyes open," or (3) "I'm not happy here, can I schedule an interview?" Of course, we never tried to "steal" employees who were content. But we felt good about providing opportunities to those who were in looking mode.

Look under your nose. The lowest person on the totem pole often carries the tribe on his shoulders. I always put that theory to test in the field. When I walked in the front door of one of our stores I greeted the guys in sales and management, then headed right for the service bays. I was searching for sleeping stars the manager had squirreled away. In Cedar Rapids, Iowa, I hit the jackpot in a technician so gregarious and sharp that I ran to the sales floor and told our personnel guru, Wayne Shimer, "You've gotta meet this tire tech. He's really something." We spent forty-five minutes talking to the guy. Within days we moved him to the sales floor. A year later he was managing his own store.

Fall in love with internal promotion—it'll return the favor in spades. Career Awareness Day was the linchpin of our retention success. Once a year in our support center, employees who were considering career changes moved among booths representing every department. "You've got to find that diamond in the rough who's already drawing a paycheck," said Wayne, "and further his career." Tire techs, for instance, discovered opportunities in the warehouse. Sales staff combing the want ads found openings in, say, customer service. "Every department had somebody who was getting a business degree," recalled Wayne. "We discovered people's hopes and dreams, but just as important is what their hopes and dreams weren't." It's like the guy who sold his home to travel the world in search of fortune only to hear later that one of the world's largest diamond mines was discovered on his old property. "We cultivated our field all the time," said Wayne. "We knew if we didn't, we'd lose 'em. We'd just be a stop-over point instead of a career point."

We retained hundreds of people by steering them into better career choices. I didn't mind losing good people if they truly couldn't find fulfillment with us. But to lose them through our own negligence was inexcusable.

Don't forget the ol' tried and true. Sure, it's more exciting to dig for buried treasure off the beaten path. But don't overlook the jewels hiding in plain sight. Network at universities and vocational schools, a sure way to tap into a consistent flow of leads. Relationships with search firms and employment agencies produce bumper crops of qualified candidates; we hired about three people at every job fair we attended. Attend trade shows and industry meet-and-greets. Subscribe to newsletters. Scour the business section. Whatever methods you choose, implement them promptly. Your competitors are reading this guide, too.

PART II

EMBRACE YOUR HIRE POWER

Making the Magical Match

What do the hiring process, a romantic dinner, and walking a tightrope have in common? A rush job produces dire consequences. Hiring after one interview—no probing, no references, no work-history review—is like hopping a red-eye to Vegas to get married after one date. It's impulsive and expensive, and your chances of long-term harmony are abysmal.

The more time invested on the front end, the less likely the chance of getting bitten on the back end. Shortcuts are tempting, especially when a candidate's personality, resumé, and references are intoxicating. The swoon is like puppy love, like they've been delivered by divine decree. Watch out. In my haste to eliminate "fill vacancy" from my to-do list, I've committed the old college sin of "wishing 'em beautiful and willing 'em brilliant." In my zeal to upgrade my top execs, for instance, I blundered. I assumed that seasoned vets from Corporate America would have more knowledge and skills than people already on my team. Yes, it may be necessary to recruit heavy hitters for a specialized slot like CFO. But big-company outsiders, particularly those prone to bureaucratic thinking—numbers over names, politics over performance, lack of urgency—often clashed with our caring, service-oriented, entrepreneurial culture.

Take the vice president we lured from a Fortune 500 firm. He floored me one day with a passing remark. "Oh, I forgot to tell you," he said, "Darren, the manager of our Richfield store, told me he wasn't happy about some things. I told him if he wasn't happy he could find another place to work." I'm almost certain steam began pouring from my ears. "You've gotta be kidding," I said, barely controlling my anger. "'Like it or lump it' is not the way we do things around here. That's a clear violation of our mission, vision, and values. Darren's a big-time performer and he's the last guy we want to lose. If he's got complaints we need to hear him out." I called Darren as soon as I could. It was too late. He had just accepted an offer from another company.

Serves me right. I never should have hired that veep in the first place. He blinded me with his credentials, charisma, and championship schmoozing. I even circumnavigated our own rigorous hiring process. Not that he was without talent. He could shuffle paper, crank out memos, and market himself like a Madison Avenue pro. Man, did he snow me. It took me a year and a half to realize he never actually did any real work. After I asked for his resignation I discovered that everyone else had seen right through him for some time. Wiping the egg off my face, I vowed to never again flip-flop that wise old adage, "Hire slow, fire fast." Even if the gaping hole you're trying to fill grows wider by the day, don't panic. Take the prudent approach. Plugging the wrong person into a key position is like applying a Band-Aid to an infected wound. By the time you realize you're in trouble, the damage may be irreparable.

Seat-of-the-pantsers typically put mediocre employees in charge of hiring. Big mistake. It takes a sharp person to recognize a fellow thoroughbred—and to be delighted, not intimidated, by their star power. Leverage the street smarts of some elite performers by placing them in the interviewer's chair.

Fear factor: some managers don't *want* their socks knocked off. Sure, it's only human nature to feel threatened by someone who can do your job better than you can. But the only way to build a strong team is to hire the best people you can find. Sharper people challenge you to grow *and* make your business more productive, and guess who will look smarter then? If you only hire people you feel intellectually superior to, you'll wind up holding yourself hostage to a bunch of deadwood subordinates who won't even sharpen a pencil until you approve it. And that sets the dominos in motion. Inevitably, the really good people leave, the really bad people are fired, and all that's left is a hot, steaming pile of mind-numbing mediocrity. If that's your idea of paradise, why are you reading this guide?

FIVE

QUALITY QUESTIONS

Stripping the Guesswork Out of Hiring

Interviewing a job candidate is like asking your teenager how school was that day. You won't find out what's worth knowing until you ask just the right questions in just the right way. When playing "The Hiring Game," it's crucial to arm yourself with probing, open-ended questions. Why? Most job seekers know the drill inside and out. They're skilled at telling you what they think you want to hear and, more importantly, suppressing details they *don't* want you to hear. But that, my friend, is exactly the information you need to know.

Before launching into a friendly grilling, level the playing field a bit and ease into the conversation. I'd thank a prospect for considering us and acknowledge that she was interviewing us as much as we were interviewing her. I'd emphasize that we'd each benefit from total candor, noting that important details that didn't surface could come back to haunt us later. I'd promise not to oversell my offer and ask her to return the favor. After stating our company's mission, vision, and values, I'd pepper her with thought-provoking questions arranged under eight themes. I'd encourage her to go with the first response that popped to mind and let her do 70 percent of the talking.

Brian Collins

11-13-2018 9:58AM

Item(s) checked out to Collins, Brian.

TITLE: By the seat of your pants : the n
BARCODE: 30379100547878lolbg
DUE DATE: 12-04-18

Cincinnati State Library
Check college email for library notices!

Here's the checklist:

1 **Job history.** Start with the basics and add a twist. To understand a prospect's experience, ask about her last three jobs.

- What was your job description, and what did you actually do?
- What did you love about the job, and what did you hate?
- How would you rate your boss, and why?
- Did you leave the job or did the job leave you? What exactly happened?

The kicker? Don't ask what her last supervisor thought about the quality of her work. Instead, ask, What will your supervisor say about you when I call? Odds are you'll get a more honest, revealing answer because she's probably thinking, Uh-oh, I better come clean.

2 **Hard work and initiative.** These questions determine a job seeker's capacity to work hard *and* smart.

- Walk me through a typical day at your most recent job (or the one most relevant to the position under discussion). How did you feel about each element?
- Tell me about the times you underperformed. What did you do about it?
- What were your biggest contributions to your last employer?
- What are some on-the-job examples of your going beyond the call of duty?
- What is your understanding of what this job requires?
- How many hours did you work at your last job, and how many do you expect to work at this job?

3 **Integrity.** Don't pass up the opportunity to stress your zero tolerance for unethical behavior. Why? People with integrity deficits assume that everyone else shares their twisted concept of right and wrong. That's how they rationalize ethical shortcuts. Weed out the bad apples with these questions:

- Everyone has bent or broken a rule at one time or another. What was one of your recent transgressions, and what did you learn from it?

- Are all rules valid?

- If you felt a rule was unfair, what would you do about it?

- Have you ever broken a rule to satisfy a customer? If so, how?

- Which is more important, customer service or making a profit? Why?

4 **Judgment.** These four questions help you judge the maturity of a candidate's thought processes and the quality of her decision making.

- Tell me about a few good decisions you made recently.

- What was the toughest work-related decision you've made?

- Describe the biggest calculated risk you've ever taken.

- Why would this be a good place for you to work?

5 **Ambition.** My eyebrows raise when a prospect makes even a modest attempt to define her career dreams. It makes me more confident that she's selective about the job she wants. Suddenly, an image of a hardworking, productive employee snaps into focus. These questions help you glimpse a candidate's career vision.

- What are your short-term and long-term career goals, and why?

- How are you going to accomplish them?

- What alternative careers are you pondering, and why?

- Why did you apply for this position?
- How does this job help you meet your career goals?

6 Personality. My hiring philosophy is simple—avoid surprises. With the interview now more than halfway through, remind her that the more you know about each other the better. Agreement secured, ask a series of tough, unorthodox questions to gauge her emotional and psychological maturity.

- What's the happiest you've ever been, and why?
- What makes you sad?
- What scares you?
- What makes you laugh?
- What really made you mad at your last job? What did you do about it?
- Describe a poorly handled encounter with a colleague. What would you do differently today?
- How would you react if a colleague or customer yelled at you?
- How well do you work under pressure and deadlines?
- When do you find you are not a team player?
- What is your greatest accomplishment?
- Tell me about your most spectacular failure.
- Tell me about three big changes you've made in your life and what you learned from each.

Prior to my triple trauma of relationship, health, and cash-flow upheaval, I wouldn't have been able to extract much value from the preceding questions. As a card-carrying seat-of-the-pantser, I was in no position to analyze somebody else's emotional or psychological well-being. Fortunately, the sunlight of self-mastery strategies (chapters 45–52) burned off the fog of dysfunction.

A touchy issue to keep in mind: I was a big proponent of standardized psychological testing for high-level managerial positions. Even though there are legal risks to consider, it's a good way to make sure a candidate's personality, world view, temperament, and work ethic match the rest of the team's. If a prospect was a square peg who would fit snugly into our square hole, I knew we could train and integrate her.

7 **Self-analysis.** You need clarity about a candidate's strengths and vulnerabilities to know if she's a magical match. Generic, open-ended questions like *What are your greatest strengths?* yield only marginally useful information. Instead, list a dozen or so topics—organizational skills, computer proficiency, time management, customer service, reaction to change, work ethic, teamwork—relevant to the open position. Begin with the first subject and ask her to rate her skill from one to ten. Follow up with, *What will it take to get you to a ten?*

8 **Compensation.** With two questions you'll zero in on a salary you'll both be comfortable with. First, ask, *What would you like to make?* After she gives a figure, ask, *What's the minimum you'd feel good about?* It's a question rarely asked. She'll hesitate. Be patient while she runs through a quick analysis in her head: *If the number's too low I'll cheat myself. If it's too high he'll lose interest in me.* I call this the "Goldilocks Strategy" because people feel compelled to shoot you a number that's juuust right.

It's worth noting that we never hemmed in people with strict salary guidelines. If we settled on above-market pay, we told new hires we expected above-market productivity. After all, it's not what you pay that's important, it's what you get for what you pay. Which would you rather have—nine highly productive self-starters earning 11 percent more than average, or ten average performers earning an average salary?

By this point in the process, I'd have a sense of whether I wanted to shift the interview into higher gear or hit the brakes. If the light was green, I'd give her the hard sell on the career opportunities *we could offer her.* Why? A drop-dead candidate has likely wowed other suitors. If you're impressed, throttle up to make sure she's just as impressed with you. First, repeat your company's mission, vision, and values. Then connect the dots from that corporate DNA to information gleaned from the interview: "You said you had a passion for serving customers. That's great, because it's an important part of our mission." Finish up by giving her a tour and introducing her to others she'd be working with. Helping her begin to feel at home will reduce the stress that accompanies a career move.

SIX

DIGGING DEEPER

Squeezing Even More Secrets Out of Interviews

These extra steps give you more bang for your interviewing buck.

FUNNEL DOWN

Inquiring about past jobs and money, let alone poking around under the psychic hood, may cause a candidate to hide behind pat answers. Soldier on. The greater the resistance to answering a question, the more important it is to question the answer. Keep going deeper. If she hesitates, whether from pondering the question or not wanting to share the answer, it might be tempting to fill in the silence. Don't. An awkward pause (and I've seen them go on for an eternity) usually gives way to a valuable outpouring of information. Thanks to the Funnel Technique, I quickly terminated an interview with "Janet" and saved both of us valuable time.

Me: How did you like your last position, Janet?

Janet: Oh, it was okay.

Me: Was there anything about it you didn't like?

Janet: No, I liked it all right. It was pretty good.

Me: There was nothing at all you didn't like?

Janet: Well, maybe my boss.

Me: Well, bosses can be that way. What didn't you like about him?

Janet: He was too requiring.

Me: What do you mean, too requiring?

Janet: Oh, he really worked me hard.

Me: Yeah, sometimes bosses can do that. How many hours a week did he want you to work?

Janet: Forty!

Me: Forty, huh? (*Red light. After a few more questions it was a wrap.*) Well, it's been good talking to you, Janet. I wish you luck in your ongoing job search.

GET REAL WITH ROLE-PLAYING

Can you imagine a director casting an actress in a starring role solely from listening to her talk about how talented she is? I don't think so. He needs to see her in character. That's why our hiring honchos asked candidates to act out theoretical—but real-world—situations they might run into. For a customer-service job, for instance, the interviewer assumed the role of an angry customer. Or, if the candidate was trying to crack management, we thrust him into an employee conflict or budget dilemma. Sales? We asked him to sell us a tire or chrome-plated valve stem. We weren't looking for the next De Niro, we just wanted to toss it back and forth for a few minutes.

Some applicants I interviewed were tentative: "Well, in that situation, I guess I'd say . . ." I'd stop him and say, "No, I'm the customer and you're the salesman. Let's get in character." After a pause, he'd start again, "Okay, here's how I would handle it..." Again I'd interrupt. "No, I don't want you to *tell* me how you'd handle it, I want you to *show* me how you'd handle it." Nobody ever walked out on me but some found it difficult to get in the spirit of the exercise. I paid attention to that. An unwillingness to project into a different mindset spoke volumes about a prospect's comfort zone, creativity, and ability to think on his feet. No matter what the response, every "audition" yielded valuable information.

ANTICIPATE COUNTEROFFERS

If your new hire is as good as you think he is, you may have to fight a counteroffer from a jealous employer in the throes of re-falling in love. This sample script can help prep the prospect and get a stronger seal on the deal:

You: John, just curious, how would you react if your company promised you the moon to keep you?

John: Oh, I don't think anything could change my mind.

You: John, I have to advise other candidates for this position that we've filled it. So, I have to ask. Is there any possibility you could be influenced by new promises? Because if you tell me later you've reconsidered, that puts me in a very tough position. I would have to call back my second choice—and nobody wants to be second choice.

John: No, Tom, this is firm.

You: (*Extend your hand*) Great, I'm really glad to have you on the team.

It only takes a minute. Don't pass up the opportunity to cement the commitment with a verbal agreement.

SOLICIT FEEDBACK

Refine your hiring process by gleaning info from:

The candidate. After the interview, ask him what he liked and disliked about the process at other companies he's interviewed with. Simply posing the question is flattering. Most people will be happy to share their experiences.

Your employees. Ask them to grade your hiring process. Now that they're in the fold, they'll fill you in on what surprised them and what made them sweat.

The ones that got away. Respectfully ask decliners for their reasons. Chances are you'll get some worthwhile feedback.

SEVEN

HR HOOPS

Building an Employee-Friendly Framework

HR is like Ellis Island. Everyone—your newly hired huddled masses, yearning for a paycheck—passes through the human resources department to enter a new world of opportunity. Some seat-of-the-pantsers see HR as a profit-draining department existing primarily to distribute paychecks, produce manuals, and answer benefits questions. Hey, guys, wake up and smell the new century. HR is now regarded as a strategic partner that pumps up the people side of your business via policies and programs aligned with your mission, vision, and values. Count on HR to deliver a consistent brand message to employees, and to work with top execs to shape cultural values and recruit and retain star performers. (Those topics and other HR functions are covered thoroughly in other chapters.)

You'll find a crackerjack HR staff at large, leading-edge firms. But many companies outsource some basic HR functions while maintaining an in-house presence to coordinate programs and maintain standards. Consultants and outside agencies help with everything from benefits, payroll, and workers' comp to recruiting, hiring, and even "employee leasing." Based on your own circumstances, ask your HR reps to mix and match the following tips to make sure you're welcoming new hires with a solid safety net of employee-wise policies and programs.

Make sure your employment-law attorney knows her stuff. A good labor-law expert should be considered an extension of management. She'll iron out wrinkles should your corporate culture clash with state or federal legal requirements.

Optimize your full-service insurance broker. Large insurance firms often employ HR specialists who manage claims, update policy manuals, and provide benefits resources (on-site seminars, administration of 401(k)s, disability). They also administer risk-management services (OSHA compliance, on-site safety meetings, training) and offer access to HR attorneys.

Sign on with an EAP. Employee assistance programs offer phone banks staffed by trained counselors. Your people can call for help with nearly any issue—emotional health, family crisis, financial stress, chemical dependency. Any one of these can turn ugly, let alone affect job performance. Many EAPs also offer management consultation to guide you through legal landmines.

Stay up to date. Business & Legal Reports (www.blr.com) offers HR news, white papers, and federal and state 411 on employment law. For online training, check out www.skillsoft.com and www.hrclassroom.com. The U.S. Equal Employment Opportunity Commission (www.eeoc.gov) provides the scoop on legal issues, from age, sex, and religious discrimination to litigation stats and education programs. The U.S. Department of Labor (www.dol.gov) provides state-specific information.

EIGHT

HIT THE GROUND RUNNING

Welcoming New Hires

With the zeal of proud parents welcoming a new daughter-in-law, we warmly, if methodically, welcomed new employees into the fold. New hires acquired a "buddy" who gave them a tour of their new home along with scouting reports on the people and culture. We introduced new associates with a group e-mail detailing their career history, family background, hobbies, and interests. That info helped break the ice with new teammates: "Hey, I love softball, too! What position do you play?" Those efforts built camaraderie, trimmed learning curves, and minimized unproductive, profit-draining downtime.

We assimilated new hires into our coaching culture as quickly as possible. Their department head asked open-ended questions to draw them out, build rapport, and establish healthy communication: "What do you see as the biggest challenges in your new position?" "What new skills would you like to develop?" "What can I do now to help you succeed?" Our orientation sessions briefed new hires on what was expected of them—and what they could expect from us—regarding attitude, ethics, and behavior.

Making new teammates feel valued from day one reaped a big competitive advantage. As a service outfit, our success hinged on hiring and keeping great personalities. We understood that the first week is crucial—that's when people decide whether they see a future with a new company. The time and money you'll spend welcoming new hires is a pittance compared to the revolving-door cost of constantly hiring and training new employees to replace those who were unhappy and unproductive.

THE LAW OF DIMINISHING DEDICATION

Ever been so fired up at a leadership seminar that you were champing at the bit to race back to the office to test things out? You were still pumped up when you got back to your desk. Then the regular stuff began crowding out your time. The days rolled by. Enthusiasm for what you learned began to wane and, finally, what was once so fresh in your mind had faded into a distant memory.

So it goes with a new job. Most people show up for their first day all gung-ho and eager to contribute. With luck, they'll be greeted by a wise, effective team leader and a healthy corporate culture. Otherwise, bureaucratic roadblocks, turf wars, inefficient systems, and the hypnotic comfort of daily routines will blunt their passion and lull them into mediocrity. It's as quiet and insidious as radon poisoning.

To avoid the Big Sleep, I personally talked to new recruits during week-long orientation courses at the company school. Young minds are impressionable. I set aside six hours to distill for them our mission, vision, and values. I urged them to keep up their guard should they happen across a rebel teammate. Even though we were vigilant about sustaining a positive, enlightened culture, I occasionally saw a new hire sabotaged by a negative colleague.

How do you combat that? I stressed there are best practices for everything, from heart surgery to piloting a plane, and that sticking to our system was the fastest route to success. I cautioned that they might get ribbed for following procedures so closely: "Aw, look at the rookie. Here, kid, lemme show you how we do it around here." Call me obsessive, but we also role-played a way to handle those encounters. I suggested something like, "Thanks. Sounds like that works for you but I'm going to go by the book so I can catch up to your level some day." Reaching new levels—and staying excited about the journey—is what the rest of this guide is all about.

NINE

FULL CIRCLE

Pointing Underachievers Toward the Exit

It's only natural to close a section on hiring with a few words on firing—or, as I like to call it, freeing up someone's future for more suitable work. In the early days, I was so doggedly caring and loyal that I terminated people only for serious underperformance or egregious offenses. It was a major shift to realize that welfare management—failing to adequately hold people accountable and allowing the wrong people to stay in key positions—hurts everyone. It took years to learn to be both compassionate and tough. Once I balanced my personal resolutions with my professional responsibilities, the termination process took on a life of its own. In fact, it often culminated with an underachieving employee offering to terminate himself.

Take one of my former top execs. A nice guy, he had been with us for years but repeatedly failed to provide accurate, timely reporting on critical issues. After one too many broken promises, I called him into my office. I asked how important he thought it was to consistently produce these reports. He agreed it was essential. He also nodded that we had established mutually defined objectives and that he had consistently fallen short of the mark. I then asked, "What do you think should happen here?" Crestfallen but with honor intact, he replied, "I think I should probably leave." I hesitated for a moment, to acknowledge how difficult this was for him. "Yes," I said, "I think you're right. Congratulations for that awareness. I really appreciate everything you've done for this company, and we'll do everything we can to make this a smooth transition." Visibly relieved, he left to type his resignation letter. We supported him until he found another job.

My corporate Darwinism also generated a boomerang effect. The more I challenged others to grow, the more I was challenged myself. I told my executive committee that if my own skills couldn't keep pace, I'd do the honorable thing and bow out. As majority shareholder and chairman, I had the power to replace myself as CEO and president and was fully prepared to do so.

These same standards also apply to business partners. During that fateful lunch with Best Buy's Dick Schulze, I told him our longtime CPA firm was a small regional shop. "That's also a problem," he said. Again, Dick was dead on. Before the month was out I interviewed four accounting firms. I was astonished when I saw what we'd been missing. But we didn't just tie the knot with the best-looking firm. We treated each vendor like a potential hire and made sure they shared our vision. We ended up switching to a larger firm with invaluable retail-chain experience.

Deciding whether to free up someone's future demands a detached viewpoint. Detachment does not imply callousness. It simply means caring deeply, but from an objective place. Ask yourself, *Does this person have what it takes to get the job done?* Hopefully, you're now better equipped to answer that question. Personnel pioneer Robert Half had a nice way of putting it:

> *There's something more scarce than ability;*
> *it's the ability to recognize ability.*

KEY POINTS: HUNTING THROUGH HAYSTACKS

Finding the Best People

✔ **Hold people accountable for performance.** A commitment to kindness and compassion must be complemented by tough love. Require outstanding results and challenge people to raise their competency ceiling.

✔ **Think of yourself as a top talent scout.** Landing the hot hire requires diligence and resourcefulness. Keep a lot of balls in the air—work your business contacts, offer referral bonuses, hit schools and hiring fairs, consider search firms. Make sure your culture attracts and retains good people.

✔ **Don't let stars in your eyes cloud your vision.** Don't assume that heavy hitters on other teams have more expertise or will fit seamlessly into your culture. Do your homework—and don't make exceptions to your standard hiring process.

KEY POINTS: EMBRACE YOUR HIRE POWER

Making the Magical Match

✔ **Develop a good game plan.** Job interviews are like "Hide and Seek." Candidates try to hide their faults—you seek to discover them. An established drill helps avoid the irritation of watching new hires turn into misfires.

✔ **Funnel past pat answers.** Ask probing questions that reveal a candidate's personality, maturity, strengths, and vulnerabilities. The greater the resistance to answering a question, the more important it is to question the answer. Keep funneling down until you hit pay dirt.

(continued on next page)

Key Points: EMBRACE YOUR HIRE POWER

✔ ***Audition applicants.*** Don't just have a job seeker *tell* you how she'd handle a real-world situation, have her *show* you. This role-playing exercise yanks people out of their comfort zone and provides a glimpse of how they'll actually conduct themselves.

✔ ***Make it mutual.*** It's just as important to impress applicants as it is for them to impress you. If she knocks your socks off, chances are she's wowed other employers, too. A perfect fit? Get an offer on the table ASAP (after her references check out).

✔ ***Counter the counteroffer.*** Expect a star candidate's current employer to sweeten the pot to try to keep her. Firm up her commitment with a verbal agreement that tackles the issue head on.

✔ ***Cover your HR bases.*** Welcome new hires with a framework of employee-friendly policies and programs. Make sure your benefits package is current and competitive. Provide resources and training for personal, work-related, and legal issues.

✔ ***Welcome new hires.*** Make employees feel comfortable from day one. Assign them a "buddy," introduce them to colleagues, build rapport with management, and brief them on what's expected from all sides. A healthy, team-oriented, systems-disciplined culture prevents newbies from drifting into mediocrity.

✔ ***Avoid "welfare" management.*** Letting wrong people stay in important positions hurts everybody. Employees who don't measure up to mutually agreed-to expectations have got to go. Lay the groundwork correctly and the termination process moves by its own volition. In the end, the underachiever often tenders his resignation.

III.
GROW THE
CULTURE

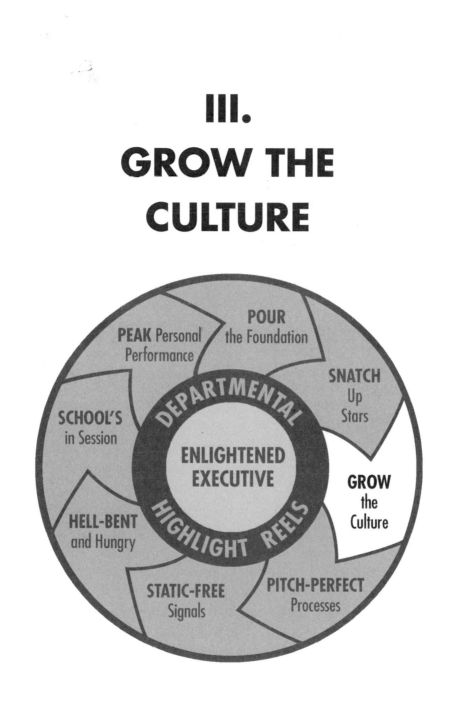

PART I

WORK SWEET WORK

Creating an Enlightened Environment

Employees are like plants. They need to be rooted in the rich soil of a nurturing environment in order to bloom and thrive. They need to be watered with care and attention, and warmed by the sunlight of appreciation. Yet, too many seat-of-the-pantsers, unskilled in the art of human horticulture, treat their people like so much cactus. They expect them to flourish in an arid, remote atmosphere. Those leaders are in for a culture shock.

By design or by default, every business has a corporate culture. But I suspect most business folks would be hard-pressed to describe theirs in any detail. By my lights, "culture" (some prefer "climate") is an umbrella term defined by

- the conditions and standards under which employees work;

- employees' shared understanding of team dynamics and how they fit in;

- the "tribe's" acceptable behaviors, dress, appearance, and rituals;

- the team's collective personality and identity.

Whether you can describe it or not, you sure as heck know a good one when you see it. In a healthy culture, people

- look forward to coming to work;
- feel pride in being part of the team;
- consider their co-workers friends;
- are excited by the organization's vision;
- gladly go beyond the call of duty when required;
- are personally satisfied when the team does well;
- are in sync with the organization's operating values;
- believe their work contributes directly to the team's success.

The leader who neglects to grow his organization's culture does so at his peril. Yes, changing an existing culture is difficult, but doable. The pressure of running a company or department can easily siphon attention away from employee-related issues. That it's difficult to stay focused on the satisfaction of employees, however, makes it no less necessary. The less attention paid to people's basic desire to offer value and feel valued, the faster spins the revolving door of turnover. (Of course, enlightened executives realize that, without a healthy bottom line, morale may become a moot point.)

The best people—productive, creative, passionate—won't settle for less than an energized, ethical shop abuzz with a spirited team attitude. John Lasseter, executive vice president of Pixar Animation Studios, would agree. Under his direction, the studio's animated blockbusters (Monsters, Inc.; A Bug's Life; the Toy Story films; Finding Nemo) generated worldwide grosses of more than $2.5 billion through 2004. As Newsweek noted:

> With such success, you might think all the competing studios
> would have plundered Pixar like an unguarded vault—which,
> technically, it is, since unlike at every other studio nobody
> besides Lasseter works under contract. So far everyone is
> staying put. "A piece of paper won't keep them here,"
> Lasseter says. "You want their heart here. So you make
> them creatively satisfied."

TEN

LAND OF THE FREE

What Employees Really Want

This is not your father's workplace. The once impenetrable barrier between work and home has crumbled in the wake of the baby boomer-fueled, personal growth movement. In the span of a generation, a hunger for meaning that grew even more ravenous after 9/11 has spurred an unprecedented demand for integration (within an employee's own life) and interconnectedness (with the lives of others).

High-tech wizardry is also contributing to blurred boundaries. It's now commonplace to e-mail extra work home for relaxed, after-dinner analysis; to use your firm's high-speed Internet connection to monitor your stock portfolio, place bids on eBay, and e-mail your kids instructions for dinner; to "tele-vacation" from a sandy beach in the tropics; to placate customers on a cell phone in your pajamas. (Closed circuit to Groucho: *How a cell phone got in your pajamas, I'll never know.*)

The cultural aftershocks rippling from these psychological and technological tremors—employees clamoring for fulfillment *and* flexibility—are leaving seat-of-the-pantsers out in the cold. Enlightened executives, however, apply the **HEAT**:

Honor the innate dignity of every employee.

Expect greatness and set high standards.

Accommodate employees' personal needs.

Trust employees' integrity and verify their progress.

Honor employees. During a routine visit to a Tires Plus store in 1995, I asked a young salesman named Gabe Lopez how things were going. "To be honest with you," he said, "not too well." Gabe said he had recently clocked a seventy-hour week only to be told after the fact that he had been "promoted" from an hourly to a salaried position. He felt chumped, like he was owed the overtime money. He methodically climbed his grievance up the corporate ladder but felt his protest had fallen on deaf ears.

On the spot, I called our human resources head and asked for an explanation. Gabe's situation was a "gray area," I was told, and we had a good case for not paying him the overtime cash. If there's a gray area, I told her, the employee should be given the benefit of the doubt; after all, that's what we do for our customers when there's a dispute. I hung up and apologized to Gabe. He got his check the next day. "I was just a nineteen-year-old kid out of high school working in an entry-level position," recalled Gabe, now a Tires Plus assistant district manager. "The fact that Tom took the time to listen to me and resolve the situation without hesitation really wowed me. It's something that will always stay with me. If not for that, I would have left the company. Tom later pulled me aside a number of times to tell me I could really go far in the company. He made me feel valued as a person, and I wanted to show him his faith in me was well-deserved."

Gabe's story illustrates why you can't leapfrog your employees—your internal customers—and focus solely on pleasing your external customers. It's a simple matter of connecting the dots. Honor your people and genuinely care about their well-being and you'll be rewarded with deeply loyal employees who set a new standard for customer service.

Expect greatness. Don't worry about setting expectations just beyond the moon. Expecting people to give their best will pull the best out of them. Jim Pascale, our vice president of franchise operations, saw this concept in action. "Working for Tom was like playing for a coach who says, 'We expect to win the championship this year,'" said Jim. "You find out what you're made of. You rise up to that level, you practice harder, and you have higher expectations. We were all fueled by Tom's ambition to grow, by his enthusiasm and energy."

But watch out. Setting high standards can actually undermine productivity and morale unless individual expectations are clearly defined *in relation to team goals* and the players appreciate how the two are related. That's why the strategic planning process (chapter 20) is critical. It establishes a clear, logical, measurable relationship between organizational objectives and individual goals.

Accommodate family priorities. Contrary to seat-of-the-pants mythology, putting family first in a systems-disciplined, achievement-oriented environment will actually *enhance* productivity, not diminish it. Countless times I've seen grateful employees tackle their work with renewed vigor after returning from a family-related absence. Maybe parents don't need to take in every single soccer game, dance line performance, or spelling bee, but a high attendance rate is important to them and to their child. Keep their bodies at work and you'll lose their hearts and minds.

Remember, output equals quantity of hours worked multiplied by the quality of those hours. Allowing your people, whether single or married, to play hooky for important family events—ones in which their absence would overshadow the event itself—is a goodwill gesture sure to boost morale. It's also a competitive advantage that may prevent otherwise resentful employees from seeking more family-friendly pastures.

Seat-of-the-pantsers typically don't connect the dots between how they treat employees' families and those employees' loyalty and performance. I'll never forget the time my wife and I were visiting my buddy and Shell Oil colleague, Art Davis, in Dayton, Ohio, over thirty years ago. The phone rang and Art's wife went in the kitchen to answer it. Eight seconds later she was back. It was Art's boss. After Art left the room she said, "That jerk, he doesn't even bother to say hello Just, 'Is Art there?'" Now really, how hard is it to say, "Hi, Judy, this is Bill, how are you?" Think about it. A spouse has more influence over your employee than anyone else. I wasn't surprised when, less than a year later, Art told me he had found another job.

Trust employees to deliver. One afternoon each week, for seven summers, Larry Brandt left work early to cheer at his son Andrew's baseball game. A key Tires Plus exec and our third largest shareholder, Larry also ducked out occasionally to root for his other son, Barett, as he worked his way up to a black belt in karate. To compensate for his absences during the work day, Larry worked at night and on weekends.

We had a caring, family-oriented culture, but also a very hard-working culture. The two naturally go hand in hand. Of course, we also had systems in place, like weekly reports and one-on-one coaching, to ensure that employees stayed on track to achieve their goals. If people didn't live up to their end of the bargain, their privilege parameters were tightened a bit. Honoring and valuing your people and going out of your way to accommodate their personal needs—not to advance your own agenda but because it's the right thing to do—produces dedicated employees and a positively charged environment.

Remember, quality employees want to be trusted, and they want balanced lives. That's why Best Buy designed ROWE (results-oriented work environment)—to attract top-notch candidates. The program, which was still being rolled out as 2005 began, goes light-years beyond typical flexibility benefits like condensed work weeks and telecommuting. People are free to work when and where they want. All that matters is results—did the job get done? Surveys and anecdotal evidence suggest that appreciative employees are living up to their end of the bargain.

In stark contrast, a seat-of-the-pants environment drains and frustrates employees. The only thing they look forward to is giving their two-week notice. Moving from that kind of fear-based, spirit-deadening atmosphere to our company gave Doug, one of our top execs, a severe case of culture shock. Doug had spent nineteen years at a well-known national company. "The executive vice president of operations was confrontational with his staff and pitted his managers against each other," said Doug. "Because he was unwilling to make a decision he could be held accountable for, we were left to figure out for ourselves what direction our divisions should go." The inevitable turf wars that followed caused some capable managers to bolt. Even though these were smart, sought-after pros, Doug's boss spun every loss as a victory. "He would boast to the board that he had weeded out another malcontent," recalled Doug. "That created a culture of managers who were afraid to make decisions, take risks, or offer creative suggestions. It just became a very stressful place to work."

Moving to Tires Plus gave Doug the intrepreneurship and growth opportunities he craved. "Management encouraged risk taking, team decision making, and information sharing," said Doug. "I didn't know a darn thing about the tire business but I felt like my opinions mattered. If I asked a dumb question somebody would take a minute to explain. Tom was an encourager, a humane manager who sought input, asked opinions, and accepted challenging comments. If we didn't agree with one of his decisions, it was still appropriate to ask questions and make suggestions."

ELEVEN

EXTEND A HEALTHY HAND

Fostering Healthier, More Productive Employees

A healthy culture requires healthy employees. My executive committee objected when I proposed building a fitness center, massage area, and meditation room in our new suburban Minneapolis headquarters. "Why waste valuable square footage on luxuries?" some argued. "They're not luxuries, they're necessities," I said. "When we take care of our people we take care of ourselves." They weren't the only skeptics. Dave Wilhelmi, our vice president of marketing, was dumbfounded. "Our home office was going to include a meditation room, an exercise room, a basketball court, and afternoon classes on dieting and yoga?" said Dave. "My first thought was, *You've gotta be kidding me, we're in the tire business, aren't we?*"

Yep. And it didn't take long to win Dave over. "When I think back," he said, "I remember the swelling pride I felt in showing off all those features to a group of out-of-town guests and watching their eyes pop as I toured them around." Dave explained why we offered those amenities, along with an in-house university with mock showroom and service bays, and a hundred-seat break room furnished with a state-of-the-art kitchen. Visitors were especially impressed with the grand staircase that cascaded down to the two-story glass windows overlooking a wooded pond. "I wasn't the only one who was happy to be working there," said Dave. "The pride among our employees was apparent to many visitors."

Pride and productivity aren't easy to sustain when you feel ill, physically or emotionally. Common sense tells you productivity suffers if employees don't exercise; if they eat too much junk food; if they're stressed out and sleep-deprived; if they don't feel good about themselves. Now, I'm not suggesting that you pry into personal lives. Even casually telling people what they *should* be doing crosses the line. With that caveat in mind, I came up with a three-step process that, over the years, inspired hundreds of employees to make healthier lifestyle choices.

1 **Model healthy behavior and habits yourself.** An overweight, cantankerous boss who chain-smokes and guzzles sugar-water all day long broadcasts a very different message than a fit, energetic, and emotionally grounded leader with a ready smile and encouraging word. But don't wait till you're a paragon of healthy habits before you send out the positive self-care vibe. In fact, employees may relate better to someone who's struggling with, and taking responsibility for, their own unhealthy behaviors.

2 **Encourage others (gently) to take better care of themselves.** When an employee was noticeably sleep-deprived or lethargic, I'd say, "Gosh, Ken, are you doing okay? You don't seem to be your usual energetic self." Judging from his response, I'd urge him to get caught up on sleep or to take time to exercise regularly, even if it meant working a little less. Of course, if he wasn't receptive, I'd wish him well and move on. Too many seat-of-the-pantsers send an unspoken message: "What's this nonsense about going to the gym and eating 'better' food? What do you think this is, a resort? We pay you good money to work your butt off." The enlightened executive understands that when employees devote a few hours a week to self-care, the hours they do spend at work will be more productive.

Seat-of-the-pants cultures are also notorious for discouraging people to take sick days. Hello? Coming to work sick often extends the illness and may put other employees at risk. If someone is sniffling, shivering, and sneezing, thank her for her dedication but tell her to go home, get some rest, and get healthy.

3 **Create opportunities for employees to make healthier choices.** Our corporate wellness program, led by an in-house wellness coach, wasn't limited to nutrition and exercise. It covered everything from stress reduction, weight management, and smoking cessation to back care, emotional health, and substance abuse. Info and programming were accessible through on-site workshops, brown-bag classes, newsletters, e-mail alerts, our intranet, an in-house library, and an EAP (employee assistance program). Once a week, everyone from computer jockeys in the home office to in-store mechanics could sign up for a fifteen-minute Shiatsu massage for a company-subsidized five bucks.

Sure, not everyone took advantage of the opportunities. But the benefits were dramatic for many who did. People dragging by lunchtime returned from a workout invigorated. Employees struggling with emotional challenges had a better shot at beating them thanks to internal support and professional help. A lot of people simply didn't know how to take the first step toward a healthier lifestyle. It was a joy to watch them take the ball and run with it.

Results of wellness initiatives are hard to measure. Conservative data I've seen estimates a three-to-one return on investment. It makes sense. The benefits are obvious—health-care costs and absenteeism go down; creativity, efficiency, and performance go up. And they're programs people enjoy and appreciate, which translates into better employee relations. Bottom line: it's a no-brainer.

TWELVE

FUN, FRIENDLY, AND FLEXIBLE

Loosening Up Keeps Grumbling Down

Your employees are on board the mission train, they're stoked about the vision, they feel honored and valued, and their wellness needs are being met. With a little more effort, you can crank up the culture and make the place so enjoyable that people wouldn't dream of working anywhere else. As Herb Kelleher, the pioneering former CEO of Southwest Airlines, put it:

> *If people come to a place that they regard*
> *as fun, entertaining, and stimulating, their*
> *minds are turned on. They're looking for*
> *solutions and they'll find them.*

Start with yourself. Fair or not, your relationships with people under your watch set the tone for the entire staff. My dad and his World War II army buddies told me, "There were some leaders we'd gladly follow out of a foxhole into battle. But there were others we wanted to shoot in the back." It's no different in the corporate foxholes. The commander in chief can make every day feel like a slice of heaven or a glimpse of hell.

Crack open the window of your life and connect more deeply with people. Let your guard down. Be accessible. Listen. Every so often, start a meeting by asking everyone to share something interesting going on in their personal life. Or, start with a humorous, self-deprecating story. Ever spill food on yourself at an important business dinner? Make a boneheaded play in a softball game? Lock yourself out of the house in your bathrobe?

Your gentle humor and humility encourage others to follow suit. Build on that. Every so often, organize a potluck lunch or have take-out food delivered. If weather permits, make it a picnic lunch. Breaking bread is a wonderful way to bring people together and strengthen bonds. Before you know it you're cooking with team chemistry. Filling people's stomachs is also a good way to show you appreciate great work. Every year, our executive team donned aprons and served lunch to the employees. During huge snowstorms we tried to keep our crews fueled up with pizza while they worked sixteen-hour days to serve panicked drivers.

Don't stop there. Sponsor a softball, golf, or bowling team. Maybe a volleyball or archery league. Gardening or chess club, anyone? Welcome spouses of employees and former employees—whoever wants in on the fun. Some of these things might spill into company time, but that's okay. It's not wasted time. People who sit anonymously in rows of cubicles can get to know their neighbors better in one afternoon at a bowling alley than by exchanging three years' worth of hallway hellos.

That camaraderie is priceless, especially when leaders also participate. I was a force to be reckoned with on the company basketball team, played in our annual company golf outing, and took on countless ping-pong challengers determined to beat the boss. By keeping "rank and file" diversions like this at arm's length, management promotes an us-versus-them mentality. If nothing else, show up on the sidelines once in awhile. I had a blast cheering on our softball team with my bleacher buddies.

Enlightened executives also recognize that most employees have busy, complicated lives. Do what you can to reduce their stress. If circumstances allow (and often they don't), provide flexible start and finish times. Let people run errands during the workday now and then. As long as the work gets done, and gets done well and on time, loosen the rules and give people the freedom to be responsible adults.

Want to be a hero to your employees and help them consistently hit their targets? Convert an underused room into a nap space. It's a common sense solution—an exhausted employee is an unproductive employee. *The Art of Napping At Work*, by William Anthony, director of the Center for Psychiatric Rehabilitation at Boston University, and his wife, Camille, argues that losing just one hour of sleep a night for a week slashes work productivity. And when American workers feel sleep-deprived, 51 percent say they do less work and 40 percent admit the quality of their work suffers, according to the International Labour Organization (ILO). I know many executives will think on-the-job napping is a bit goofy but the concept is catching on; 16 percent of workers surveyed by ILO were allowed to take naps at work. I expect that number to grow. Employees who take catnaps make fewer mistakes, are more productive, and—here's the best part—are eternally grateful they work at such an employee-friendly company.

Creating a can't-wait-to-get-to-work-on-Monday culture not only helps retain people, it can even lure them back once they've left. Before a departing employee slipped out the exit door I made sure he saw the WELCOME BACK sign taped to the other side. We thought of former employees as "lifetime alumni," and invited them back for special events like it was high school homecoming week. We also regularly checked in with them to see how they were getting along (we knew once people had a taste of our culture it was hard to settle for less). If a former employee was happy at his new company, I was happy. But if he felt like a fish out of water, I'd jump at the chance to reel him back into our pond.

Once, a larger company offered our director of loss prevention, Eric Randa, a major boost in salary and responsibility. After reviewing the facts, I shook his hand. "I hate to lose you, Eric," I said, "but you're obviously making the right decision." Almost five years later, we had grown from forty stores to one hundred fifty. I got a wild hair, called Eric, and asked if he'd like to come back, as a vice president, with stock options. "I was fairly content where I was," recalled Eric, "but the new job hadn't been nearly as enjoyable. At Tires Plus, I had put in long hours, but I learned a lot and it had been a lot of fun. It didn't take long to accept Tom's offer. It was a breath of fresh air to come back."

Maintaining cordial relations with ex-employees was an important part of our culture. It wasn't just because we hoped they'd return; it was also one of our values. If I heard an employee badmouth a former teammate I slammed on the brakes. "You're glad he's gone?" I'd say. "That's not okay. Yes, he made some mistakes. But don't we all? Overall, he's a good person, he contributed, and I hope he's happy at his new company." Speaking well of former colleagues shows your people your concern is authentic, and that you won't treat them like yesterday's news should they leave. That authenticity is the glue that binds a healthy culture together. You can't fake it any more than you can put a price on it.

Okay, reality check. No matter how much effort you put into making your office a fun, stimulating place, a small pocket of employees are still going to grouse. It's always left me scratching my head—the happier most people are, the unhappier other people seem to get. But that's okay. It isn't possible to please all the people all the time.

Changing your culture is hard, but rewarding, work. There are no quick fixes. But take heart. Once you begin engaging hearts and minds with the idea that work can be exciting and enjoyable, the process takes on a life of its own. As Stanford University professor Everett M. Rogers noted: "When approximately 5 percent of a population adopts a new idea, it becomes 'embedded.' When it's accepted by 20 percent of the people, it is unstoppable."

THIRTEEN

THE MUSKETEERS MODEL

Developing Team Spirit

Our esprit de corps was impossible for visitors to ignore. During one of my talks at a company gathering, a tire vendor whispered to Brad Burley, a regional manager, "Does Tom make you all drink the same punch, or what?" Brad laughed as the vendor went on. "You guys all talk the same. You don't have 'problems,' you have 'opportunities.'" Brad took it as a compliment. "It was recognition that the tone of a culture is set from the top down," recalled Brad. "It was fun to be a part of because that attitude bled into everything we did, from executive team meetings to the way customers were treated." Many seat-of-the-pantsers prattle on about teamwork but few walk their talk. Yes, individual expression is highly prized and indispensable, but getting everyone on the same page is equally important. My six-pronged approach to team-building transforms a collection of individuals into a collective "team ego."

1 **Saturate the environment.** Our offices pulsated with team-building. Anyone in a position to coach was trained to model team-oriented traits and preach that every employee's success depended on the sum of our parts. Egomaniacs stuck out like cutoffs at a cocktail party. Now, that doesn't mean we wanted everyone to think alike. In fact, it's important they don't. General George S. Patton said it best: "If everybody's thinking alike, somebody isn't thinking."

2 **Talk the walk.** Talk isn't *always* cheap. We asked our people to call their colleagues "teammates." It reinforced the Three Musketeers motto, "One for all and all for one." It also made a world of difference when our managers told their people, "Here's what the team needs," rather than, "Here's what I need." When an outsider knocked the company we took it personally—as in taking personal responsibility if fixes were in order. After all, a company isn't a corporate seal on a piece of paper, it's a team of people. And all those people have a common goal—making the organization better than it was yesterday.

3 **Hire team players.** We asked job candidates questions like, "Where do you rank as a team player on a scale of one to ten?" and "When do you find you are *not* a team player?" Invariably, they would leave the interview with our mission statement plastered on the billboard of their mind—*"Deliver caring, world-class service to our guests, our community, and to each other."* We took special care to draw attention to the last four words. The message was plain—lone wolves need not apply.

4 **Recognize and reward it.** If you don't actively promote teamwork, you may as well endorse selfishness. Toss out a "Way to go!" whenever you catch someone in the act of team-building. Good moves were greeted with kudos—and occasionally cash awards—at staff meetings. That was just the tip of our incentive iceberg. A big portion of our bonuses rode on achieving team goals. We even built a baseball-style "farm system" to reward skilled coaches. For instance, if Store A needed an assistant manager and was eyeballing a promising sales staffer over at Store B, then Store A had to "draft" the up-and-comer. The manager who tutored the hot prospect was owed something. So Store A had to pay $3,000 to Store B for the honor of picking up the future assistant manager. That fee in turn pumped up Store B's profits, added to the bonus kitty split among staff, and encouraged the team to continue to develop strong talent.

5 **Embody it.** You can hold a pep rally seven days a week, but it's merely platitudes and pom-poms unless leaders demonstrate the highest standards of teamwork. Early on, I'm embarrassed to admit, it was always about me, me, me instead of we, we, we. As I shed my seat-of-the-pants ways I came to my senses, and John Hyduke, a vice president, noticed. Our executive team had been deliberating about strategic timing for planting our flag in an array of new markets. "Tires Plus was a private company and Tom had majority interest," recalled John. "He had every right to make decisions while shaving in front of the mirror." John appreciated that I weighed my opinions against those of the rest of the committee, and rarely exercised a veto. "We all shared a sense of ownership in the decisions," said John. "So, whether or not a store was successful, morale was never a problem. We didn't stand around second-guessing, we just moved on."

6 **Celebrate achievement.** We celebrated all the time at Tires Plus. "Tom was a stern taskmaster," recalled Brad Burley. "But he wanted us to feel good about what we accomplished." Establish traditions to mark hard-earned victories and bolts from the blue—hand out cigars, pop the cork on the Dom, give the team the afternoon off. Announce triumphs—a successful product launch, blowing past projections, landing the huge account—while blaring Queen's "We Are The Champions."

FOURTEEN

LEADING OUT LOUD

Cultural Leadership Laws

Break these twenty laws of cultural leadership and your culture surveys will be graded D for dreadful. Renounce your seat-of-the-pants ways and be an A+ leader. Here's how:

1 **Be authentic.** Regrettably, employees view bosses through a distorted lens; they see execs as subhuman and devoid of feelings. It gives employees an excuse to downplay their boss' good side and exaggerate his bad. Then, when job frustration hits critical mass, they can feel justified in checking out emotionally. Unfair as it is, too many business owners perpetuate the stereotype. Let go of the notion that signs of emotion or fallibility are unprofessional. My relationships with employees grew healthier when I started admitting mistakes, revealing more of the real me, and being more caring.

2 **Hand out all-access passes.** Imagine you're a kid again. Somebody treats you like dirt, yet your parents won't listen to your grievance. You're frustrated and resentful. As a boss, you've got to recognize that you're a surrogate parent for many employees. Make yourself available to employees *when they need you*. Give them your full attention, and their appreciation will show up in the simple metrics of productivity and turnover. "Anybody in the company, from a store manager to a tire technician, could meet with Tom about anything," recalled Dave Urspringer, one of our top managers. I did have two stipulations. An employee had to first address the issue with his superiors (assuming it didn't involve family or health troubles). Second, he had to bring me at least one solution for the problem. "It was an ironclad rule," said Dave, "that you come prepared with at least some idea about how to make things better. Knowing we'd be listened to at the highest level, that we'd be treated like our ideas really mattered, was one of the biggest secrets to our success."

3 **Project a positive image.** An egomaniac inspires a lot of feelings, but loyalty and passion aren't among them. He's followed only reluctantly. Ditto negative and insecure leaders. An enlightened executive projects the right mix of confidence and humility. She's serious about life and work but doesn't take herself too seriously. "Tom carries a pretty good-sized ego," testified Trent Stoner, our director of public relations and marketing. "But at the same time he's so giving and caring that it doesn't put people off in any way. Tom leads with his mind and his heart and that's inspired me to always go with my instincts regardless of what anyone else says."

4 **Beware your impact.** I still remember the huge crush I had on Linda Harness in high school. No clue was too minor to crack the case on whether she liked me, or, you know, *liked* me. Did she smile? Was she looking over my shoulder when we talked? Like it or not, that's how your employees think of bosses (minus the romantic part, I hope). It's not fair, and it may even be a bit odd, but that's reality—one wrong look from the boss can ruin someone's day. It's a fault line to keep an eye on but there are limits to your vigilance. Take the time I forgot to bring my eyeglasses to a sales meeting. The next day I learned that a young sales associate was smarting because he had nodded and smiled at me from across the room and I failed to respond. I called him right away and joked that without my glasses I could only make out blurry outlines of people. He laughed and accepted my apology. And I never forgot my glasses again.

5 **Snoop like Columbo.** An enlightened executive roots out the truth like a gumshoe. If key details are missing, you can't make the right choice, solve the big problem, or launch the stinger strategy. When employees told me things were fine, I dug deeper: "Anything I can help you with?" "If you ran things, what would you do differently?" Sooner or later, the answers spilled out. "When Tom hit the field, we'd do everything in our power to make sure the stores were firing on all cylinders," said Jim Pascale, our first Iowa regional manager. Before one of my visits, Jim asked all his store personnel—over and over—the questions I typically asked. "Sure enough," recalled Jim, "Tom ended up asking the same questions I had. But he got twenty new answers!"

Be relentless. Employees instinctively withhold bad news from the boss. Some try to protect underperforming colleagues, or hide embarrassing details. Other times, the truth remains elusive because no one's connected the dots between problem and root cause. I methodically drill like a west Texas derrick to the core of problems. Beware, though. I sometimes hit nerves instead of veins. "There were times," recalled Wayne Shimer, head of retail operations, "when I wanted to reach out and say, 'Stop!' But, ultimately, Tom was right because everything was out on the table all the time. And I don't care what anybody says, that's a healthy culture to work in."

6 **Practice the accordion.** The best decisions emerge from a process that's neither exclusively top-down (leader calling the shots) nor bottom-up (rank-and-file referendum). It's gotta be a collaborative effort I call "the accordion." You can argue that top-down decisions are smarter because upper management commands a broader view of economic, cultural, and mission-related factors. Yet, management is too often out to lunch on the down-and-dirty details, if only because employees hate delivering bad news. The remedy: raw intel, gathered from as many sources as possible. I'd tell people, "If something needs to be said, don't minimize it or dramatize it. Just flat out say it."

In too many shops, input from the floor is either ignored or discounted. The rationale is predictable—*Hey, if my employees were smarter than me, I'd be reporting to them.* Perhaps a common military axiom will shed some light: "Battle plans never survive contact with the enemy." Without a constant feedback loop from the front, plans hatched by the top can be comically naïve or fatally flawed. That's why Wayne Shimer's store inspections started in the service bays. Why did he talk to the guys with grease under their fingernails first? In high school, Wayne had worked construction for a family friend named Mel. Every morning, Mel pulled up in his station wagon and headed straight for the welders. One day Wayne asked him why he spoke to the foreman last. "Wayne," said Mel, "after talking to the guys, I knew if the walls were going up at the right pace, I knew if the sand was being delivered, and I knew if the cement guy had been by. So by the time I got to the foreman he couldn't snow me."

7 **Eliminate obstacles.** My first day at Shell Oil in Chicago was electrifying. I was twenty-one and ready to take on the world. I wanted just one word to come to mind when my boss thought of my performance: *spectacular*. I never lost the desire to do great work, but, bit by bit, a bloated bureaucracy and stifling daily routines blunted my gung-ho edge. Naïve as I was, it was obvious to me that a company's procedures and systems have gotta be user-friendly. I also learned not to jerk people from one can't-wait-another-minute project to the next, and not to call a meeting unless I absolutely had to. People can't soar when they're bogged down in systematic sludge.

8 **Keep people in the loop.** One reason I left Shell Oil was I didn't know whether I was making a difference. Every nugget of information was closely held. That didn't make sense to me. Leaders at all levels need real numbers to make smart decisions and inspire people to hit their targets. Information sharing is also a valuable insurance policy. Take Al, one of our veeps, who felt alienated by his old employer's top-secret culture, where strategic initiatives and financial results were shared on a need-to-know basis. At Tires Plus, all department heads knew the revenue and expense flow of every unit, and everyone cross-advised everyone else's departments (And all store personnel knew details of their store's profit-and-loss statement.) "Without that culturally ingrained information sharing, we would've been badly hurt had we lost a key manager to injury or illness," said Al. "We may not have been able to step in seamlessly to run their division but it wouldn't have floundered either."

All employees should be briefed on the enterprise's performance and plans. Keep them up to speed with the company intranet, group e-mails, internal newsletters, and team meetings. Transparency inspires loyalty. As entrepreneurial icon Sam Walton pointed out:

> *Communicate everything you possibly can*
> *to your [employees]. The more they know,*
> *the more they'll understand. The more they*
> *understand, the more they'll care. Once they*
> *care, there's no stopping them.*

9 **Face the facts.** My passion for a project has been known to derail my common sense. I'd just want the darn thing done, the heck with the details. As *New York Times* film critic A. H. Weiler quipped, "Nothing is impossible for the man who doesn't have to do it himself." Sometimes it took me months to realize a delegated project was doomed. Once I told Wayne Shimer to get popcorn into all fifty of our stores. He scratched his head, duly priced out the machines and supplies, and researched popping big-quantity corn. He also took every opportunity to tell me that popcorn wouldn't lure customers, never mind that managers had better things to do. "Tom kept hounding me for six months to finish the popcorn project," remembered Wayne. "One day I dug in deep enough to get him to understand we'd need a food license, which meant regular city food inspections and plastic gloves for the sales staff. Finally, he threw up his hands and said, 'Fine, I give up.'" A year later, I recognized a familiar look on Wayne's face when I handed him a new project. "This is another popcorn project, isn't it?" I laughed. That became our inside joke. "When something was too bizarre," said Wayne, "we'd look at each other and laugh, 'That's a popcorn project.' And we'd blow it off."

10 **Talk it through.** Larry wanted to thaw the tension at his small Minneapolis packaging firm. "I just don't understand why people here don't get it," he told me. "I tell them what to do but they don't seem capable of following simple instructions." After talking to his employees, I broke it to Larry that *he* was the one who didn't get it. I was told that Larry often snapped, "Because I said so," or "Just do it, okay?" when his methods were questioned. "That just doesn't fly with people," I told Larry. "They'll tune you out and do things their own way." Be direct, I said. Ask the employee what she would do differently when she disagrees with your decision. If her suggestion makes sense, tell her you'll consider it and get back to her. If it's impractical, explain why. If she's still upset, say something like, "I know you don't agree but I think it's the right thing, so I hope you'll support it for the good of the company." Even if she doesn't agree with you, it's more likely she'll accept your decision if you weigh her input and explain your rationale.

11 **Look with "fresh eyes."** The status quo is a work in progress. One question always on the tip of my tongue was, *What did you learn?* "If you didn't have a good answer," recalled regional manager Brad Burley, "you got a little tough love. Tom and I would visit stores together, and knowing he was going to ask me that question at the end of the day kept me very focused." Another question that yanks people out of their daily grind: *Let's assume there are flaws in our customer service procedure (or ad-approval process or flextime policy). If we were starting from scratch, how could we make it more effective?* The question often lit the fuse to innovation.

It's up to you to lead the fresh eyes charge. Unfortunately, leaders are conditioned to project a know-it-all facade. Escape that trap. Admit when you're stumped. Listen *to* new ideas, not *against* them. It'll influence your people more than any lecture. Remember, the more you say, *I don't know,* the more you'll hear back, *Let's find out.*

12 View mistakes as opportunities. In the heat of frustration, it may be tempting to rub employees' noses in their mistakes. I used to do just that. It should be obvious, but there's a whiff of sadism in shaming somebody who is already beating herself up. Besides, morale and confidence spiral downward when the boss chews you out, especially if it's done in a mean-spirited way. Enlightened executives pose thoughtful questions until the light of understanding flicks on. Here's how to use question-based coaching to convert a miscue into a teachable moment:

You: So, John, how'd you feel when you heard we lost that order because the form was filled out wrong?

Employee: Pretty lousy.

You: Yeah, it's tough. This has happened before, hasn't it?

Employee: Yeah, a few weeks ago.

You: What happened then?

Employee: I dunno. I guess I was just rushing and got a little careless.

You: Same thing this time?

Employee: I guess so.

You: Well, let's look at this a minute. If you find yourself rushing again, what will you do differently?

Employee: I guess I'd tell myself to slow down and get every detail right because one wrong digit can really screw things up.

You: Yeah, your job demands dotting all the i's and crossing all the t's, doesn't it? Do me a favor and grade yourself on attention to detail.

Employee: Probably C-minus.

You: Okay, that's honest. And where would you put your desire to get better? Low, medium, high?

Employee: High, definitely high.

You: That's what I was hoping. Now, are you willing to put in the effort to upgrade your skills and get organized?

Employee: Absolutely.

You: Excellent. Let's put our heads together on an action plan to make it happen.

Partnering with an employee creates solutions both parties own, as opposed to one side feeling lectured to. Partnering takes a little extra time but it preserves dignity and helps lessons sink in. And when employees use their own noggins to find solutions, they're more likely to execute them with gusto. It's human nature. People *want* to expand their capacities. They *want* those "Aha!" moments.

Of course, sometimes action speaks for itself. The story goes that Thomas Edison and his crew worked twenty-four hours straight to complete the first working light bulb. Exhausted, Edison placed the precious orb in the hands of his young assistant to carry upstairs. The nervous boy was shaking so badly that he dropped the bulb on the way up. The team spent another twenty-four hours making a second bulb. Come time to carry it upstairs, Edison smiled and again handed it to the boy. Confidence restored, the kid ferried the bulb upstairs without incident. The simple gesture earned Edison the boy's loyalty for a lifetime.

13 **Be tough, not rough.** One day a shipment of high-performance tires arrived at one of our stores instead of its true destination—our chief competitor. Dave, the manager, quietly accepted delivery, only to be busted later during a routine audit. Pressed for details, Dave confessed that Jerry, his district manager, advised him to hang on to the $700 tires. I happened to be visiting my mother in Indiana, and was patched into a hastily called teleconference. Deliberations were rough. My heads of HR and loss prevention urged termination for both Dave and Jerry. It was as if they had broken into a rival's shop and stolen the tires, they reasoned. Two other execs argued for suspension because Dave and Jerry had clean records and years of exceptional customer service.

I broke in with a challenge: "I want the person who's never accepted too much change at the bank or grocery store to speak up, please." Silence. "Is what they did wrong?" I asked. "Absolutely. Should there be consequences? Of course. But it *isn't* just like breaking into another company's store. And don't tell me this is worth trashing the careers of two decent men. That's overreacting. Who among us has never needed a second chance?" We returned the tires to UPS and slapped Dave and Jerry with two-week suspensions. Both men literally broke down when they learned we had spared their jobs. My management team also learned a lesson—big decisions that impact the lives of our people ought not be made in the heat of the moment.

14 **Slip on those moccasins.** A few months after launching the company, we moved our "headquarters" out of the back room of a gas station and into a small suburban office building. Cash was tight, so I persuaded the building owner to let me install a vending machine in the community break room to help defray rent. I filled the machine with granola bars, nuts, and fruit, expecting to rake in about half the rent. It soon became clear that I was the only one dropping in coins. Puzzled, I asked the other tenants if they knew about the vending machine. Sure, they said, but it wasn't stocked with anything decent like Snickers, Hershey bars, or chips. Click. On went the light bulb. Wasn't there a touch of arrogance to my assumption that, if I wanted healthy snacks, everybody else did, too? Gee, what a concept—*not everybody thought like I did*. My "me-ism" and lack of empathy were grimly comical.

15 **Huddle up.** We were getting ready for the grand opening of our first store in Minneapolis' bohemian Uptown district. Flanked by a couple of key execs and the store manager, I saw an opportunity. "Hey, everybody," I said, "let's huddle up on the marketing plan." Gathered around a stack of tires, we ping-ponged ideas over the suggestion net. In twenty minutes we produced a grassroots marketing campaign complete with a dozen action steps.

Seize opportunities for spur-of-the-moment brainstorming. When I was talking to a store sales team about a big issue, I'd often call a timeout and pull in the mechanics. Everyone stopped work for fifteen minutes to hash things out, then returned to work energized because they had a chance to weigh in on a big decision. Huddle up on everything from marketing and operational issues to personnel conflicts and general malaise, or simply to communicate need-to-know info. If I sensed tension in a department, for instance, I didn't hesitate to pull everyone together and ask what was going on. Often, all it takes to reverse negative momentum is a forum for people to speak their mind. Caveat: a brainstorming huddle only works if you're truly seeking input, not simply validation for decisions already made.

16 **Respond rapidly.** Back in the day, whenever a subordinate asked me to do something—review a draft, powwow over a big issue—my reflex was the same: *Hey, I'll get back to you when I feel like it, pal. I'm the one who calls the shots around here.* Inevitably, deadlines came and went and I got mad. I'd ask people where their reports were, and they'd explain that they were still waiting for info from me. It took awhile but the message finally sank in. First, these were things I had asked them to do. Second, it's intimidating to ask the boss for something more than once. Last, the faster I got things back to people, the faster things got done. *Man*, I thought, *whenever somebody needs something from me from now on, I'll hit the ball back into their court ASAP.* It was as if I had rolled a huge boulder out of the road to allow traffic to pass. I, of course, had been the boulder.

17 **Make amends.** During an executive committee meeting, Neil offered a suggestion I didn't think much of. I was in a foul mood and jumped all over him. It was not one of my best moments. When I returned to my desk, the devil on my right shoulder urged me to forget it. "So you were a little rough on him," he said. "You sign his paychecks. He'll get over it." But the angel on my left shoulder wouldn't let it go. "That was inexcusable," she whispered. "How would you feel if you were treated that way? Go to his office and apologize." Gulping down a big slice of humble pie, I coached myself on the danger of letting my ego—the size of a championship watermelon—get the better of me. I had to pry myself out of my chair; my legs felt weighted down with lead. Swallowing hard, I knocked on Neil's door. "Neil," I said, "I am really sorry for the way I embarrassed you. It was inappropriate, and I promise it won't happen again." Fortunately, Neil accepted my apology.

For some reason, the words "I'm sorry" are kryptonite to leaders. But they're also two of the most powerful words in the leadership lexicon. They're a tonic for employees who feel wronged and cling fiercely to their resentment. Only a heartfelt apology can cleanse the hurt and repair the relationship. We all make mistakes, but not owning up to them ranks among the biggest mistakes of all.

18 **Don't play favorites.** Signing John Leach to a consulting contract was like the New York Yankees signing A-Rod. John was an all-star with great instincts in the field and a mind that saw the game from thirty thousand feet. He had been head of Western Auto Supply Company, a division of Sears that owned Tire America and NTW, two of the country's largest tire chains. Soon after John began attending executive committee meetings, however, two members approached me independently and accused me of knighting John "The Golden Boy." They claimed I valued his advice above theirs. At the next meeting I asked if anyone else felt that way. They all did. I fought off the urge to justify my favoritism. Instead, I bit my tongue and looked through their eyes.

Humbled, I pleaded guilty to the charge of poor leadership. Few things are more deadly for morale than a "star system." Sure, cashing in on the fresh eyes of new teammates is a given. But I overdid it. Listening to one person at the expense of others pains the entire room. Certainly, you can't treat every idea equally. Nor should you suppress enthusiasm for a great one. But find the healthy middle ground. Avoid the appearance of consistently valuing the opinion of one teammate, or outside consultant, at the expense of everybody else.

19 **Express gratitude.** Few things are appreciated like the balm of a heartfelt thank you for a job well done. It's what loyalty is built upon. I thanked my execs with annual birthday notes—like this one to our treasurer, Jim Wolf:

> *Jim, happy birthday. Thanks again for your dedication to our team. Your contribution is very important: lowering interest rates, critical budgets and projections, handling cash, and profit improvement team, among a few biggies. You do all this with a sense of fun as well as discipline and focus—a great combination. Great attitude. Thanks and take care, Tom.*

Little did I know that Jim saved every letter. "A handwritten note like that," recalled Jim, "with specifics about my performance, told me Tom really took the time to think about what he was writing." Eric Randa, our loss-prevention czar, had never worked at a company where the president handwrote letters of appreciation. "It was one of the best pats on the back I ever had in my life," said Eric. "I now do the same thing at my new company. One of my managers just told me it meant the world to him to read the kind words I had written." The difference between thanking people and taking them for granted is only a minute or two. Go out of your way to let people know you value their work, and you'll soon be fielding an all-star team.

20 **Congratulate publicly.** Wayne Shimer, a sixteen-year colleague, never complained, never got defensive—he just rolled up his sleeves and blasted away. To Wayne, a job well done was its own reward. In 1992, a grueling but rewarding year, I started handing out a Most Valuable Player Award at our annual convention. It gained instant Oscar-like stature in our little tire universe. I had been riding Wayne hard all year but we had made a good profit, and I bestowed the inaugural award on him. "Out of the blue," recalled Wayne, "in front of five hundred people, Tom calls me up and gives me this award. I couldn't even talk afterwards I was so emotional."

Wayne may have been surprised by his reaction but I wasn't. People crave recognition, not only for results but also for their ideas. Applaud their efforts (literally when possible) every chance you get—in team meetings, informal settings, group e-mails, and news-letters. When Scott McPhee, our retail operations chief, suggested we create a "head of automotive services," I never let him forget it. Years later, I was bragging on Scott's RBI (Really Big Idea) to anybody who worked with him. "You're the man, Scott!" I'd say, turning to the others. "Do you know how much money this guy made for us?" Sure, people may turn beet red when you pour on the praise, but don't be fooled for a second. They can't get enough of it.

PART II

GETTING PERSONAL

When Personal Issues Affect Personnel

Joe was half human, half cyborg. The guy was a rock, a street-smart, twenty-year veteran with a friendly smile who ran his Tires Plus store in Iowa by the book. Sales were always near the top of the charts. So I was more than a little puzzled when I saw his numbers plummet over the course of three consecutive months. When complaints from customers and employees began rolling in, I knew we had a serious mystery on our hands. I scheduled a quick trip south and set aside a little extra time for his district manager and me to take Joe to dinner. Joe was wary. By the time the appetizers arrived, however, he had let his guard down and confessed he was in the midst of a messy divorce. No wonder he could barely function at work; he was distracted, disoriented, and depressed.

No stranger to a painful breakup, I asked him what he was doing to take care of himself. Nothing, he said, he was just trying to tough it out. Joe was a man's man, a real blue-collar guy who viewed asking for help as a sign of weakness. I asked if he cared to hear how I got through a similar rough patch. He nodded, so I told him how counseling had helped. I recommended he consider it. He was skeptical, but recognized what was at stake. He promised he'd think about it. Joe's next two monthly store reports showed him moving in the right direction. The month after that looked even better. A few months later, he called and told me about the "shrink" he was seeing. "Wow," he said, "that's powerful stuff." He went on and on about how much he appreciated my feedback, and promised he wouldn't cause me any more fitful trips to Iowa. He was a man of his word.

It always astonishes me that business leaders can look the other way when an employee's personal life interferes with his performance. Even worse is barking out orders like, "Get your act together or heads are gonna roll!" It calls to mind clueless Americans abroad who assume that the louder they speak the better the natives will understand.

Dysfunctional behavior is a deadly serious business issue, yet it's rarely dealt with. The consequences are staggering, both in the emotional toll leveled against brittle employees and in cold, hard cash. Mind/body research performed in the last decade has proven conclusively that, without intervention, emotional or psychological turmoil can weaken the body's immune system and lead to physical illness. The upshot? More absenteeism, a productivity plunge, rising health insurance costs, and high turnover.

As the old proverb goes, "For want of a nail the kingdom was lost." Likewise, one employee's personal problems can set in motion a chain of events that could threaten the health of an entire organization. It's your responsibility to smash the snowball of employee personal problems before it begins rolling down the hill of neglect and picking up speed. Act wisely early or prepare to be bowled over.

FIFTEEN

BAGGAGE CHECK

Dealing with Dysfunctional Behavior

Joe's struggle over the last two pages illustrates a crucial point. Whether it's marital crisis, illness in the family, or demons dragged around since childhood, everyone's personal baggage spills out at the office. Does that mean you have to be an amateur psychologist? Maybe. Let's revisit the definition of enlightened executive: *A tough-minded, warm-hearted, systems-disciplined leader who inspires people to actively embody the organization's mission, vision, and values.*

By my lights, it's impossible to be a master motivator without a minimal understanding of what makes people tick. All leaders would do well to learn the basic tools psychologists use to help clients work through problems. What I gained through self-study has made all the difference. After all, I wasn't blessed from birth with the skills to recognize warning signs in the next guy, or to follow up with open-ended questions, or to coach him toward a healthier attitude and lifestyle.

Why is a chapter that's basically about psychological health in a business guide? Because the most troubling and potentially dangerous challenges in the workplace aren't caused by knowledge gaps. They're caused by behavior. There isn't an honest person alive who hasn't unconsciously indulged in mind games at one time or another—control freaking, defensiveness, intimidation, workaholism, sabotaging, perfectionism, procrastination, displaced anger, victimology. Take a second to study this list. They're games being played *right now* by your employees, many of whom feel perfectly justified in playing hardball.

Consider asking key employees to take a standardized psychological test (consult first with a corporate attorney). Tests like the Myers-Briggs Type Indicator or Riso-Hudson Enneagram Type Indicator can help you interact more effectively with various personality types. As your grasp of interpersonal dynamics grows, these tests become less important.

I can't overstate it—it's incumbent upon leaders to compassionately confront workers who are underperforming and over-annoying. You do it not just because you're concerned about their welfare but also, frankly, because doing nothing incurs enormous costs. Every flare-up by a drama king or queen dents productivity and peace of mind.

You'll find that employees are often relieved to tell you why they've been acting up. More often than not, as in Joe's case, it doesn't demand heavy lifting from you—just a question or two here, a suggestion or insight there. When you finally penetrate a dysfunction barricade and make caring contact with the human being on the other side, you help an employee find confidence and courage. You also strengthen your professional relationship.

Occasionally you get lucky, and a few minutes of probing sweeps away years of secrecy and shame. After a few frustrating encounters with Mike, one of my mid-level managers, I suspected he was playing dumb about a key issue he should have been fully aware of. During our next one-on-one, when he feigned ignorance about an important detail, I quizzed him, gently but persistently, until he boxed himself into a corner. With tears running down his cheeks, he confessed he had been lying. "I'm sorry to break down," he said. "Mike," I said, "this isn't a breakdown, it's a breakthrough. Congratulations."

After composing himself, Mike explained that he was raised by a cold-hearted father. Whenever Mike did something wrong, his father relentlessly interrogated him until he extracted every last humiliating detail. Then Mike was punished mercilessly. His survival instinct quickly taught him that lying was a good form of protection. I assured Mike that this was a safe place, and he could feel free to talk about anything without fear of reprisal. The look of relief and gratitude on his face was a joy to behold.

One extreme, but effective, method I've used with employees is the Two Chair Technique. I don't know anything better for clearing the clouds on pressing personal or professional storms. One afternoon, one of my v.p.'s was depressed and questioning his value as an employee and human being. "Mark," I said, "you're such a hard worker and you do so many things right. Now, this may sound strange, but if you're willing to have a conversation with yourself and also look at things from a positive perspective, we can try something I learned from my therapist. It helped me bounce back when I was thinking like you are now."

With a look of both alarm and amusement, Mark shrugged. "Sure," he said, "what the heck." I arranged two chairs facing one another—a "negative" one and a "positive" one. He chose the negative chair, of course. Now, I said, imagine you're also seated in the positive chair. I told him to make the case to his other, positive, self that he was a failure. Given his mood, that wasn't difficult. He said things like, "You're bad news, Mark. You keep on screwing up. What's the point of even trying anymore?" Then I asked him to change chairs and respond to what Mark in the negative chair had just said. Addressing the negative chair, Mark pointed out all his positive qualities and all the great things he'd done. It wasn't exactly trial-lawyer quality, but it was a convincing argument. Fifteen minutes later, Mark felt energized after realizing he was a good guy after all. Over the following months, Mark confided that the Two Chair Technique had also helped him resolve some personal problems. Last I checked, he was still reaping the benefits.

SIXTEEN

RULES OF ENGAGEMENT

Connecting Personally with Employees

Don't hesitate to speak up, whether an employee is fighting with a colleague, struggling with a personal issue, or just in a funk. "How ya' feeling these days, Jenny? You sure? Feels like something's not quite right." When she acknowledges she's not on top of her game, try a little commiseration: "Yeah, we all have days like that. Any way I can help? Anything you're comfortable talking about?" Granted, some people won't budge when it comes to revealing their inner lives. That's okay. Don't force it. You'll find that a lot of people *will* tell you what's on their mind, as long as you follow these tips.

Earn trust. People will open up if they sense they can trust you. They need to know you care, and that the personal information they're sharing won't come back to them from another source. Establishing that trust begins today—right now—through respectful interaction. That way, when an issue does bubble up, an employee will trust that his secret will be safe with you. As former Secretary of State Colin Powell observed:

> *The day people stop bringing you their problems*
> *is the day you stopped leading them.*

Stop, drop, and listen. When an employee needs to talk, stop thinking about business, drop what you're doing, and give him your full attention. Reading the words of Brad Burley, one of our regional managers, brought tears to my eyes. Brad's three-year-old daughter had been having earaches and developmental problems that stumped her doctors. Touring the stores one day, I asked Brad how she was doing. "Normally, Tom was very focused on business while we were driving around," recalled Brad. "But I bet he spent an hour and a half with me sitting in a store parking lot talking about alternative medicine options and giving me the names of doctors who may be able to help. He even told me that if I couldn't get in to see them, to call him and he'd help me get an appointment." Brad and his wife tried a few dietary changes I suggested and noticed some progress. Eventually, their daughter's ears healed and her health improved. "That was pretty powerful," said Brad. "You know, for a leader to spend that much time talking about one of my kids, well, it was an impression that will last the rest of my life. Tom wasn't a perfect person, but I think of him like one of my big brothers. I feel like I can open up to him about anything. I just miss being around the guy."

Be humble. Joe's story a few pages back showed that employees respond better to an empathetic leader than to an imperious autocrat looking down his nose as if to say, *Do what I say because I'm more successful than you.* Sharing my vulnerabilities with Joe by telling him how therapy helped me deal with my own painful divorce bridged the boss/employee gap and enabled us to forge a deeper connection. Imagine if I had allowed my ego to maintain the distance between us and had simply told him to go see a therapist. I doubt Joe would be lighting up the charts in Iowa today.

Eliminate barriers. Step out from behind your big, imposing, all-hail-the-boss desk and sit toe-to-toe with employees as equals. If you have two extra chairs in your office, that'll do. Or stake out neutral territory—perhaps an empty conference room or cafeteria table.

Get permission. The introduction of personal issues into a workplace discussion requires—unequivocally—the employee's consent. How to get it? Recap the underlying performance issue, then empathize: "Any roadblocks preventing you from doing the great work we both know you're capable of?" "Are you comfortable sharing whatever's affecting your performance?" "I'm sensing there's a deeper issue at work here. How do you feel about discussing it?" My batting average was about .800. That's a far cry better than .000, which is what you'll be looking at if you don't ask how you can help.

Step back. It's admirable to want to help employees work through difficult issues. But remember, you're their coach, not their best friend. Be caring, be authentic, but be sure to keep a professional distance.

Stay objective. If you've struggled with a similar issue, don't assume your fix is universal or that your recovery timetable is relevant. Sure, your experiences are good points of reference. But recognize that the circumstances and rhythms of your employee's life created a very different animal. Proceed with caution. Be patient. And be open to their point of view.

Walk the talk. It's one thing to assure people they can tell you anything; to tell them you'll respond with understanding; to tell them you'll help them work things out and regain their footing. But you cripple your credibility if you respond in a way that puts the lie to your assurances. You can't be judgmental, you can't be condescending, you can't trivialize their concerns. Breach that trust *even once* and it'll be served up as the main course by the gossip gourmets in the office for weeks to come.

Do right by your teammate. Your goal as coach is to maximize each employee's value. To do that, never lose sight of the fact that her well-being takes precedence over her work responsibilities. Heresy? Only to a boss running the shop by the seat of his pants. Putting the health and happiness of employees first unquestionably benefits an organization in ways both measurable and intangible.

Be ready with outside resources. Sometimes you have to call in the professional. The time will come when the issue is over your head—chemical dependency, anger management, clinical depression, marital strife, physical abuse. The first step is to subscribe to an EAP (employee assistance program), a phone bank staffed by trained counselors. But don't stop there. Compile a list of programs, support groups, and organizations whose mission is to help people who are severely stressed out or consumed by a full-blown crisis. Post the list in the office (on your intranet or bulletin board) and remind people it's there. Encouraging your staff to consider outside help adds credibility to those options and may take the edge off their shame. Remember, troubled employees don't always know which way to turn. Pointing them in the right direction might be a lifesaver.

PART III

NO SHORTCUTS ALLOWED

Gaining the Ethical Advantage

Unethical behavior is the seductive narcotic of corporate America. It can produce a quick high, but it inevitably—and insidiously—rots the tapestry of your life's work. You feel invincible until that hopeless, horrifying day when your reputation and aspirations unravel before your eyes. It begins with that first puff. Pocket a few pens from the supply room here. Slide personal mail through the postage meter there. It's easy to rationalize minor transgressions—"Nobody will notice. It's just a few bucks. They don't pay me enough anyway."

But a tiny crack in the glass gradually expands until it threatens the integrity of the entire windshield. That is, one dishonest action, no matter how slight, can compromise our sense of right and wrong and leave us vulnerable to the allure of more dangerous temptations. Especially when we're under pressure to make those high mortgage payments, to get our kids into the best schools, and to own a luxury car befitting our standing in the community.

We never intended to cross the line. But that's what we do when we cut corners on quality to save a few cents per unit. Or when we dodge environmental regulations. Or cook the books. Smart business decisions, we tell ourselves. Before we know it, security is escorting us out of the building. Or, worse, we trade in pinstripes for prison orange. Feel yourself edging up to a slippery slope? Take an ethics check. Ask yourself how you'd feel if your behavior was broadcast on the local news. Would you make the same decision if your family were standing at your side? Some may consider this litmus test naïve and overly simplistic. They'll argue that situational ethics are too complex to be boiled down to such shirtsleeves decision making. I disagree.

Enlightened corporate responsibility demands that business leaders recognize a common interest other than their own self-interest. In 1776, the American Revolution coincided with the publication of Adam Smith's *Wealth of Nations*, which revolutionized economic theory. The Scottish philosopher and economist theorized that the "invisible hand" of the market transmutes the individual pursuit of self-interest into a public benefit. One hundred ninety-nine years later in Switzerland, the Caux Round Table took a more practical view. In recognition of the complexities of the modern world, this annual gathering of business leaders from Europe (Alfredo Ambrosetti, chairman of the Ambrosetti Group), Japan (Ryuzaburo Kaku, chairman of Canon), and the United States (Winston Wallin, chairman of Medtronic) endorsed a set of ethical practices. These seven Principles for Business are rooted in the western ideal of respect for human dignity and the Japanese ideal of *kyosei*, which asserts that human beings should strive to live and work together in harmony for the common good. In other words, self-interest alone doesn't cut it.

Don't get me wrong; I'm a staunch defender of economic and intellectual liberty. I agree with philosopher Ayn Rand that a free mind and a free market go hand in glove. But as the implosions of Enron, WorldCom, and Tyco clearly illustrate, our capitalist system is riddled with loopholes easily exploited by unscrupulous pros. The rash of corporate scandals in the early 2000s angered large swaths of America, to say nothing of the millions of ethical businesspeople who felt tainted by association. It's incumbent upon each of us to act, at all times and in all ways, ethically, responsibly, and with the common good in mind. A heroic effort is required to earn back the respect of employees, the confidence of shareholders, and the trust of the public. I'm confident we can answer the call.

SEVENTEEN
TRUTH OR CONSEQUENCES
Pitfalls of Unethical Behavior

Like narcotics, unethical behavior can have lethal side effects. Three to consider:

1 You're being watched. Think again if you believe the people who report to you aren't watching your every move. Not only is every eye on you, you're expected to meet an extraordinarily high standard of conduct. One slip and you're instant fodder for the gossip mill. But that's not the worst of it. Employees model their leaders like children model their parents. Swipe a few pads of Post-it™ notes and people will interpret that as open season on the supply cabinet. I gave my assistant Dorie an ongoing kitty of $100 or so to pay for my personal expenses—snacks, postage, whatever. I obeyed every rule set for employees and received the same discount on tires and car repairs as everyone else.

2 You'll know it. Maybe you can convince yourself that a dubious decision is justified. But deep down, where the best part of you lives, you'll know better. *New York Times* columnist William Safire nailed it:

> *The right to do something does not mean
> that doing it is right.*

Take the time my company car's lease expired. I upgraded to a more expensive model. Profits were below expectations that year and the entire company was in belt-tightening mode. Even if nobody so much as raised an eyebrow, it didn't feel right to force the company to take the hit for my new higher car payment. So I asked human resources to take the extra $300 out of my paycheck each month. Every year I also asked HR to compare my compensation against our CPA firm's national CEO market survey to ensure we were in line.

Those times I did compromise my conscience cost me, often in subtle ways—not being fully present around others; sensing that peace of mind was just beyond my grasp; wondering why that lump in the pit of my stomach wouldn't go away; not allowing myself to fully appreciate successes; sleeping poorly. The result? Polluted thinking and impaired decisions.

Feeling guilty about past decisions? You're not alone. To the extent you can, forgive yourself for past errors. Tell yourself you know better now and resolve not to make the same mistake again. Tomorrow is a new day with new opportunities to act honorably. You already know that doing what's right for the sake of doing what's right is deeply rewarding. So take the high road. There's less traffic there.

3 **You're gambling with your good name.** When news broke that Arthur Andersen shredded Enron documents and committed other crimes and misdemeanors, the "Big Six" accounting firm's sterling reputation was forever tarnished. Not so long ago, the overnight collapse of a mighty global corporation was unimaginable. Now, there are days when the business section of the newspaper reads like a rap sheet.

We live in a transparent age. Corporations have glass walls. Disgruntled employees can e-mail incriminating documents around the world faster than you can say, *Not guilty, your honor.* If you bend the rules even once, you're asking for trouble. Same goes for your personal life. After the sale of Tires Plus to Bridgestone/Firestone was made public, I received an unsolicited call from a well-known accounting firm we weren't doing business with. They told me I could save several million dollars in taxes on my proceeds from the sale by setting up an offshore account. But, they added, while the loophole was legally defensible and wasn't likely to ever face a court challenge, it wasn't an option for the faint of heart. Now, I don't like paying a penny more in taxes than I have to. But I do feel good about paying my share in recognition of the opportunities I've been given to earn a good living. So when I hear the word "loophole" or "offshore," I walk the other way. I've worked too hard for too long to run the risk of staining my reputation. It's not a question of faint-heartedness, it's a matter of right-heartedness. The dollar amount was irrelevant. You can't put a price tag on a good night's sleep.

EIGHTEEN

ACCOUNTABLE ETHICS

The Three Pillars of Ethical Leadership

Compelling evidence points to a direct link between ethical leadership and higher profits. So states the Center for Ethical Business Cultures (full disclosure: I'm a board member) in its 2001 study, *The Ethical Advantage: Why Ethical Leadership is Good Business*. Certainly, ethical leadership offers no protection against a badly flawed corporate strategy. But a fundamentally solid organization stands to gain an ethical advantage by developing three traits.

1 **A balance of stakeholder interests.** Enlightened executives recognize that their firm fits into a larger community. Its relationships—with employees, customers, business partners—are intertwined. Doing business in an enlightened social context is both a predictor and a consequence of superior financial performance. A firm generates this virtuous circle when it honors employees, who in turn produce a higher-quality product, which in turn pleases customers so much they stand on a hilltop to direct others to your door.

Whenever our executive team voted on a big issue we first mulled over its effect on our constituencies. Our three-word litmus test— *Is it fair?*—exposed flawed analysis and produced better decisions. When voting on our company insurance programs, for instance, we tried to balance what was best for the company and what was best for the employees.

2 **Leadership integrity.** From the start, Tires Plus stores were upscale, with cappuccino machines, prints on the walls, TV and movies, toys for kids, and shiny, clean floors for them to play on. The industry was tagged as unprofessional, so I wanted to set Tires Plus apart by presenting a clean-cut, professional image. Some team members thought we went too far. An internal survey showed that 60 percent of our sales staff hated wearing white shirts and ties. The issue came to a vote at an executive team meeting. I voted yes. Everyone else voted no. I vetoed the team's decision, one of only a handful of times I overruled everyone.

Enlightened executives tune out the grumbling. They're purpose pleasers, not people pleasers. They're less concerned about who is right than what is right. They base decisions on what's best for all stakeholders. They know that long-term benefits are worth the price of short-term pain.

A leader's primary role is to ensure that all decisions uphold the company's mission, advance its vision, and express its core values. She sets the ethical tone by modeling the West Point cadet prayer:

> *Make us to choose the harder right instead of*
> *the easier wrong, and never to be content with*
> *a half truth when the whole can be won.*

3 **Process integrity.** Process integrity (or institutional integrity) is a reflection of how deeply a company's ethics are ingrained in its core processes. Every element must be held to the same high standard. And people, as well as processes, must be held accountable for results. In an environment like this, employees feel free, and perhaps obligated, to report individual and organizational breaches of conduct. They follow their scruples, even at the cost of profits.

These principles have guided Reell Precision Manufacturing Corporation, a manufacturer of electromechanical components (primarily clutches and hinges), for more than thirty years. When fears of a recession plunged orders and revenue in 2001, Reell executives asked employees to take a temporary pay cut to avoid layoffs. Workers readily accepted the proposal because the dozen senior execs had already stepped up and slashed 16 percent off their own pay. Reell saved half a million dollars—and dozens of jobs.

That's business as usual for the Vadnais Heights, Minnesota, company, which was awarded the 2002 Minnesota Business Ethics Award. Reell's institutional integrity is strengthened by its *teach/ equip/trust* style of management—as opposed to *command/direct/ control.* The results show up on the assembly line. Workers are typically hired with no particular skills, but they learn every stop on the line, from scheduling and assembly to quality checks and failure analysis. Product is shipped only when the line worker signs off—without inspection other than periodic audits.

The goodwill between Reell's management and labor propels the company's virtuous circle. "Turnover is almost zero," said Reell cofounder Bob Wahlstedt. "The most important reason for enriching the production jobs is to benefit the workers—they're happier and more fulfilled. But from the company's standpoint, encouraging and educating employees to develop mastery in their work, and to take pride in it, makes for a consistently better product." Reell's faith in its people and processes produce stratospheric quality achievements. Of the roughly half a million units Reell shipped annually to Xerox, not a single one was rejected during a four-year span.

Times of crisis magnify a firm's ethical advantage. When everyone—employees, customers, business partners—categorically trusts a firm, they're more likely to pitch in to help it weather a storm. Six months after Reell's pay cut, the company restored salaries and returned to profitability.

KEY POINTS: WORK SWEET WORK

Creating an Enlightened Environment

✔ **Culture requires constant nurturing.** Sustaining an energized, team-oriented atmosphere is an ongoing process. It begins with ethical leaders who authentically model the organization's mission, vision, and values. Attention must be paid to people's social, physical, emotional, and motivational needs.

✔ **Honor your people and accommodate their priorities.** Great employees seek fulfillment and flexibility. They expect to be held accountable. They welcome challenging and meaningful work. They put family first. And they hate being micromanaged.

✔ **Give employees opportunities to be healthier and happier.** Establish a wellness program and encourage camaraderie through humility, humor, and occasional diversions. The better you take care of your people, the better they'll take care of business.

✔ **Mold individual egos into a team ego.** There's nothing so heady as being on a winning team. Use formal and informal channels to communicate that long-term success depends on harmony with co-workers. More importantly, lead by example.

✔ **Apply the twenty laws of cultural leadership.** Great leaders are born—and made. Seat-of-the-pants bosses can begin improving their leadership skills today by putting these essential laws—practice the accordion, huddle up, respond rapidly—into practice.

KEY POINTS: GETTING PERSONAL

When Personal Issues Affect Personnel

✔ **Realize that personal issues spill into the workplace.** People are human beings first and employees second. That means nobody sails through life without the occasional crisis that impairs their performance. Recognize warning signs so you can direct people to appropriate resources.

✔ **Be more concerned with dysfunctional behavior than with general competence.** Skills can be upgraded with modest investments of time and effort. But unhealthy behavior that goes unchallenged insidiously threatens morale and productivity.

✔ **Don't hesitate to ask if everything is all right.** Keep in mind that people who act dysfunctionally believe they're justified in doing so. Consequently, many are receptive to probing. Others, however, force a smile and deny that anything's amiss. That's okay, you're not a miracle worker. All you can do is coach people who are open to it and keep a compassionate eye on those who aren't.

KEY POINTS: **NO SHORTCUTS ALLOWED**

Gaining the Ethical Advantage

✔ *Honesty is an all-or-nothing proposition.* No matter how it's justified, a single unethical act may ultimately collapse the house of a good name. Ask yourself if you would make the same decision if the details made the local paper.

✔ *Enlightened executives base decisions on more than self-interest.* Healthy pursuit of self-interest often leads to parallel public benefit. But, as the Enron and WorldCom scandals demonstrate, lax ethical principles and social concerns can topple corporate giants, ruin lives, and cause enormous economic damage.

✔ *Ethical leadership and sound business practices increase profits.* A company gains an ethical advantage, which translates into a competitive advantage, when it demands integrity from its leaders, processes, and stakeholder relationships.

IV.
PITCH-PERFECT
PROCESSES

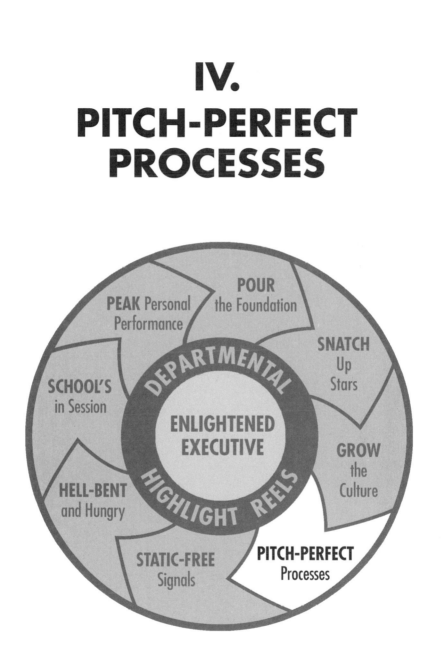

PART I

ALL SYSTEMS GO

Building a Systems-Disciplined Organization

Imagine you're at the Kentucky Derby, the Run for the Roses, the Super Bowl of horse racing. Betting is brisk. The horses are champing at the bit for the electronic gates to fling open. The jockeys position their steeds. The flag goes up, the bell sounds, and the gates—stay closed. The jockeys curse, the horses bray, and track officials scramble. Propriety unravels as minutes tick by. The crowd's grumble swells into a roar. It's an unbridled nightmare.

You can be a walking billboard for your company's mission, vision, and values. You can have a stable stocked with talented, motivated thoroughbreds. You can take pride in your enlightened, healthy culture. But if you don't have the right systems in place, nobody's going to be galloping anytime soon.

Quality guru W. Edwards Deming declared that 80 percent of all errors are systems errors. While Deming was referring chiefly to manufacturing processes, the essence of his statement is applicable to any system. Even if that percentage was halved, it's clear that developing sophisticated, user-friendly processes—for everything from strategic plans to meeting management to monitoring employee goal attainment to phone etiquette—can help you blow past your competitors. Structural integrity makes it easier to

- define roles, responsibilities, and relationships;
- coordinate, communicate, and decision-make;
- allocate and deploy resources;
- convert strategy into reality;
- respond to change;
- develop employees;
- provide stability.

A structural linchpin of any size business is the "org chart." Keep it current and visible so everyone knows who does what and who reports to whom. Even if everybody in a small firm wears three hats, the org chart still lets everyone know how their piece of the puzzle fits into the big picture. The flatter the org chart—meaning more people reporting directly to you—the better. The more levels between you and department heads—and between you and your customers—the more communication snafus you can expect in both directions. For instance, CEOs often have IT (Information Technology) and human resources—functions critical to overall success—report to the CFO. That lack of direct contact makes it more difficult to stay dialed in to front-page issues. Don't worry, having more report-tos won't be a drain on your time, *if* you're doing everything else right, like hiring the right people, empowering them, and regularly meeting one-on-one. (While an org chart is the official power grid, it's just as important to know who wields the unofficial clout. For instance, a CEO's executive assistant often has more influence than some high-level execs.)

Without a framework of precise processes, any organization—corporation, government, nonprofit—is doomed to mediocrity and chaos. A taut system is like a trampoline—it keeps you bounding forward. Slip up, it lets you bounce right back. Yet, relying heavily on processes is a leap of faith for creative, right-brained leaders who view well-defined systems as ingenuity-squelching bureaucracies.

The challenge is to find the sweet spot between too much and too little bureaucracy. Large corporations tend to be top-heavy with regulations while small businesses often run by the seat of their pants. It's easy to see why. Many entrepreneurs start their own businesses because they feel suffocated by bulky bureaucracies. But they tend to overcompensate by going from too many rules to too few. That's why inefficiency and waste are common causes of death for small businesses.

Just make sure employees focus on all the options and freedom within your structural parameters rather than on what's not allowed. A long list of don't do's—accompanied by incessant harping—can stifle creativity. Worse, fixing attention on what not to do can bring about the very result you're trying to avoid. Karl Wallenda, founder of the Great Wallendas, a daredevil circus troupe famous for performing death-defying feats without a safety net, inadvertently illustrated this truth on March 22, 1978. At the age of seventy-three, he attempted to "walk the wire" between two hotels in San Juan, Puerto Rico. His widow said afterward that, for the first time in his life, her husband had "put all his energies into not falling rather than walking the tightrope."

NINETEEN

THE BEST NEVER REST

Continuous Process Improvement

Success has many fathers, as the saying goes. One sire to my company's exponential growth was our obsession with improving the way we did things. We were fanatical about identifying roadblocks, unearthing errors, and fine-tuning systems. Part of our crusade was benchmarking what the highfliers did; one way we did that was an occasional intel-gathering field trip. For instance, we once chartered a twin-prop plane for our regional managers, Wayne Shimer, and me to investigate a top national chain's Omaha locations (those were its stores nearest us). The company had a great reputation and did a lot of things right—and they were about to invade our most lucrative market. We split into three teams, rented cars, and went shopping. We got oil changes at every store and watched their M.O. "While we waited," recalled Wayne, "I'd say to the manager, 'That looks like a great computer system. How does it work?' And he'd explain the whole thing in detail." We flew home fat with process improvements that we immediately clicked into place, like installing windows between the bays and the lobby so customers could watch the progress on their cars. "Looking back," said Wayne, "the cost and the time to load us all onto a charter and fly us back and forth to Omaha, I mean, that's crazy. Or is it? It takes a lot of passion and drive to be the best."

Many big corporations pursue structural precision via Lean Enterprise, a hybrid offspring of TQM (Total Quality Management) and JIT (Just In Time). Essentially, Lean Enterprise integrates quality commitment, waste elimination, and employee involvement within a structured management system. Its primary objective is to perform all functions—from product development and production to sales and customer service—so that actions that don't ultimately create value for the end user are eliminated, and those that do are allowed to flow unimpeded in a continuous value stream. Clearly, Lean Enterprise demands a thorough understanding of customer needs, as does Six Sigma, a rigorous, measurement-based method of eliminating defects in all processes. Six Sigma, conceived by the late Bill Smith, a reliability engineer at Motorola, defines a defect as anything outside of customer specifications. General Electric claims that Six Sigma produced $10 billion in benefits in just five years.

There aren't many companies *saving* $2 billion annually. But you can save plenty on process issues by troubleshooting the disease rather than the symptom. Seat-of-the-pantsers do the exact opposite—they focus on the errors (symptoms) caused by the process (disease). Don't have a formal process improvement strategy? Get in the game by taking these steps.

- ✔ Seek **employee input**. They're in the thick of the action, so every month ask each person, "What's working and what isn't?"

- ✔ Implore employees to **report all errors** as soon as they happen. Welcome mistakes with open arms. Finding and fixing errors prevents major headaches down the road.

- ✔ **Abandon any process** as soon as a better way emerges.

- ✔ Set up a **hotline number.** Some employees aren't comfortable making even the smallest wave. Partner with a loss prevention company to provide a hotline for employees to confidentially offer suggestions and point out problems.

- ✔ Establish **process improvement committees** to hunt bottlenecks in your systems, from machines and materials to communication and training. Do whatever it takes to repair broken links.

- ✔ **Partner with a consultant** specializing in Lean Enterprise, Six Sigma, or some other highly regarded process improvement system.

TWENTY

STRATEGIC SUNRISE

Laying Out the Strategic Plan

We went from contender to champ the day we implemented a strategic planning system. The (drum roll, please) strategic plan is the sun in your systemic solar system. It illuminates the purpose of every proposal, every process, every project. Everything revolves around it. Everything radiates from it. The strategic plan flows into team objectives, which flow into operating plans, which flow into individual goals, which flow into action plans, which, finally, flow into results. "Our strategic plan put us all on the same page," said Jim Bemis, our CFO. "It made everyone accountable and helped us work more cohesively together. Without it, the level of success we achieved would have been unthinkable." It's not too much to say that every choice, every decision, every single action traces back to (drum roll) the strategic plan.

Seat-of-the-pantsers, particularly in smaller organizations, pooh-pooh strategic planning as a waste of time. Markets change too rapidly, they say. It's true—long-term plans are subject to the whim of unexpected events. And strategic planning is conceptual at best when planning out five to seven years. But short-term and mid-range strategic planning are absolute necessities. Certainly you can't plan for every possibility, but failing to methodically look out a year or two can be fatal.

Show me a leader who's resistant to planning and I'll show you a leader who's resistant to change. It's human nature; grooves are safe and comfortable. I can't argue that—except for the "safe" part. But too much comfort dulls the senses. An antelope whose reaction time has slowed is no match for a young lion in hot pursuit. Hey, it's a jungle out there. And every business today lies directly in the path of the river of change; the trick is to flow along with it rather than fight against the current. Anticipate change. Embrace it. Integrate it into the strategic planning process. Twice a month, at executive committee meetings, we had people report in on what was new and different. What new products and services were competitors offering? What did customers want that they didn't want a year ago? What new tipping-point technologies were in play? Don't be caught flatfooted, like New World Pasta. The nation's largest maker of dry pasta products declared Chapter 11 bankruptcy in May 2004, three days after Krispy Kreme Dough-nuts slashed its earnings forecast (two weeks later, the doughnut giant reported its first quarterly net loss—$24.4 million—since it went public four years before). The chief culprit? The low-carb diet craze, which a New World Pasta veep had called "a fad" that would soon fade. Ignore cultural cues and it's your company that will do the fading.

Strategic planning is a straightforward process. Frame it with a searching question: *How can we take advantage of our strengths and opportunities and neutralize our weaknesses and threats?* In other words, fix your eye on your SWOTs (strengths, weaknesses, opportunities, threats), and you'll design the operating plan that's right for you.

Here are the eight steps:

1 **Identify SWOTs.** You need clarity on every issue you're facing. In July (or six months prior to the next fiscal new year), schedule a series of two-hour brainstorming sessions with reps from every group of stakeholders, from department heads and customers to vendors and the rank-and-file. Each group has its own point of view. Collect plenty of observations—macro, micro, and everything in between—about internal strengths and weaknesses and external opportunities and threats. Keep it simple—ask every-one to fill out a single sheet listing the four SWOT categories. Then merge the results into one report.

2 **Set priorities.** Come September, gather the executive committee and other key people for a daylong priority-setting meeting. (The "executive committee" in smaller shops may simply be the owner and her three top people.) First, establish context by summarizing industry trends, competitor activity, last year's performance, and this year's financial forecasts. Next, vigorously debate which issues (gleaned from your SWOT list exercise in step one) deserve priority in the coming year, and which make the list over the next two to four years. (Best use a pencil for anything more than eighteen months out.) Simplify both lists by grouping similar issues under the same macro heading (approve no more than eight macro issues per time period). Now that priorities are set and ranked, assign them to the appropriate leader.

3 **Taskforce it and plan, plan, plan.** Each priority earns its own taskforce, composed of the company's natural subject-matter experts. For the next two months, they research the priority and design an action plan that assigns responsibilities and accountabilities, sets deadlines, allocates resources, and establishes controls.

4 **Present action plans.** Schedule a review meeting (a day or two) in early November that includes the same folks from the early-September gathering. Here, taskforce leaders present their action plans. Each presentation is like a Ph.D. dissertation— it must be defended. That means respectful disagreement is essential. It pushes the taskforce to thoroughly prepare benchmarking protocols, ROI projections, and other necessities.

With the taskforce plans presented, start green-lighting. Some plans will be good to go; others will be modified based on availability of resources. (Plans requiring revision should be redistributed within two weeks.) Of course, each strategic objective is generally multi-departmental—hence the team approach. If the goal, for instance, is to open a dozen new stores, the exec in charge of real estate secures locations and oversees construction. Meanwhile, the CFO arranges financing; the retail operations people groom new store managers;

marketing folks study the markets, develop a plan, and negotiate ad rates; IT analyzes and preps data systems.

Now that action plans are established, incorporate them into the annual grand strategic plan. The strategic plan—ours ran ten pages—has two major sections. It kicks off with the company's mission, vision, and operating values. Fundamental business plan issues follow—product and service offerings, the marketplace and how you'll target it (much of this is carried over year-to-year with minor tweaks). The second section explores the company's SWOTs, and details its action plans. (It may be counterintuitive, but the strategic plan is not a top-secret document. Portions can be an ideal calling card for bankers, vendors, and potential partners.)

5 **Present departmental operating plans.** Now, break each action plan into pieces and parcel them out to the right people. Those employees who have others reporting to them create individual operating plans to execute the pieces assigned to them. Department heads collect these operating plans, approve them, and roll them into departmental operating plans. In December (or the final month of your fiscal year), round up the same group to review and approve these departmental plans. Example: *The accounting plan looks good except we need the financials two days earlier.* Departmental and individual operating plans are then updated.

6 **Budget it.** Start the budgeting process in early November. All four parts of the corporate budget (projected P&L statement, projected monthly cash flows, projected balance sheet, capital expenditure plan) are built off departmental operating plans.

7 **Follow up.** A poorly executed plan isn't worth the spreadsheet it's printed on. Follow-up is critical. After all, enthusiasm can wane. Attention can be diverted. Here are three ways to monitor results:

✔ Six months after approval (and again six months later), convene the executive committee for an operating plan review. Each department head introduces her key reps (from the accounting department, it may be the controller, treasurer, and accounts payable manager) to present progress reports comparing accomplishments to operating plan goals. The presenters, and the department chief, grade their own performance. The group's accomplishments and grades (later factored into employee annual bonus calculations) are open to compliments and challenges. The department head wraps things up with a summary of successes and shortfalls over the last six months as well as expectations for the next six months. Once complete, all but the department head who sits on the executive committee are excused, and another department files in.

✔ Each manager keeps the operating plan humming by meeting one-on-one two to four times a month with everyone who reports to her (chapter 31).

✔ Regular, one- to three-hour executive committee meetings throughout the year—once a week to once a month, depending on team experience and the pace of change (ours was every two weeks)—also keep the strategic plan on track. The agenda typically includes

- mid-month review of P&L, including department-by-department response;

- monthly review of key departmental metrics;

- brainstorming on inter- and intra-departmental challenges;

- round-robin sharing of new ideas or recent successes;

- competitive updates;

- introduction of new enterprise-wide policies and programs.

8 **Team update.** Gather the entire company for a few hours each month or quarter to motivate, inform, celebrate, and educate. Have department heads update people on wins and losses, what needs to be done over the next period, and how the audience can make it happen. Solicit ideas and questions. It's also a good time to salute birthdays, births, and employment anniversaries.

At first blush, the creation and execution of a strategic plan appears as complicated and overwhelming as learning a foreign language. Sure, it takes discipline and hard work—but following these eight steps can deliver you to the promised land. After upgrading our strategic planning, our profits increased tenfold and revenue soared from $40 million to $200 million in just eight years. Coincidence? I think not.

TWENTY-ONE
EXECUTION EQUATION
Making Sure It's Done Right

The best operating plans aren't worth a plugged quarter (even clichés need to keep pace with inflation) without thorough execution. My four-step Execution Equation helps employees hurdle obstacles and pick themselves up when they stumble:

1. Define expectations
2. Inspire
3. Teach
4. Follow up

It's deceptively simple. Let's say an employee blames lack of execution of a piece of her operating plan on colleagues who failed to fill out a form correctly and on time. That calls for a checklist check:

- ✔ First, did she **define the expectation**? Ask if she spelled out what needed to be done and by when. Did she write a clear memo (bullet-point format with key points bolded)? Did the subject line or first sentence clearly convey her key message?

- ✔ Second, did she **inspire**? Ask if she explained why it was important to completely and accurately fill out the form, and why speed was essential.

- ✔ Next, did she **teach**? Ask if she demonstrated how to fill out the form. For more complex issues, did she resort to the Confucius Checklist (chapter 41)?

✔ Last, did she **follow up**? Ask if a system was in place to ensure accuracy and timeliness. If so, does it call for instant feedback for noncompliance?

Did she answer yes to each question? If not, tell her you'll be happy to listen to what somebody else needs to do *after* she's done what she needs to do—execute all four steps. Until then, the ball remains in her court.

TWENTY-TWO

MEETING REQUIREMENTS

Running Tight, Productive Meetings

It's been said that a meeting is an event where minutes are kept and hours are lost. So why have meetings at all? Because of the huge payoff. They leverage your time—you can impart vital information to many key people at once, so everybody sings from the same song sheet. They tap into the power of brainstorming—one plus one can equal three when viewpoints converge. And meetings tamp down turf wars—when a group solves each other's problems, people magically become less turf-conscious. Yet, you'll waste a year of your life in meetings—unless you announce agendas and expectations with a bullhorn. Get tough. Set tight parameters. Otherwise, you'll be listening to disorganized people ramble on deep into the weeds about God-knows-what. Here are my battle-tested protocols to get you in, out, and back to your desk before all the muffins are snatched from the conference table.

READY

- Cancel it. Or, at least, ask yourself whether the meeting truly needs to happen. So many issues can be handled via memo, e-mail, or a quick one-on-one.

- Still gotta do it? Okay, but invite only the A-listers. And make sure you've got a quorum.

- Confirm the meeting room's availability and be darn sure the necessary audio-visual gear will be assembled and working.

- If it's a teleconference or video-conference, confirm timing with the vendor. E-mail the agenda, handouts, and step-by-step access instructions to all participants (noting start time in both your time zone and theirs). Add a note to remind teleconference participants to identify themselves before speaking.

Set

- Prep an agenda that includes time limits for presentations and discussions. Circulate it via e-mail, clearly laying out the meeting's date, time, and place.

- Remind presenters to come armed with handouts that minimize questions and note-taking.

- Appoint a time sheriff to signal you whenever people run long.

- Designate a note-taker to record the action steps produced by agenda items.

Go

- Start on time, to the minute. It enforces promptness. George W. Bush was known to lock the door when he began his meetings. Starting ten minutes late sends people a bad message—that it's okay to mosey on in whenever they feel like it.

- We'd sometimes start with sixty seconds of quiet time to just breathe and relax (some people needed to catch their breath after running to get there on time). It's amazing how this simple exercise can get people grounded and ready to go.

- If it feels natural, go around the table for (very) brief updates on everyone's personal lives. It promotes esprit de corps.

- Devote thirty seconds to the meeting's objective and importance. Don't assume that everyone takes their seat ready to hand over their full attention (even after a breathing exercise). You need to capture the attention of the woman who just finished arguing with her husband. And that guy frantically dousing a departmental fire? You need him, too. A quick pep talk energizes and focuses everyone.

- Quickly review the agenda, then ask for late-breaking additions or deletions.

PICK UP THE PACE

- Firmly, but tactfully, bat away remarks that stray from the meeting's target. Positive comments get the point across without embarrassing anyone: "Sue, that sounds important. Why don't we get that on the agenda for next time?"

- Urge ramblers, even when they're on message, to keep it moving: "Hey, Tony, FYI, we've got five more minutes for this segment. Better finish up so we have time for questions." And if time is running out: "Hey, Tony, great point. Can you bottom-line it?"

- Beware "piling on," the tendency we have to toss in our two cents even if they're wooden coins. Rather than allow everyone to say the same thing in slightly different ways, ask people to call out ditto to signal agreement.

- Deep-six side conversations by looking directly at the talker and injecting his name into what you're saying: "So this solution, Jim, should solve that problem."

- Drawn-out discussions make it hard to wrap up an issue. Bring it to a head by saying, "We've got two minutes. What are our action steps?" If that's not practical, either defer the topic to the next meeting or appoint a committee to explore it. I know, committees have a bad rap. As former House of Commons clerk Sir Barnett

Cocks delicately put it, "A committee is a cul-de-sac down which ideas are lured and then quietly strangled." But when they're quarterbacked with discipline, committees save time and produce results.

STRETCH RUN

- Think high-stakes poker. Hold your cards close and betray nothing with your facial expressions. Why? Play your cards too soon and the pot won't have time to grow. In other words, a leader's opinion influences others' opinions, the mental equivalent of a pile of chips. Keep a poker face and you're more likely to draw out the quiet types and make it hard for the sycophants to parrot your ideas. (Ask a trusted team member to cue you if you're too quick to seize the reins.)

- Get everyone to ante up. Don't let the Silent Sams get through a meeting without contributing. Call on individuals if you sense they're stifling their ideas. Resort to the round-robin technique if too many people are holding back.

- Use secret balloting when serious issues require a vote. When I staked out a position, I found others were sometimes reluctant to openly vote against me. Still, you may occasionally have to trump an outcome by playing the executive-privilege card. In the end, you're the protector of the company's mission, vision, and values.

- Ask open-ended questions. You'll get thoughtful (and often revealing) answers.

- Indulge wisecracks. You're keeper of the tone, and laughing and kibitzing with everyone else keeps it light and fosters strong relationships.

- Stand and stretch every hour or so to keep people invigorated and focused. Allow people to stand if they begin to feel uncomfortable or fatigued.

Finish line

- Close out every issue by defining action steps: "Okay, exactly what are we going to do, who's going to do it, and when are they going to do it?" Skip this critical step and you waste everyone's time. Plus, the next meeting will have a bloated, déjà vu agenda.

- Try putting the meeting "on the couch" every so often for post-game analysis. Ask the group what they liked about the meeting, and if they have any ideas for making the process better.

- Finally, schedule the next meeting.

Cooling down

- As people leave, strike up a conversation with anyone who was straying during the meeting: "Hey, Jim, good distribution idea. But I couldn't help noticing you strayed off the mark a few times. That's not like you. Everything all right?"

- Ask the designated note-taker to e-mail attendees a bulleted action-step summary within twenty-four hours. Succinct bullet points will be read more thoroughly than long paragraphs.

- The note-taker also updates the Meeting Follow-Up Log, a list of items whose progress you want to assess during subsequent meetings.

Tight team meetings generate two powerful side effects. First, you teach participants by example how to efficiently conduct their own staff meetings. Second, you broadcast a message that reverberates through the entire culture: *We value efficiency and teamwork, and we need your help to solve our problems.*

TWENTY-THREE

QUICK FIXES

Helping Individuals and Groups Solve Problems

Blame, shame, panic, pander—enlightened executives don't do any of that to employees or units that miss their marks. Sure, these execs may be frustrated. But they're cooperative and exploratory, not combative and accusatory. They know that a disciplined attitude, tight procedures, and plenty of intellectual elbow grease can make problem-solving more like piecing together a puzzle than pulling teeth.

For instance, say your department's sales report reveals that Bill's in free-fall. When you ask Bill what's up, he points to a deskful of factors beyond his control. "I'm doing everything I can," he insists. "But the deck's been stacked against me for weeks. Business is down all over, man. Those new guys are really underpricing us. And the weather!"

The stage is set for the one-two knockout punch—*external comparison* followed by *internal analysis*. Be direct and upbeat. Express curiosity, not condescension, or you may plant seeds of anger and resentment. "Really?" you might reply. "According to this report, Debbie and Max hit their numbers in the same environment. Let's take a look at how well you're following the system. The plan calls for you to make twelve to fifteen cold calls daily, and I only see a handful of calls on your cold-call sheet. Why is that? By the way, have you notified your customers about the specials we posted? I only see checks by half the names on your log. Sorry, not to belabor the point, but your new-account follow-up matrix only has a few chicken scratches on it. What's up with that? Sure you're doing everything you can?" What can he say? He's cornered, and he knows that you know that he knows. Hopefully, this jolts him out of denial. After he takes responsibility, nudge him with some kind words: "I know you've got what it takes to do a lot better than this, Bill. If you plug back into the program you'll be back on track."

Drawing a distinction: a streamlined system is invaluable for *process problem solving*, but useless for *people problem solving* (chapters 15–16). Dealing with emotions and feelings are beyond the range of precision-guided procedures.

Not all problems can be solved one-on-one. That's why it's important to master my group-coaching process. When I hit the road for store visits it was actually a fun challenge to identify and resolve roadblocks as a group. The process can yield a big harvest wherever you roam in your organization.

The seven steps look like this:

1 **Build rapport.** Learn or confirm everybody's name: "Nice to meet you, Mary, glad you're on the team." "Great to see you again, George, you're looking good." Ask about spouses and kids, and whether anyone's had recent accomplishments or adventures. Genuinely making the effort to connect, one human being to another, builds the bonds of an effective working relationship. The goal here is to get everyone to chill and loosen up. Maybe start with a self-deprecating story and see if you can't coax others to do the same. A lighthearted clubhouse atmosphere teases out the creativity essential to problem solving.

2 **Offer assistance.** Confirm that everyone's getting all the support they need. Somebody's almost always thinking, *How can we take on something new when we can't even get support for what we're doing now?* Maybe one employee isn't receiving an important report on time. Perhaps marketing isn't providing someone else with enough lead time on promotions. Promise you'll check into things and get some answers. Some people hesitate to mention irritants to higher-ups because they don't want to be branded a complainer. But they'll open up if you demonstrate a willingness to diplomatically unplug blocked channels. Later, when you do discuss concerns with the appropriate managers, *do not* name names. If you absolutely must reveal a source, positively frame her suggestion: "Jill had a terrific idea for how we can make this process even better. But I need your help."

3 **Review the numbers.** Ask for stats—revenue, customer satisfaction surveys, ad-response rates—that reflect the group's performance. For instance, I'd ask the store manager for last month's profit-and-loss statement and up-to-the-second key indicators. That info provided valuable, problem-solving context. It's also a reality check to the *Everything is great!* syndrome (phony optimism is a huge red flag).

4 **Compliment and congratulate.** Recognize and praise individual and team successes. Get the applause meter jumping. In exceptional cases, promise to pick up the tab for a team outing. Praising people in front of their peers pumps up the team and sends the message that excellence is expected, appreciated, and rewarded.

5 **Identify roadblocks.** Ask everyone where improvement is most needed and where they see obstacles. In an atmosphere of trust and security, it's amazing how a simple question like "What's going on?" produces all sorts of valuable info. At the first hint of a problem, drill down with "Columbo"-like questions until you hit a gusher. If revenues are lackluster, for instance, find out if basic protocols were followed. In our stores that meant pulling work orders and asking questions: "Were the brakes inspected?" "Was it noted on the inspection sheet?" "Was the customer told?" "Was her response recorded properly?" Remember, the answer to every problem is in that room.

6 **Cast the net again.** Just to be safe, hand out blank sheets of paper and ask everyone to anonymously describe the best things about the unit and its biggest challenges. This always produces eye-openers. If it's a small group, collect the responses and mix them up to preserve anonymity. Then address them one by one, cheering the positive ones and digging into the challenges. For large groups, schedule a follow-up meeting so an assistant can merge/purge the comments and distribute the results. No matter how supportive you are, however, some employees may still hold back, especially if the issue involves singling out a colleague. So wrap up with a reminder that you're always available to discuss sensitive issues one-on-one.

7 Get commitments. It's natural for somebody to be embarrassed when they're identified as a roadblock in front of their teammates. Disarm the situation by warmly pointing out what the person is doing right and framing the matter as a teachable moment: "I'm really glad this came up because it's a great reminder that every single step in our process impacts customer service, store earnings, and, ultimately, your bonuses." Gently ask the employee how he can make things right. If you're satisfied with his answer, agree on a course of action. Then—and this is pivotal—ask for a commitment to make it happen and set a date for a progress report. Finish with a dollop of genuine praise: "Great, John. You're a sharp guy and I know you can do it. We're all cheering for you." You'll get great results, as long as the room doesn't feel like someone's just been offered up as a sacrificial goat.

The magic of candid group sessions can illuminate every angle of a problem. That leads to better decision making and deeper support for your decisions—and for procedures already in place. It was a rare brainstorming session that failed to produce effective solutions. It's like Voltaire said:

> *No problem can withstand the assault of sustained thinking.*

KEY POINTS: ALL SYSTEMS GO

Building a Systems-Disciplined Organization

✔ ***Build a solid framework of internal processes.***
Dedicate yourself to continuous process improvement.
You can embody your company's mission, vision, and
values and be blessed with a talented, motivated staff. But
it takes the right processes to rise above mediocrity.

✔ ***Focus on strategic planning.*** It's the cornerstone
of a proactive, healthy organization. Don't let the
process intimidate you. Strategic planning exploits your
strengths and opportunities and diminishes your weaknesses and threats.

✔ ***Execute in four steps.*** Define expectations, then
inspire, teach, and follow up. The Execution Equation
helps employees avoid obstacles, or get back on track
when they do trip up.

✔ ***Manage your meetings.*** Disorganized meetings waste
time and drain energy. Productive meetings run on tight
pre-meeting preparation and strict protocol.

✔ ***Methodically solve problems.*** When an individual
or department underperforms, don't blame, shame, panic,
or pander. Cooperate and explore, don't fight and accuse.
The right attitude and the right systems turn problem
solving into no problem at all.

V.
STATIC-FREE
SIGNALS

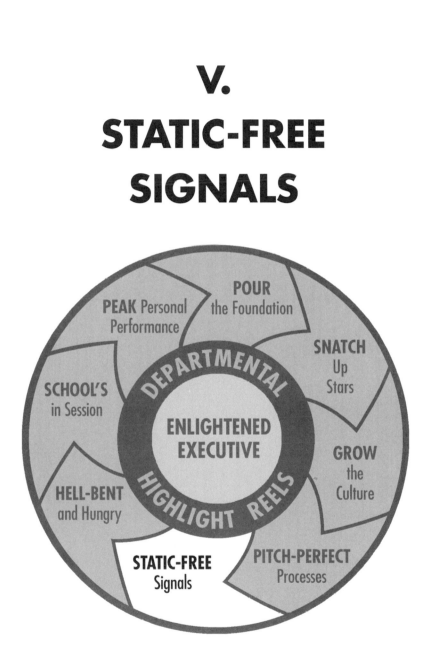

PART I

CAN YOU HEAR ME NOW?

Communicating Effectively

During an orientation session, I'd ask new hires a few simple, if unorthodox, questions: "What percentage of all people say they're in love when they get married? And what percentage of couples divorce?" Their answers were predictable—100 percent are in love; 50 percent divorce. Then I'd ask, "What percentage of all people like their employer on the first day? And how long do people typically stay in a job?" The answers were generally 100 percent, and three years. Heads would start bobbing at the obvious parallels.

Why the disconnect, both at home and at work? "Why do so many of these relationships start off so good and end up so bad?" I would ask. Someone usually volunteered the correct answer: "It's a communication problem." More bobbing heads. "Right," I'd say. "Does anybody here have regrets about the way they communicated—or didn't communicate—in a past job or relationship?" Every hand shot in the air. "Are you ready to break unhealthy patterns and commit to communicating more effectively?" You bet they were.

It's not easy, of course. These unhealthy communication patterns are ingrained in our culture. Our schooling may have taught us to present to a group, but where did we learn the finer points of listening and responding? In business, information flow is hindered by excessive management layers, personal agendas, and clogged communication pipelines. Diversity in the workplace, while a huge plus on most fronts, presents unique challenges— imagine what can be lost or misinterpreted in a simple exchange between two people of different genders, age groups, and socioeconomic and cultural backgrounds. Mix in unprecedented levels of change, stress, and multitasking, and it's no wonder so many workers are so scattered.

Even so, few of us acknowledge—or are even aware of—our communication chinks. I remember seeing a survey showing that 80 percent of all people consider themselves above-average drivers. I suspect just as many people have a blind spot about how well they communicate. This self-awareness deficit is often the difference between operating a business efficiently and running it by the seat of your pants.

TWENTY-FOUR

BUILDING BRIDGES

The Secret to Successful Relationships

Back in 1968, I graduated from Indiana University into the human resources department of Shell Oil Company's midwest regional headquarters in Chicago. At twenty-one years old, it was my job to ensure that proposed salary increases were commensurate with corporate policy. I threw myself into the fray with all the youthful, bullheaded passion of an idyllic, fresh-faced college grad. I kicked up a storm, to put it mildly. After I butted heads with department leaders for a week, my manager, Neal Pettit, was deluged with complaints about me.

Thank God Neal saw the uproar as a teachable moment. He asked me to tag along as he visited a few poodles I had turned into pit bulls. Neal put on a diplomacy clinic. He started with a smile and some small talk, then eased into inquiring about the logic of the raises I had rejected. He listened intently and praised each supervisor's approach. But he didn't hesitate to scratch his head over a few things that didn't track for him. It was a humble, help-me-out-here approach (like Peter Falk's M.O. in the old detective show *Columbo*). Neal patiently worked with each manager to explore options and find solutions. I was amazed at how effortlessly he patched up relationships I had so recklessly trampled over. I wasn't mature enough to fully appreciate and articulate what I was witnessing, but eventually I distilled Neal's approach into the Alphabet Rule:

Always Broach Conflicts with Diplomacy, Empathy, Friendly Gestures, and Humility.

Neal taught me two simple but important lessons. First, it takes great communication skills to build and manage relationships. Second, every single thing you do requires building and managing relationships. After all, it's the quality of your relationships that ultimately determine the effectiveness of your communication, and vice versa. This four-word mantra will enhance both your relationships and your communication skills: *Less egotism, more empathy.*

Egotism and empathy are opposites. They repel each other as surely as like poles of magnets. The more you pour ego into your consciousness, the less room there is for empathy, and vice versa. Unfortunately, our culture rewards big ego a lot more than big empathy. If you could see the thought-bubbles floating through America's cartoonish executive suites many would contain variations of, *The world revolves around me; my needs come first.*

If you're quarreling with colleagues, step back for a moment. Think of yourself as a complex communications network that processes the messages you receive and assembles the messages you send out. Are your lines open and clear, or is the signal distorted by static generated by, say, an oversized ego? If it's the latter, you'll be locked into endless loops of miscommunication and misunderstanding.

TWENTY-FIVE

DO ASK, DO TELL

Avoiding Crossed Wires

My eye-opening lunch with Best Buy's Dick Schulze spurred me to fortify our accountability infrastructure to better define expectations, monitor progress, and measure outcomes—for every single person in the company. Employees old and new responded to this renewed sense of direction with hard, smart work. But keep in mind that purpose and enthusiasm have the shelf life of sushi. Further, the law of diminishing dedication (chapter 8) states that malaise develops when employees aren't regularly educated, inspired, and challenged. Clear communication is the ultimate antidote. That's why I developed the four-step Ask/Tell Technique. It keeps you informed and connected, both with people who report to you and with people to whom you report. More importantly, it's the foundation for one of my bedrock business principles—no surprises. Here's how it works:

Ask: "What are your expectations?" Know each team member's needs, desires, and expectations—both as they relate to their job and their career goals. Do you know what each employee under your watch values most? Is it making more money? A promotion? Meaningful work? Time off for family responsibilities?

Relationships, personal or professional, break down if they're taken for granted, if we focus exclusively on meeting our own needs. In business, this is called "turnover." Don't kid yourself, turnover is always about employees' needs going unmet. Ask your people what they need from you and from the organization, and then do what you can to give it to them.

Tell: "Here are my expectations." Do your people know exactly what's expected of them? If there's a chance you're not on the same page, don't wait till the end of the book to confirm it. Get clear by committing your expectations (whether operating plan-related or task-oriented) to paper and defining how you'll measure their fulfillment. Then ask employees to sign off on them, literally or figuratively. Writing down specifics prevents wires from getting crossed, and builds benchmarks for future reference.

Think that formally defining expectations is overkill? Just the opposite is true—it's liberating for people to know what's expected of them. Done with care, clarifying mutual expectations stokes initiative and leads to professional growth. It also sets the stage for a continual exchange of constructive feedback.

Ask: "How am I doing?" We're imperfect creatures. Daily brush-fires can divert our attention and dilute our commitments. Checking in with others helps us stay on track. But be realistic. Don't expect employees to rattle off opinions when you ask how you've been doing as a leader. Sure, some may respond without reservation. Others will be reluctant, even if a laundry list of gripes is burning a hole in their back pocket—unless you've demonstrated an openness to hearing honest feedback. Even then, you may have to resort to the Rule of Three Technique; generally, we need to ask for feedback three times, digging deeper with each request, before we get honest answers.

If he hesitates, but you can see the wheels turning, resort to the reliable ASU strategy—*Ask and Shut Up.* Just smile and look him in the eye until he's able to express himself. People get an energy boost when they empty the buffer between what's on their mind and what they're hesitant to say. It frees up their psychic energy so they can focus on their work in a more positive, constructive way. A typical exchange:

> **Request One:** Is there anything I could do differently to improve how things work around here?

Response: Uh, no, not really.

Request Two: I really value your opinion, Scott. You're telling me there's *nothing* I need to change?

Response: *(Pause)* No, everything's fine.

Request Three: *(Now get specific.)* C'mon, I bet you can name three things I'm doing right and three things I could do better.

Response: Well, yeah, I guess I could think of something. It's no big deal, but you always seem to have broccoli stuck in your teeth.

Asking about your interfering behavior shows you value his opinions and encourages him to be open and candid. You also benefit, because not asking the question is like swerving your car into the next lane without checking your blind spot. A quick, friendly honk from your people avoids messy pileups.

Tell: "Here's how you're doing." Remember the three cardinal rules of coaching:

1. Mold, don't scold.
2. A spoonful of sugar helps the criticism go down.
3. Leave people feeling empowered, not embittered.

Corrective feedback is more likely to be taken to heart if it's imparted with care and—this is critical—accompanied by kudos. That's to say, shy away from striding up to an employee, brusquely pointing out an error, and warning it had better not happen again. Any short-term productivity gain will be offset by a steady decline into hostility. And for heaven's sake, don't ever reprimand anybody in front of their colleagues. Not only is it demeaning, it leaves employees seething. I don't care how busy or moody you are, it's inexcusable to disrespect people. Call it corporate karma, but if the day comes when you find yourself flailing away in the unforgiving grip of career quicksand, it's the dead weight of all your damaged relationships that will be dragging you down.

The Ask/Tell Technique also helped me monitor how the people who reported to me were dealing with the people who reported to them. Every so often I asked my executive committee to list the names of everyone on their team. Then I asked them to grade each relationship based on four Ask/Tell questions:

1. How well do you understand her needs, desires, and expectations?

2. Do you think she perfectly understands what you expect of her?

3. Is she comfortable letting you know her likes and dislikes?

4. Are you giving her regular feedback?

For grades lower than A, I didn't even bother to ask why. My execs knew the drill. They immediately busted open their planners to schedule meetings with the employees they needed to communicate with better. Nobody knew their people better than Wayne Shimer. He was master of what I called the "inner-view," chatting up employees in the hall, during lunch, or before getting down to business around the conference table. It's nothing more complex than a series of simple inquiries: "What's up with your kids?" "How's your dad feeling?"

Wayne read his people like sports fans read box scores. "Full-time or part-time, sales or mechanic," said Wayne, "I want to know your name, whether you're married, got kids, pets, and anything else I could learn about you. I knew if somebody was ready to quit, and why, long before their manager did." Good inner-viewers don't just go through the motions. People knew I genuinely cared about them. "With just one question, Tom could get people to open up and tell him what was going on in their lives," said Brad Burley, a regional manager. "He always looked you straight in the eye and you could tell he was listening, that he really did want to know. That was the key to Tom's success: caring."

Point the Ask/Tell Technique either up or down the corporate ladder. It also works with external business partners. Best of all, it keeps employees zeroed in and streaking toward their targets like heat-seeking missiles.

TWENTY-SIX

NICE AND CONCISE

Precision Matters

One day our vice president of loss prevention, Eric Randa, dropped off a three-page memo. I scanned it and called him back into my office. "Eric," I said, "this is a great memo but I need you to condense it and make it simpler. In fact, write every memo like it's for the president of a company, someone who has to read a hundred memos a day and doesn't have time to read two pages, let alone three." Eric did exactly that. At the next executive committee meeting, I handed Eric's memo out and said I wanted all memos done in that format—short paragraphs, subheads, crisp writing, *and lots of bullet points*. "Tom called it the 'President Randa format' and everyone had a good laugh," recalled Eric. "From then on, every memo was short, sweet, and to the point."

Clarity and precision are just as critical in verbal communication. I recall a high-level team meeting where a key exec stated a "fact" that threatened to reverse an important decision we were about to make. I asked if she was sure about her accuracy. "Absolutely," she replied. That's not the way I recalled it, so I asked for supporting documentation. Sure enough, she had erred.

My tolerance for sloppy communication is low. Bad information creates chaos and sabotages team goals. Recognizing, however, that this exec was already embarrassed by her mistake, I reined in my frustration and stressed to the team that success hinged on airtight info. Effective immediately, I said, we need to be precise with our language and extraordinarily careful not to confuse "probably" or "pretty sure" with "absolutely." My executive's red face and my own exasperation were a small price to pay for purifying the process.

TWENTY-SEVEN

LISTEN UP

Practicing Active Listening

"Hi, my name is Tom and I'm a talkaholic." That's right, if there were a support group for dialogue hogs I would've been a charter member. I used to see every conversation as a race—first one to get their point across wins. But cutting off a conversation without considering what the other person can offer is like tearing up a lottery ticket after checking only the first two numbers. One of the most memorable seminars I ever sat through was *Active Listening* by C. J. Hegarty in the mid-1980s. That's when it finally clicked: hearing is involuntary but listening is an acquired skill.

Some Hegarty highlights:

Seek first to understand before seeking to be understood. These nine simple words, from the timeless prayer of St. Francis of Assisi, are powerful to behold. Challenging myself to view things through another person's eyes expanded my powers of perception and deepened my connection to—and appreciation of—others. It was further proof that empathy trumps ego. Another benefit: the more you listen, the better informed you are when it's your turn to talk.

Be a human mirror. People are more comfortable talking to people who talk like they do. If a colleague, for instance, thoughtfully chooses every word, your brilliant idea might zip by her if you spew sentences at the speed of light. The same goes for decibel level; your pithy points may not register if you overwhelm her soft-spoken sensibilities with bluster.

Value the speaker as well as the speech. It's easy for people to tell when their boss is listening *against* them instead of *to* them. A dead giveaway is the wall he throws up—leaning back in a chair and folding his arms across his chest. No matter what comes out of his mouth all they're going to hear is, *I have nothing but contempt for you and your ideas. Stop wasting my time.* If this sounds like you, you won't be crowned Mr. Motivation anytime soon—people are certainly not going to share all their great ideas just to see them shot down. Conversely, a caring approach—a smile, leaning into the conversation, eye contact—lets employees know they're taken seriously. The mindset is *What's right with what she's saying and how can I learn from it?* rather than *What's wrong and how can I object to it?* A leader who actively listens sets the tone for the entire department or company; people he listens to will listen to their people more carefully, and so on down the line.

Hear the unspoken. Scott McPhee, one of our top execs, learned the tough way that people care not only about *what* is said but *how* it's said. One afternoon, Scott's colleague teared up as she confided to me that Scott's body language proved his disdain for her. She feared for her job. I called Scott in for a briefing. "When Tom explained it to me," said Scott, "I thought, 'Wow, I've heard the same thing from my wife.'" That insight helped Scott understand the impression he left on people. He apologized to his colleague and repaired the damage.

As Scott discovered, subtle messages flow through facial expressions, body language, and tone of voice. That awareness came in handy during store visits when I queried customers about our service. I recall one typically over-polite Minnesotan who called the service "fine." But her steady foot-tapping and the restless way she flipped through her magazine told a different story. So I pressed her. "Are you sure?" I asked. "Anything I can help you with?" She paused, then confessed her car was twenty minutes overdue. Information in hand, we addressed the problem.

Repeat what you hear. Try not to ape the speaker, of course, but play back your interpretation of what you heard. Paraphrasing her message shows you listened carefully, and gives you both a chance to clear up miscommunication. (Remember that one of our deepest desires is to be heard.) Skipping this step can set off a chain reaction of misunderstanding that culminates in dented feelings and awkward apologies.

Active listening is grounded in courtesy, empathy, and a desire for clarity at all costs. You don't have to agree with what you hear. But your attentiveness and attitude speak the unspoken: *I want to understand where you're coming from. Tell me how you see this.* Practiced conscientiously, active listening engenders trust, reduces errors, and encourages people to speak their mind.

The same dynamics apply to groups. My colleague Eric Randa left the company and returned four years later only to notice a distinct change around the conference table. "There had been a tendency for some executive committee members, including Tom, to go for the jugular," recalled Eric. "It made people feel lousy and drove wedges between team members." Eric's right. Thankfully, I wised up. I told the team that corrosive, vindictive behavior was no longer acceptable. I reminded them that our mission statement and operating values called for caring, respectful interactions. "Once Tom put a stop to that kind of behavior, things really turned around," said Eric. "Nobody dreaded meetings anymore. We all realized that challenging each other in a professional way would help us all grow."

TWENTY-EIGHT

CAST A WIDE NET

Soliciting Employee Ideas

Hoping to grab a pre-flight bite one night, I scanned the slim choices at an airport concession stand—chili-cheese dogs, chocolate muffins, ice cream sandwiches. Nothing remotely qualified as healthy. I suggested to the kid behind the counter that he urge the owner to add veggie burgers to the menu. His blank look morphed into a laugh. "Are you kidding?" he said. "The boss would never listen to anything I said." That's a portrait of a boss taking a pass on success. Employees in constant contact with customers are like the wait staff at a small-town diner. They know the inside scoop on just about everything.

Fresh ideas are the lifeblood of any organization, and it's often the non-managerial players on the front lines who come up with the biggest corkers. But woe to the employee who tells a seat-of-the-pantser how to do things better. Those firms all have legends of The Transfer to Siberia. So problem-talk is just passed among peers rather than handed up to management. The cure? Keep the ideas flowing and the heart of your operations pumping with clear, convenient channels of employee communication. The poet Mark Van Doren understood this perfectly when he wrote:

> Bring ideas in and entertain them royally,
> for one of them may be the king.

I can't count how many times I mined employees for ideas. Take the time during a long road trip that Scott McPhee, a key exec, suggested that we create a new executive position—head of automotive services. I knew he was right the second the words left his mouth. Tires Plus was known more for selling tires than for selling the "plus"—shocks, brakes, batteries. The time was ripe to expand our expertise and brand into the service arena. Sure enough, Scott's idea sprouted a lucrative profit center.

Do not, however, get so caught up in popping champagne corks that you overlook the occasional squashed grape. Every culture, no matter how enlightened, has success-sabotaging roadblocks lurking in the shadows—the incompetent employee, inappropriate Internet surfing, a weak link in the production chain. The longer you wait to root out the problem the more entrenched—and costlier—it becomes. The challenge is breaking the code of silence among employees, without wreaking havoc on morale and solidarity.

To excavate the gold of employee intelligence:

Forecast brainstorms for staff meetings. A fun part of our meetings was when I'd say, "Give me your RBIs" (really big ideas). One by one, around the table we'd go. One person might propose a new policy or procedure. Another would pass along an idea suggested by a customer or vendor. Somebody else would describe a team member's recent innovation. People were encouraged to build on every idea. The brainstorms were torrential, and livened up the place. If you try it, vary the format and occasionally provide incentives to keep the creative juices flowing. For the best RBI of the day, we often awarded a dinner certificate or small cash bonus.

Poll the people. Our annual culture/climate survey asked employees what they liked about our operation, what they thought we could do better, and what they would do if they ran the place. HR sorted the feedback by topic and presented summaries to the executive team. Some suggestions were good and others comically bad, but some were organizational Eureka! moments. The e-mail we sent to employees broke it all down: "Based on your recommendations, here are some things we'll be changing . . ." and "We won't be able to implement the following suggestions because . . ."

We also surveyed the troops during our annual strategic planning process (chapter 20). We asked them to list our greatest strengths, weaknesses, opportunities, and threats. We then asked for ideas on how we could take advantage of those strengths and opportunities and neutralize the weaknesses and threats.

Ask departing employees. Here's an overlooked resource. Simply ask, "What do you think we need to change around here? What do you think is unhealthy?" Take notes. A person packing up his office has nothing to lose, and typically is only too happy to tell you what he thinks. For best results, have the soon-to-be-ex-employee talk to his boss and, separately, to his boss' boss.

Be prepared to hear things you don't want to hear, but need to. Employees who had given their notice occasionally said their manager had paid little attention to them, that they hadn't been given enough responsibility. I'd immediately remind my executive team that staying connected to our people was Priority 1. "Tom often said a little bit of attention, a little bit of love, goes a long way," said Wayne Shimer, a key v.p. "But Tom was realistic. When you have sixteen hundred employees scattered throughout ten states, all with different personalities and supervisors, some are going to slip through the cracks." Wayne may be right but that didn't stop me from trying to caulk every last crack. Good employees are hard to find and costly to train. I never missed an opportunity to hammer home that point.

Query new recruits. You'd be surprised by the ideas you can glean from asking new hires what they'd do differently. They have the fresh eyes of a consultant, without the enormous price tag. But get them before they're stained by the status quo—*This is the way things are done around here.* Tapping newbies for advice makes them feel valued, which engages and motivates them. Even if their suggestion is a stinker, react positively so feedback channels stay open.

One morning a new salesman in one of our suburban Minneapolis stores mentioned that he sensed a rift between the mechanics and sales staff. "The tire mounters come across as pretty resentful," he said innocently, "like they think we've got a cushy job." Ten minutes later, when I met with the store manager, I asked how things were between the mechanics and the sales team. Reluctantly, he acknowledged some brewing tension. "Oh, really," I said. "How do you think we can fix that?" He and I brainstormed a few minutes and decided to call a huddle to find out what people were thinking. It was like a group therapy session. Grievances were aired and addressed and, voilá!, cooperation improved.

When you reel in suggestions, criticisms, and company secrets, be sure to:

- ✔ Show appreciation no matter how surprised or upset you may be.

- ✔ Ask how the person would resolve the situation. People are more likely to back a solution they helped create.

- ✔ Keep it confidential. If it's impossible to conceal your source, make it clear to everyone that you sought out— and will continue to seek out—information to improve the organization and everyone in it.

Break these rules even once—by going ballistic, imposing unilateral solutions, or identifying your source of information— and your intel pipeline will run dry. Worse, resentful employees may retaliate against the whistle-blower.

TWENTY-NINE
PODIUM POINTERS
Harnessing the Power of Public Speaking

Enlightened executives know that delivering key messages to an entire staff or department leverages the power of their words like nobody's business. Seize every opportunity you can to address your troops in a group; achieving the same impact via dozens of one-on-one meetings is inconceivable. The same goes for outside engagements; speaking to community groups extends your company's goodwill. All leaders can benefit from polishing their public-speaking skills. My top ten tips:

1 **Get organized.** Ask yourself three questions: *What's the goal of this talk? How can I take the audience from here to there? What might block their understanding or acceptance?* Use the answers to prepare a killer bulleted outline. If you write your speech out to get more comfortable with it, hear yourself speaking the words as you write them. "Speaking" your speech instead of writing it is the difference between sounding conversational and sounding wooden.

2 **Practice with a colleague.** Or, stand in front of an empty chair representing the audience. Speak conversationally. When you're finished, do it again—over and over until it's second nature. (Helpful hint: take a Dale Carnegie course or join Toastmasters for real-world speaking practice.)

3 **Don't hide behind the podium.** It's a home base, not a planting pot. A wireless lavaliere microphone lets you roam through the audience.

4 **Cut the cord.** Jot key words on recipe cards to trigger thoughts and stay on track. Or, go with a PowerPoint presentation (be sure there's a small screen in front of you as you face the audience).

5 **Get real.** Keep your head up. Maintain as much eye contact as possible. Trust that the words will come. Better to skip a point or stumble occasionally—and come off as spontaneous—than cover every point reciting from a canned script.

6 **Slow down.** Novices often jabber at warp speed, making it hard for audiences to digest their message. Don't discount the value of a pause.

7 **Make it personal.** Smile and use audience members' names when appropriate.

8 **Illustrate points with examples.** Interesting, real-life stories lodge in people's memories better than facts and figures.

9 **Interact.** Pepper your talk with questions to individual audience members and to the group as a whole: *What would you do in that situation, Erin?* Perhaps role-play with a volunteer—showing drives home the point better than telling.

10 **Start and finish strong.** Save your best stuff for the beginning and end. It's what audiences will remember most.

PART II

FACE TO FACE

Keeping the Feedback Flowing

Enlightened executives help their people correct course and work through roadblocks. Just be careful to avoid coming off like Judge Judy, CEO. In other words, give feedback that's welcomed rather than dreaded. Take the time regional manager Brad Burley and I drove north a few hours to Duluth, Minnesota, to inspect a store. It took all of ten minutes to understand that the store manager was just skating by. I was more than a little disappointed, in both Brad and the manager. "To his credit," recalled Brad, "Tom didn't take it out on the manager—that was my job. He chose to have the coaching moment with me."

Brad and I walked to a gas station across the street, grabbed something to drink, and planned the next move. "First," said Brad, "Tom looked me in the eye and said, 'You're too good to allow this to happen.' Then, before we covered what I needed to do, he talked through everything I was doing right." Before leaving, I made sure Brad was in the right frame of mind. "Hey," I said, "you *can* do better and you *will* do better because you've shown me you can. Don't let this guy get away with it."

Hammering away at how Brad had screwed up would have left him wallowing in negativity, unable to think clearly and creatively. Instead, a positive spin left him fired up and on top of his game. Today, Brad uses the same M.O. with his managers—and his family. "When I'm upset with my kids," said Brad, "the first thing I tell them is how great they are and how much I love them. Then I single out the specific behavior that isn't acceptable. I look them straight in the eye when I'm doing it. I learned that from Tom."

Delivering timely feedback to everyone who reports to you may sound overwhelming. That's why I broke it down into four manageable pieces. They help transform the process from grating and stressful to gratifying and successful.

Level One: Weekly meetings to review status of projects (chapter 31)

Level Two: Quarterly twenty-minute reviews (chapter 32)

Level Three: Biannual operating plan reviews (chapter 20)

Level Four: Annual performance review (chapter 43)

Each level reminds people what's expected of them and redirects them when they stray off course. Now, mind you, this sort of structured feedback doesn't lift your obligation for quick, floor-coaching critiques whenever opportunity knocks—both on what an employee is doing well and on what I call NTIs (needs-to-improve areas). Don't worry about overkill. Artfully delivered repetition is the backbone of effective coaching. It can take months to change habits, so be that broken record. Human nature demands it.

THIRTY

THE SANDWICH TECHNIQUE

Delivering Corrective Criticism

As a consultant, I'm often running into leaders who are wildly inconsistent with reprimands. They manage to restrain themselves when someone makes a huge mistake, only to erupt later over a penny-ante infraction. That's when you see employees shaking their heads (or muttering, "What a psycho."). Well, that was me back in my seat-of-the-pants days. I didn't hesitate to light into employees who had messed up and hurt the company. But, I'm embarrassed to say, I blew my fuse over lesser offenses just as often. It was classic "React in haste, regret in leisure" behavior. Why the outbursts? Running a growing company felt like I was saddled up on a bucking bronco, holding on for dear life. Patience was a luxury I could ill afford.

In time, thankfully, I got a better grip. Instead of breaking people's spirits, I learned to make them soar. How? By serving up the Sandwich Technique, which slides the meat of the matter between two slices of organic praise. Before Sandwiching, remember—one of the basic expectations you established through the Ask/Tell Technique (chapter 25) is that you're in continual coaching mode. That means every matter on the coaching continuum is in play, from job performance to co-worker interactions to the employee's state of mind.

Sandwiching looks like this:

A positive slice. Ask if she's open to hearing a concern. Look her in the eye to establish intimacy and trust. Smile and pay her a bona fide compliment: "Sally, I can't tell you how much I appreciate the care you put into your work."

The meat of the matter. Ask a question or two about the issue at hand to get her take on it. Then, focus on *your* feelings and what *you* see rather than *her* behavior. Telling her she screwed up only backs her into a corner, whereas telling her how you *feel* about what she did may produce a more cooperative response. People can't help but relate to how you feel; they *can't relate* to getting smacked upside the head. Remember, egos are fragile. The second you sense a defense mechanism kicking in, clarify that you're talking about something she *did*, and that you're not evaluating her net human worth: "This has nothing to do with who you are, Sally. You know we value you and care about you very much. This is strictly a performance issue." If you can't resolve the issue on the spot, agree on when she'll get back to you with recommendations.

A positive slice. Sprinkle on a complimentary condiment: "Overall, Sally, you're doing a super job. Thanks for your efforts." Now, if you have a boss and you're talking to him, close with something like, "Thanks for listening, Jim. It's great to talk candidly about these things." This final step can mean the difference between leaving someone elated, deflated, or just plain mad.

Taste tip: take the bite out of the Sandwich from time to time. If you habitually follow up praise with a helping of corrective criticism, people will develop a Pavlovian response, and wince whenever a compliment escapes your lips. ("Oh-oh, here comes the meat of the matter!") That's counterproductive any way you slice it. (I can vouch that the praise/criticism/praise habit is hard to break; it was on my needs-to-improve list for years.) Avoid that syndrome by throwing out plenty of standalone high-fives and way-to-go's.

THIRTY-ONE

GOING ONE-ON-ONE

Conducting Regular Sit-Down Sessions

"**N**o excuses," I told Ron, a client who runs a midwestern manufacturing firm. "Meet one-on-one every single week with every employee who reports to you." His eyes bulged and he sputtered, "Where am I going to find that kind of time? I've got a business to run. Besides, I already talk to people dozens of times a day." One of the most common blunders leaders make, I told him, is believing that office drop-ins and hallway encounters are tantamount to regular one-on-ones. To cement my point, I rattled off some face-to-face benefits:

- Clears fog from mission-critical projects and speeds problem solving
- Shows you value your people by fitting them in your demanding schedule
- Straightens the paths of misguided workers
- Deepens connections and loyalty between you and your people
- Prevents brushfires and saves time and money by nipping mistakes in the bud
- Produces prepared employees geared toward weekly project check-ins
- Speeds the idea-to-implementation cycle
- Reduces interruptions by delaying minor questions until the next meeting

- Unearths deeper issues through open-ended questions and big-picture thinking

- Sharpens minds and boosts confidence of employees through focused coaching time

The meetings can be held weekly or every other week, and last anywhere from thirty minutes to two hours, depending on the employee's responsibilities and performance. The agenda is simple and direct.

The overview. Kick things off by asking how things are in general. Every three or four weeks, also ask how he *feels* about his job. Keeping tabs on an employee's state of mind yields clues about whether he's ready for a new challenge or position. Tapping into feelings also provides a window into wellness issues that could affect performance.

Next, review the employee's Goals Activity Report (opposite page). It tracks operating plan-related projects and other tasks added throughout the year. Each goal is listed along with its status and three due dates—rough draft, final draft, implementation. Career and behavioral goals are also listed (often without due dates) to keep awareness high. The Goals Activity Report is a reminder of the expectations you created together in the first two steps of the Ask/Tell Technique (chapter 25). (Should expectations need sharper definition, repeat the steps.) This document—either as a hard copy or a spreadsheet attachment to an e-mail—should be available at your request.

The Goals Activity Report is an effective way to track all the moving pieces that propel your business. Wayne Shimer, who headed up a few divisions for us, swore by it. He also at times swore at it. "Everybody was plowing full speed ahead," said Wayne. "We all had 135 things on our plate. Then Tom would go on what we called 'a ride'—visiting some stores. I don't care what region he rode in, we had to have a meeting when he came back. He'd have a million need-to-do's, all broken out by category. One by one, they'd hit somebody's Goals Activity Report for follow-up, and suddenly we'd all have 175 things to do."

After Tires Plus was sold, Wayne brought the report to his new company. "It absolutely works," said Wayne. "It shows me very quickly what each person needs from me and how they respond to priorities and timelines. Bottom line, it will make them better. They may not know it today, but they'll know it tomorrow."

GOALS ACTIVITY REPORT
Adam Lehrke

GOAL	STATUS/NEXT STEP	DUE DATE ROUGH DRAFT	DUE DATE FINAL	DUE DATE IMPLEMENTATION
Projects				
Annual re-bid of vendors (Target = 5% savings)	*Ask Bob for specs*	JUL 12	JUL 24	AUG 8
Review Yellow Page ad, reposition ad prototype	*Ask rep about costs*	JUL 5	JUL 12	AUG 1
Develop and implement Frequent Customer program	*Meet with Chuck*	JUL 7	JUL 12	JUL 21
Do market labor rate assessment, revise rates accordingly	*Strategize with team*	AUG 3	AUG 28	SEP 15
Negotiate with credit card companies for TP credit card	*Start calling for bids*	JUL 5	JUL 10	JUL 24
Develop and execute annual advertising plan	*Call account rep*	JUL 6	JUL 17	AUG 14
Plan and implement Tent Sale or 72-hour sale promotion	*Meet with Joanie*	JUL 8	JUL 17	JUL 20
Ongoing Tasks	**Frequency**			
Role-playing selling (show tread depth, ask about ride quality)	*Tuesday and Friday p.m.*			
Place weekly newspaper ads (*Star Tribune, Pioneer Press*)	*Monday a.m.*			
Monitor and report on Guest Enthusiasm Index	*Thursday a.m.*			
Weekly night-school course at U of M	*Wednesdays*			

Hot projects. For each high-priority project, ask six questions (varying the verbiage to keep them fresh):

1. How do you see yourself proceeding?
2. What roadblocks do you anticipate?
3. How do you plan to hurdle those roadblocks?
4. What do you need from others to be successful?
5. What do you need from me?
6. When do you expect to complete this? (Verify—and, if necessary, adjust—the three due dates listed.)

Next, tackle any project-specific NTIs (needs-to-improve areas): "We've talked about the importance of meeting deadlines on urgent projects. You've missed the last three due dates for this. What's happening, Joe? You're generally on time." The gravity of your reaction depends on

- the project's importance;
- the project's timeframe;
- how close the project is to completion;
- the number of warnings you've given;
- the employee's record for hitting deadlines;
- the employee's level of denial.

With each project, be generous with compliments for progress made. If he's enthusiastic about a particular assignment, encourage his passion. Wrap up this section with a dollop of praise: "It's nice to have someone on the team who's so diligent, Joe. I'm impressed with how you collected and summarized everyone's input on the new campaign."

Throughout the process, avoid yes-no questions. Open-ended questions like "What do you suggest?" give the mind room to roam and nudge him along until he arrives at his own solutions. Answer any monosyllabic responses by digging deeper. For example, if your question, "How do you feel about this project?" is met with, "Good," ask, "Good in what way?"

Feedback. Ask for questions or concerns. If he says nothing comes to mind, prompt him: "What would you do differently if you were in charge?" You may have to resort to prying him open with the Rule of Three Technique (chapter 25): "C'mon, I *know* you can give me three things you'd like to see different around here." It's the rare employee who wouldn't enjoy tweaking the status quo.

THIRTY-TWO

RAPID-FIRE REVIEW

Managing Quick-Hit Quarterly Reviews

Most people are dying to know what the boss thinks about them. I certainly was when I worked for Shell Oil Company. So I started doing my people a favor. Every few months, as a weekly one-on-one wound down, I'd ask, "Are you open to a quick review of what I think is going well, and hearing a few ideas on how you can do even better?" Now, granted, not many employees will say "No, thanks" to the boss, but I rarely sensed resistance. In fact, eyes lit up virtually every time I offered a twenty-minute mini-performance review. The boss' critique generated some anxiety, sure, but they were eager to hear what I had to say.

I started by writing bullet points on everything the employee was doing well, and salted in some detailed anecdotes: "The way you reformatted the sales report is a big help, Charleen, and it's on my desk first thing Monday morning just like I asked. I can't tell you how much I appreciate you making that happen." I relied on memory, but I also scanned the "employee highlights" pages in my planner for recent notes.

Next, I addressed NTIs (needs-to-improve areas) in quick-hit summaries only, since they were ongoing coaching issues. Remember, putting NTIs squarely on the table won't be seen as going negative as long as they're presented fairly, and offset by things the employee is doing right. But choose your words carefully. If she feels under attack, the tips you're trying to embed in her consciousness won't hurdle her hastily erected barriers of shame, guilt, and fear. There's a world of difference between "Boy, if you nail that you'll be in superstar territory" and "Damn, you really screwed up. What the heck were you thinking?"

Put a bow on the meeting by briefly putting it all into perspective: "Everyone's really happy you're on the team, Charleen. You always seem to find a way to do what needs to get done, and that's a rare quality. I'm confident you'll resolve those NTIs and continue to grow with us."

THIRTY-THREE

SAUCE FOR THE GANDER

Soliciting and Responding to Frank Feedback

It was 1994, but I can still see the shell-shocked faces of the other CEOs. In Quebec City for an American Management Association conference, I had just shared the results of my annual Roundtable Review (chapter 43), in which the six vice presidents who reported to me anonymously listed their view of my strengths and NTIs (needs-to-improve areas). The NTIs were things like:

- You're very careful of your own time but not always with others' time. You get too involved in micro issues and often cause meetings to run late.

- In quizzing deeply for problems, you come up with small, insignificant things that waste people's time on follow-up.

- You try to come across as caring but you're not always genuine. Example: you asked an employee in the presence of his spouse the name of another employee's spouse. The first spouse then heard you go up and say, "How's it going, Mary?" The two spouses got together and joked about it afterwards.

The consensus of the other CEOs: "I can't believe you let your people talk to you like that." "Hey," I fired back, "if they're thinking it, I wanna know. At least then I can deal with it." Was it painful to read the negative stuff? Absolutely. You always like to think you're viewed by colleagues with equal parts awe and admiration. But don't kid yourself. If you're committed to being the best leader you can be, you've gotta let Toto pull back the curtain and expose the flaws of the great and powerful Oz (that would be you).

Yes, the "Tell me how I'm doing" step in the Ask/Tell Technique (chapter 25) extracts some useful information, but there are some things employees just won't say to your face. Digging up the really good dirt requires three conditions:

Confidentiality. For my annual Roundtable Review, the people who reported directly to me wrote their critiques and submitted them to HR, who merge/purged the comments and presented them to me anonymously.

Receptivity. Solicited, brutally frank feedback must be accepted with grace. Early on, I often heard comments like, "You say you're open to us giving you feedback but you should see your facial contortions when we do; it's a kill-the-messenger look." They were right. My spoken gratitude belied body language that said I'd rather be walking barefoot over hot coals. I had to train myself to listen reflectively, rather than defensively, because an organization isn't healthy unless its people can speak their minds, respectfully, without fear of reprisal.

Action. Confidential feedback has to be acted upon—quickly—lest your people quit bothering to drop comments into the pipeline. I basically had three responses: "That's valid and I'll try to do better," "I hear what you're saying but this is why I do it like that," and "I totally disagree and here's why."

For the record, here's how I responded to the three NTIs listed above at the next executive team meeting:

- *You're very careful of your own time but not always with others' time.* Very valid. I am re-committing myself to be more timely and to better respect your time and schedules.

- *In quizzing deeply for problems, you come up with small, insignificant things that waste people's time on follow-up.* Some nitpicking probably occurs. I'll try to be better at backing off if there really isn't a problem. But I know that real problems tend to stay hidden from leaders and only surface after deep probing. It's a "lesser of two evils" thing, and the way I'm going about it is better than not finding the bigger problems. Therefore, I will continue to actively seek out the challenges facing our team.

- *You try to come across as caring but you're not always genuine.* With the number of employees and spouses we have, I'm not able to remember every name. I have asked, and will continue to ask, somebody's name when I don't know it. I will, however, make sure no one else hears me doing so. I would hope, though, that if someone does overhear me they would think, "What's wrong with asking someone's name?" After all, it's better than avoiding somebody or not caring that I don't know their name. (In hindsight, I think I was a bit too prickly here. I see how people might find it insincere to ask someone's name from a third party and then approach that person like an old friend. I am more straightforward today and willing to tell someone that I'm embarrassed to say I can't remember their name.)

Sure, I was occasionally hurt and frequently humbled by the criticisms I received. But I tried hard to take them to heart and change what needed to be changed in order to become a better person *and* a better businessman. Burying my head in the sand was not an option. As Winston Churchill said:

> *Criticism may not be agreeable, but it is necessary. It fulfills the same function as pain in the human body. It calls attention to an unhealthy state of things.*

KEY POINTS: CAN YOU HEAR ME NOW?

Communicating Effectively

✔ *Less egotism, more empathy.* These four words enhance work relationships because they scrub the vagueness out of communication. Ultimately, success depends on how well you communicate your ideas and how well you receive feedback.

✔ *Ask and tell.* Superior communication is the secret to keeping your people lively and engaged. The Ask/Tell Technique keeps everyone informed, involved, and connected to colleagues both up and down the corporate ladder.

✔ *Be concise.* Keep memos short, sweet, and readable. Use subheads, quick paragraphs, crisp writing, and lots of bullets. Be clear and precise in verbal communications, especially when stakes are high.

✔ *Acquire listening skills.* Conversations aren't competitions. They're only successful when both parties win. People feel free to express themselves when they feel appreciated, and nothing shows appreciation in the business world like the scarce resource of undivided attention.

✔ *Cast a wide idea net.* Fresh ideas fuel organizations. Tap your people, especially if they have direct contact with customers. Keep their rich intel flowing through meetings, surveys, and informal chats.

✔ *Sharpen your public speaking skills.* Speaking to groups internally and externally leverages the power of your words and spreads your company's goodwill. For best results, prepare a killer outline, maintain eye contact, use stories, and interact with your audience.

KEY POINTS: FACE TO FACE

Keeping the Feedback Flowing

✔ **Structure feedback.** Breaking operational reviews into varying formats and frequency (weekly, quarterly, biannual, annual) makes them manageable. Capitalize on opportunities to offer spontaneous praise and corrective critiques.

✔ **Serve up the Sandwich Technique.** Begin and end sessions with legitimate compliments to take the sting out of performance issues. Avoid predictability by looking for occasions to dole out standalone dollops of impromptu praise.

✔ **Schedule regular one-on-ones with employees.** Private meetings strengthen relationships, sharpen analytical skills, encourage attention to detail, prevent brushfires that flare up in a seat-of-the-pants culture, and allow deeper issues to emerge.

✔ **Rapid-fire review every few months.** Occasionally add to regular one-on-ones a twenty-minute review to share your thoughts on what an employee's doing well and how she can do even better. It reinforces positive behaviors and helps minimize interfering ones.

✔ **Request brutally honest feedback.** Painful as it may be, you're best off knowing what employees think of you. Keep it anonymous, accept it graciously, and offer a detailed response to show you take their input seriously.

VI.
HELL-BENT
AND HUNGRY

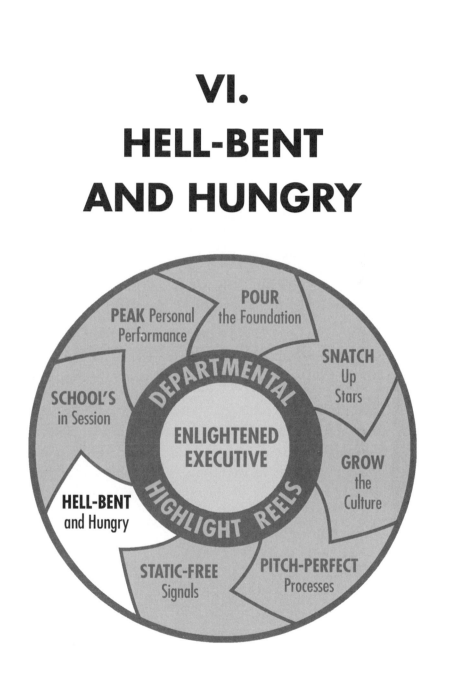

PART I

RUNNING THROUGH WALLS

Transforming Amateurs into Pros

Gabe Lopez had been on the brink of turning in his name tag when I intervened in his salary dispute (chapter 10). Over the next few years, I often took Gabe aside and encouraged him because I saw his potential. Why did Gabe stay with us and work so hard? Was it the salary? The benefits? He could've found similar deals elsewhere. Gabe supplied the deceptively simple answer: "Tom really made me feel valued as a person and I wanted to show him his faith in me was well deserved." Gabe's story touches the essence of enlightened leadership:

> *People make decisions emotionally and*
> *justify them intellectually.*

That's the first thing I share with clients who are befuddled by their inability to control employees. They're managers who shake their heads and moan, "Man, I just don't know how to deal with these attitude problems." It's difficult for seat-of-the-pantsers to realize that it takes more than raw wits or charisma to inspire employees. Whether they're big-shot execs at a Fortune 500 firm or unpaid interns at a nonprofit, people won't run through walls for you unless you've forged some sort of emotional connection.

Never forget: *people don't care how much you know until they know how much you care.*

Motivation isn't like a baggy sweatshirt—one size doesn't fit all. Your challenge is to discover what motivates each and every member of your team. For Adam, it may be money. For Erin, recognition. Jim thrives on meaningful work. Shelly's been trying to expand her power base. Ethan loves the thrill of solving a challenge. Nate wants to be in on decisions. Sure, it takes some effort on your part, but you can't melt somebody's butter until you know which burner to fire up.

Seat-of-the-pantsers are typically either Type A (dictator— hard-driving, self-centered, gets results but leaves a trail of human debris) or Type B (doormat—passive, people pleaser, tolerates less productivity). Enlightened leaders—let's call them Type E— produce uncommon, sustainable results through firm, but caring, leadership coupled with efficient business practices. Type E leaders are ever alert and nurturing. They leverage intellectual, physical, emotional, and spiritual well-being to deepen connections and inspire achievement.

The good news is, Type E leadership is contagious. The more you act like an enlightened executive, the more likely you are to infect employees with the Type E bug. Symptoms include decisive movements, a sparkle in the eye, a spring in the step. You know you're getting a great return on invested leadership when the weekly one-on-one meetings with your people become shorter and shorter. Their need for hand-holding diminishes as their energy and capabilities expand.

Enlightened executives are at the service of their employees. That means that personnel development ranks up there with locking up the store at night. When people sense you've got their best interests at heart they'll rise to the occasion, if only to justify your confidence in them. Novelist Hermann Hesse illustrated the service/leadership connection in *Journey to the East,* in which a humble servant in a mystical organization is revealed to be the group's wise and exalted leader.

Serving employees was a given at Tires Plus. "I still preach that today at my new company," agreed Wayne Shimer, our vice president of retail operations. "You will never be a good leader until you learn to put the needs of your employees first." Wayne watched me ride herd on management to serve the stores and serve them well. I insisted they return calls to store personnel as soon as possible. "If Tom heard you weren't getting back to the stores in short order," said Wayne, "I tell you what, you did not want to have that meeting with him."

The late A. Bartlett Giamatti, former president of Yale University, called leadership "the assertion of a vision, not simply the exercise of a style." Allow me to build on that. Enlightened leadership demands the *vision* that inspires followers, the *values* that earn their trust, and the *vitality* to march them to the promised land. With all three in place, a leader is like a lantern that lights the road, beckoning, *Come, follow me.*

THIRTY-FOUR

THE COACH APPROACH

Cheering and Steering, Not Domineering

Seat-of-the-pantsers, burn four words into your consciousness: *Manage things, coach people*. Manage people impersonally and they'll resent being treated like cogs in a machine. Coach them individually and they'll flourish. It's your choice—your people will either get bitter or better.

What kind of coaching are we talking about? A Lamaze childbirth coach comes to mind. Or a golf or tennis coach. Someone who stays close to the action, offers tips, and patiently corrects technique. Good coaches are incurable optimists. They view people as unique human beings, each capable of greatness. They care about their employees and accept responsibility for their professional development. They ask insightful questions and nudge people to craft their own solutions. Enlightened coaching is the best way to fend off the inertia that's enveloping today's workplace like sleeping gas.

Is the shift from managing to coaching easy? Depends. If you're a kinetic, hard-nosed boss, the kind of guy who's convinced that, dammit, a regular paycheck is all the motivation employees need, then no, it's going to be a grind. And you'll only make things worse if you apply these principles without buying into them. People can smell insincerity a mile away.

With the right attitude, anyone can become a good coach. Soon after Scott McPhee joined us as regional manager, we relocated him to Iowa, our first market outside Minnesota. We had big expansion plans, and a lot was riding on the twelve stores down there. Trouble was, a lot of Iowans were riding on tires purchased somewhere other than Tires Plus. Scott struggled, big time. He had been a hard-driving regional manager elsewhere, but his my-way-or-the-highway style wasn't in sync with our culture. "I was working long hours," recalled Scott, "but things were spiraling out of control."

Scott was a systematic guy, but a poor listener. "I didn't pay much attention to what others thought," he admitted. "I always got results by ordering employees around, but that starts to wear on people pretty quickly. The store managers I was overseeing actually started working against me instead of with me." Moribund sales and high turnover signaled me it was time to pay Scott a call. A stand-up guy, he admitted he was in over his head. I urged him again to coach rather than manage, to get to know his team and learn what made them tick. Ask more questions, I said. Partner with people instead of laying down the law. Then, Eureka! "I finally got it," said Scott. "I realized I had to transition from preaching to teaching. Instead of *telling* people what to do I had to *inspire* them to do it."

Scott went right to work and scheduled a weekly team meeting for his dozen managers, some of whom had to drive halfway across the state to attend. He kicked off the meetings with news and small talk, then coached his managers on coaching each other. "Immediately, everything changed," said Scott, "beginning with the camaraderie. They started helping each other, sharing best practices, and putting their heads together on recruiting and staffing. They got really excited about working as a team, and looked forward to each week's meeting." A few months later, Scott was back on course. Sales shot up. Turnover dropped. Three years later, Scott was promoted to vice president of retail operations.

Good coaches also know that leading is more important than doing. You may be clocking Wall Street hours on your own projects. But if you aren't also coaching your people to maximize *their* potential, you're perpetuating a seat-of-the-pants culture. Devote more of your time to inspiring and educating the people who report to you. Monitor, recognize, and applaud their progress. Otherwise, employees will feel you're oblivious to their hard work. They'll think, *Why should I knock myself out? I'll just do enough to get by. Nobody will notice anyway.* That leads to—you guessed it—lots more work for you. Worse, you'll have further proof that if you want something done right, you'll have to do it yourself.

I learned this lesson firsthand from observing one of my Shell Oil dealers in Chicago. Roger was one of the smartest guys I knew. He was also the most frenzied. Every time I stopped by, he was working his tail off while his employees pretty much stood around and watched. I remember thinking, *There's a management lesson if ever I saw one.* I wasn't surprised a few years later when I heard Roger had gone out of business.

More doing and less leading may work temporarily in a start-up or small business unit. But the problem grows exponentially as more people come on board, particularly if new employees aren't self-starters. The sooner you embrace the coach approach, the sooner your company will be flying on its own.

THIRTY-FIVE

HAVE A HEART

Caring for Employees Boosts the Bottom Line

Some of the wisest words ever written about coaching were penned by Dee Hock, chairman emeritus of Visa International. Essentially, he supersized the Golden Rule:

> Make a careful list of all things done to you that
> you abhorred. Don't do them to others, ever.
> Make another list of things done for you that
> you loved. Do them for others, always.

Reading between the lines, two of the qualities a good coach must possess are kindness and empathy. No, I'm not talkin' namby-pamby pushover—an empathetic coach is also steel-tough in holding people accountable. He's equal parts teacher and taskmaster, dreamer and disciplinarian. He's mastered the "hard" skills of leadership—everything from strategic planning to meeting management. But it's unquestionably the "soft" people skills that help him win hearts and minds.

Still not sold on the kindness component? Read on, because the stakes couldn't be higher. An undercurrent of mean-spiritedness, or even benign neglect, will produce a culture of fear and loathing. And things gradually get worse because an ill-tempered boss is usually oblivious to his impact; for every snide comment he flings out, a seething employee raids the office supply cabinet to exact revenge.

All my life, till I was forty-two, I had scoffed at the notion that kindness and empathy were bedrock on which leadership was built. I was a seat-of-the-pants guy. My faith was in ruthless efficiency and the cold, hard numbers of a balance sheet. Truth be told, I was so tough on people because I lived in constant fear that my business was teetering on the brink of collapse. It never occurred to me that caring about my employees' well-being could lead to higher profits.

Leading solely by intellect—"coming from your head"—may earn you grudging respect and build a culture of perfunctory competence. But it's leading with your heart—treating people as unique human beings first and employees second—that ignites the twin sparks of passion and loyalty, and inspires ordinary people to achieve extraordinary results.

In hindsight, I should have learned these lessons earlier. After all, it was the way I was treated at Shell Oil that motivated me to start my own company. Three incidents, all within a few months of each other, stick in my mind.

Cold water was poured on my proactive thinking. It was the dawn of a new era in the oil industry. The Minnesota state legislature had just legalized self-service gas stations, and I excitedly spent a big chunk of time researching the possibilities. I designed a plan for gas station owners to convert one of their driveway pump islands to self-service pumps. Increased volume, I calculated, would more than offset Shell's share of conversion costs. Management yawned and said the self-service concept was probably a flash-in-the-pan trend. End of discussion.

Rules were other-worldly. I organized a gala trade show at a high-end Minneapolis hotel for our Minnesota dealers. It worked. We doubled our sales goal. But John, my district manager, chewed me out for (modestly) exceeding the event budget. When I protested that I had still netted a huge profit for Shell, he spit out, "It doesn't matter. You were over your expense budget!" Hello? On what planet do profits not matter?

I got razzle-dazzled. John scored tickets to the big December clash between the Minnesota Vikings and the Green Bay Packers. A Packers fan, he asked me to book his hotel room—a presidential suite complete with fresh flowers and champagne—and put it on my expense account. But thousands of rabid Packers fans were streaming into the Twin Cities. Rooms were scarce. Fortunately, I had a good business relationship with a hotel near the stadium and managed to book precisely what he requested. A few weeks after the game (the Vikes ruled, 24-3), John held a sales meeting and announced the new corporate austerity program. It included, you guessed it, a crackdown on expense accounts. After the meeting, I walked up and joked that it was a good thing the new policy didn't apply to that football game weekend. John looked me in the eye and said, "God, I'm sorry, but it does," and walked away. I was stunned—and wound up paying for John's weekend getaway.

To be sure, my eight-year apprenticeship at Shell Oil was invaluable. I met lots of good people and sharpened my skills. But the molasses-like bureaucracy and office politics warped my youthful idealism and enthusiasm. Deliverance came when, finally, armed with a plan to start my own company, I vowed to take only the best elements of Shell Oil with me. But some of the bad ones tagged along, too. I was like the product of a dysfunctional home who rebels against his family's unhealthy behaviors only to unwittingly perpetuate them in a family of his own. I soon found myself tilting at some of the same windmills that had exasperated me at Shell Oil. I was a typical seat-of-the-pantser—I had an ego the size of Texas and was more concerned about proving how great I was than in being a good leader. The problem was obvious to others—I didn't get it. I didn't understand that I was managing too much with my head and not enough with my heart.

It wasn't until I shook off my triple trauma of personal and professional calamities that I realized that learning how to be a better leader begins with learning how to be a better human being. My own experience tells me you're never too old and it's never too late to become an enlightened executive. The first step is a commitment to continual improvement. As French critic Charles DuBois wrote:

> *The important thing is this: to be able*
> *at any moment to sacrifice what we*
> *are for what we could become.*

THIRTY-SIX

GO AHEAD, MAKE THEIR DAY

Reviving the Lost Art of the Compliment

There simply wasn't anyone better than Dorie Thrall, my executive assistant at Tires Plus. She was smart, quick, and dogged. She knew when I needed help before I even knew I needed help. One morning I called her into my office. "Dorie," I said, "I just wanted to tell you I think you're doing a super job." For ten minutes I rambled on about her skills, dedication, and cheerfulness. Her efforts meant a great deal to me personally and professionally, and I told her so. The odd thing was that Dorie, with her Minnesota stoicism, just sat there, occasionally nodding her head. All in all she looked rather blasé about the whole thing, as if I was giving a blow-by-blow account of everything I'd eaten over the weekend. *That's okay*, I remember thinking, *I just want to make sure she knows how much I appreciate her contributions*. Later, Dorie's teammates told a different story. One stopped me in the hallway. "What did you say to Dorie?" he said. "She's beaming from ear to ear and telling everyone about all the compliments you paid her."

Don't give people your attention just when they're screwing up. Add some drive-by praising into the mix. When you notice what they're doing well, your constructive criticism will then be heard in the spirit in which it's given. They'll think, *My boss is a good guy and he's always fair, so if he's got something to say I wanna hear it.*

If nothing revs an employee's motivational motor like positive strokes, why are bosses so miserly about rationing them out? (A recent Gallup Poll showed that 65 percent of workers received zero recognition for good work *in the preceding year*.) Answer: the seven deadly sins of executive excuses.

1 **Not enough time.** Baloney. It takes ten seconds to light someone's afterburners. All you have to do is pay attention to what, and who, is right in front of you.

2 **They're just meeting expectations.** Seat-of-the-pantsers think, *What, I'm supposed to congratulate people for doing what I pay them to do?* Yes, if you want those results to be repeated, if not eclipsed, and you don't want employees jumping ship. And don't wait till they cross the finish line. If someone graduates from 70 percent of goal to 78 percent of goal, hey, that's reason to celebrate. My motto was, "If you're not performing, you better be trending!"

3 **Too touchy-feely.** The sad truth is that relating to an employee on anything resembling a personal level is foreign to many seat-of-the-pantsers. In order to give someone a genuine compliment, you've got to connect, one human being to another. No disrespect, but if something's preventing you from doing that, deal with it.

4 **I get no reaction.** As I found out with Dorie, extolling an employee's virtues may elicit deadpan looks but the praise still makes a huge impact. Tell a child how wonderful he is and he beams. That joy doesn't fade as we get older; many of us are just too uptight to express it in front of an authority figure.

5 **Don't wanna overdo it.** Ever hear of somebody over-dosing on compliments? Have *you* ever been fed up with too many? Our appetite for praise is bottomless. The operative word here is "genuine." Don't bother setting a weekly compliment quota; employees will see right through it.

6 **Gotta hold onto power.** It takes a strong ego to lift up somebody else's. Too many seat-of-the-pantsers play one-upmanship with rules that assume *If I acknowledge how good you are I mustn't be as good, but if I'm putting you down I feel better about myself.* Such zero-sum thinking is both disturbing and destructive.

7 **I'll pay for it.** Let's get this straight. You think keeping your mouth shut will dissuade people from thinking better of themselves, and thus be less likely to ask for more money? Again, baloney. Motivated people perform better. That leads to a healthier culture, higher morale, and higher profits. The real cost is in *not* dishing out praise.

THIRTY-SEVEN

GOAL TENDING

Helping Employees Hit the Bull's-Eye

Without a little stretching, goal-setting can be an exercise in futility. If a goal is too easy, productivity drops off as soon as that first hurdle is cleared. Good coaches know just how far each individual can be stretched. Their people stay excited about scoring bull's-eyes because each target is freshly painted and placed just beyond their previous best effort. To turn employees into goal-getting juggernauts:

Make it mutual. Wise and all-knowing leader that I was, I used to unilaterally assign goals to people. And I remained perpetually mystified why no one was as excited as I was about reaching them. It finally dawned on me that employees would be more fired up about their goals if they had a hand in shaping them. So, we sat down together, negotiated a bit, and arrived at something we both liked. But they walked away with *their* goals, not *my* goals. And that, as poet Robert Frost would say, has made all the difference.

Don't overstretch. For too long my philosophy toward employee goal-setting was, "Shoot for the moon! Even if you come up short, you're still up there among the stars." What I was oblivious to was that my sound, sensible strategy actually created a locomotive streaking toward a head-on collision with human nature. I had assumed that people would just barrel along until they ran out of steam. But people don't work that way. A goal that's too far out of reach becomes a *demotivator*. Discouraged employees think, *What's the point of even trying? I could work 24/7 and still be light-years away* Hopelessness is contagious, and team morale is inevitably the ultimate victim.

The solution? Either scale back the goal or help your employee put it in perspective. Stretch goals don't necessarily need to be achieved in order to serve a purpose. Instead of focusing solely on the numerical target (doubling sales or slicing three months off time-to-market), shift some attention to the process you're trying to stimulate. When people came up short, I told them not to worry about it—*if* they were following our system and working hard. Whatever the outcome, stretch goals help people realize they are infinitely capable of improvement.

When it comes to motivating employees, it's not always up to you to do the heavy lifting. I often asked team members to name three ways they could improve their performance (hint: vary the question to avoid stale responses). As you get to know each individual's strengths, capabilities, and mental makeup, inspiring them requires less effort. Remember, people do things for their reasons, not yours. Learn what people want, then find a way to help them get it.

THIRTY-EIGHT
REWARDING RESULTS
Matching Incentives to Outcomes

Like all entrepreneurs who pour every last dime into their company, my cofounder Don Gullett and I got nervous early on whenever business hit the skids. What made me really nervous, though, was nobody else was nervous. *No wonder there's no urgency*, I remember thinking. *Everybody else is on straight salary. They get paid the same no matter which direction sales spike. Yet, if revenues dry up, Don and I don't get paid.*

What was wrong with this picture? It was out of focus, and that epiphany changed everything. A couple months later we activated an incentive-based compensation plan. It took awhile to work out the kinks, but we tied a portion of most every employee's salary to individual, team, and organizational performance. Suddenly, we began picking up steam. Slackers were exposed and cut loose. Productivity rose.

Yet, it wasn't all about money. The greenback barely cracks the top ten in employee motivation surveys. Consistently topping the list are intangibles like "challenging and interesting work," "involvement in decision making," "feeling respected and valued," and "the ability to make a contribution." Salary, benefits, and vacation time are closer to the bottom. Wanna know what seat-of-the-pantsers call motivators? Turn the list upside down.

By my lights, compensation lures employees more than surveys suggest and less than employers would like to think. Sacks full of cash might make people stick around, but they aren't necessarily going to be happy campers. Likewise, stimulating work at below-market wages might produce quality for a while, but top performers eventually follow the fat paycheck. The best results come from providing opportunities to flourish in an enlightened environment where extra effort equals extra pay.

Bonuses are a good way to tie it all together. I'd set a bonus target of around 30 percent above a non-administrative employee's base salary. She'd get paid below market value if she failed to reach any goals, market value if she achieved half, and significantly more if she accomplished all of them.

The X-factor here is human nature. Motivational motors sputter and stall, so you've gotta get inside people's heads if you hope to match incentives to outcomes. Your shop may have it all—a supportive culture, capable people, incentive-based compensation, the works. But you won't lift off until your empathy engine is fully throttled. Business writer Steven Kerr explored this dynamic in his classic essay, "On the Folly of Rewarding A While Hoping For B," which appeared in the esoteric *Academy of Management Journal.* "Managers who complain about lack of motivation in their workers," wrote Kerr, "might do well to consider the possibility that the reward systems they have installed are paying off for behavior other than what they are seeking." A few institutional follies:

- We hope for teamwork and collaboration, yet solely reward individual effort.
- We hope for innovation and risk-taking, yet reward the errorless status quo.
- We hope for long-term strategic thinking, yet reward quarterly earnings.

The follies sound like obvious and curable maladies until you realize how deeply they're ingrained in Corporate America. After reading Kerr I asked myself, *What behavior are we really rewarding?* whenever I saw something that just didn't seem right. This awareness led me to create the "farm system" approach of rewarding store managers for developing assistant managers (chapter 13).

Without the farm system, many of our efforts to trumpet teamwork rang hollow. Rhetoric must be backed up by reward. It's folly to tie a store manager's bonus to his team's performance, and then expect him to tell us when his best salesperson was ready for promotion. The first time he sees one of his protégés whisked off to manage someplace else will be the last. He'll keep the next little secret weapon to himself.

Human nature is a powerful force that demands to be reckoned with. Before launching a new initiative, close your office door and take a few minutes to consider its real-world consequences. Close your eyes. Slip on the shoes of an employee. Step by empathetic step, walk through—and work through—your own gut reaction to the new incentives. Ask yourself, *If I was on the receiving end of this policy, how would it change the way I do things and why?* Remember, employees see right through slick packaging to what management truly values. It's pretty simple, really. They watch what raises the boss' eyebrows. If you don't notice promptness, they're going to be late. If you focus on promptness and ignore quality, you'll have an office of punctual, mediocre performers.

Speaking of human nature, would you work as hard if you didn't have a piece of the action? When appropriate, we let key execs invest in the company. The payback was phenomenal. "My commitment and loyalty were heightened when I became a share-holder in the company," said Jim Pascale, who headed up our franchise operations. Jim's small percentage spurred a no-limits attitude. "It made me care about all aspects of our organization, not just the division of the company I was running," said Jim. "I was willing to help everybody and work more cooperatively to do whatever had to be done."

KEY POINTS: RUNNING THROUGH WALLS

Transforming Amateurs into Pros

✔ **Aspire to Type E (Enlightened) leadership.** People make decisions emotionally and justify them intellectually. People will run through walls for you once you've forged bonds. Type E leaders achieve sustainable results through firm, but caring, leadership.

✔ **Manage things, coach people.** See each person as a unique human being capable of greatness. Become a steady stream of constructive feedback. Ask insightful questions and nudge people to craft their own solutions. Coaching is the best way to maximize the potential of everyone in your organization.

✔ **Care about your people.** Yes, business leaders need to master "hard" skills like strategic planning and meeting management. But don't forget that kindness and empathy are bedrock values of enlightened leadership. Caring for the well-being of your employees has a big impact on profits.

✔ **Pour on the praise.** Sincere words of praise are necessities, not luxuries. They inspire confidence, shore up self-esteem, and reinforce good habits. People will go the extra mile when you start tossing out drive-by praisings.

✔ **Co-create challenging (not impossible) goals.** Goal-setting is part art and part science. On one hand, it's hard to squeeze motivation out of an easy goal. On the other, a goal that's out of reach can demotivate. Avoid either extreme by involving people in the process.

✔ **Match incentives to outcomes.** Examine your reward system when you find yourself wondering why you have listless employees. Ask yourself, *What behaviors are we really encouraging?* You may be unwittingly rewarding the wrong kind of conduct.

VII.
SCHOOL'S
IN SESSION

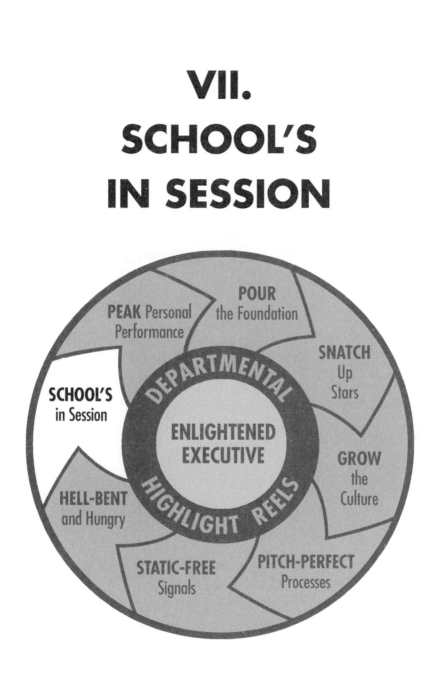

PART I

EMPHASIS ON EDUCATION

Riding Employee Development to the Top

Some years ago, a junior IBM executive lost the company $10 million when a deal blew up. Shortly afterward, CEO Tom Watson, Sr., called the young man into his office. When the contrite exec said, "I guess you want my resignation," Watson replied, "You can't be serious, son. We've just spent $10 million educating you." Elementary, my dear Watson. Whether it's Big Blue or a business of two, PR&D (people research and development) should be a big-ticket item on any company's budget.

Hard-line fiscal hawks may squawk, but yields on human-capital upgrades are better than on most other capital expenses. It's cause and effect. Educated employees are more likely to visualize a bright future, and to be able to create and execute a plan to get there.

Thanks to my company's education obsession, our competition always lagged a few steps behind. Scrambling to catch up, our seat-of-the-pants competitors imitated everything we did, from store design to our television commercials. They even swiped our phone greeting. What they couldn't copy was our people and culture, a proprietary blend of personalities and values. Whether you're teaching an employee to manage payroll or coaching him to get organized, you're doing more than shoveling information into his brain. You're equipping him with the wisdom and skills to meet your high expectations. And capable employees add up to profitable days and restful nights.

THIRTY-NINE

BEGINNERS, WINNERS, AND SINNERS

Guiding Rookies, Pros, and Fallen Stars

Enlightened leaders take into account the natural four-stage process of learning and unlearning that governs most people's career maturation. After all, as author Alvin Toffler wrote, "The illiterate of the 21st century will not be those who cannot read and write, but those who cannot learn, unlearn, and relearn." Here's my spin:

Conscious Incompetent. Out of the gate, the newbie is perfectly aware he doesn't know what he needs to know to do the job well. Nevertheless, he's determined to succeed. The excitement of a new challenge propels him to study systems, ask questions, listen hard, and follow even the tiniest rule.

Unconscious Competent. This is learning's sweet spot. He's sharpened his skills and is starting to shine. Yet, he's still humble, and eager to master every challenge that comes along. He sees with "the beginner's mind," as Japanese Zen priest Shunryu Suzuki-roshi calls it, a mind fertile for limitless learning and growth.

Conscious Competent. He's darn good and he knows it. Coaches dream of a team full of players at this stage—confident and capable, passionate and productive, a skilled professional with a beginner's mind. But beware. Once he scales the hill of success, it's painfully easy to tumble down the other side. Confidence can rot into arrogance, corners may be cut. *Sure, I'll try that* morphs into *Been there, done that.* A good coach recognizes the signs and issues a wake-up call. Half your employees will respond; the other half hit the snooze button and drift into the next stage.

Unconscious Incompetent. It's the twilight of his career (if he's not careful). He no longer knows what he needs to know in order to keep pace. The golden boy's glitter has faded, but he's too busy taking long lunches and admiring old press clips to notice. He's flying by the seat of his pants straight into turbulence—shifting trends, technological advances, competitive pressures—but he's still on auto-pilot. A good coach steers him (jolts him, if necessary) back to stage one and presses restart. If he's too proud to take a few steps back, well, I hope he's packed a parachute.

Sometimes an involuntary plunge is precisely what a former star performer needs to break out of his sense of entitlement. After years as one of our top store managers, Warren was neglecting the basics. His store's revenue and morale spiraled downward. Motivation didn't work. Probation didn't work. After eighteen months, concerned about the message we were sending to other employees about tolerating mediocrity, we were forced to go Donald Trump on him and free up his future. A few years later, Warren called and offered a heartfelt mea culpa. He said he had matured and asked for another shot. After two months of retraining, he roared back with a vengeance and reclaimed his star status.

Warren's story illustrates the importance of customized coaching. A seat-of-the-pants leader acts impulsively without seeing employees as individuals. He reaches for motivation when he should grab education. Sure, an inspired employee will leap over a moat of alligators—but you'll both be better off if you teach him how to lower the drawbridge instead. As much as the following rules have a whiff of Management 101, seat-of-the-pantsers violate them like speed limits.

	Knows How	**Doesn't Know How**
Wants To	**Delegate** (who to)	**Educate** (how to)
Doesn't Want To	**Motivate** (why to)	**Terminate** (show the door to)

- If you want something done, and know somebody who wants to do it and knows how to do it—Delegate.
- If somebody knows how to do it but doesn't want to do it—Motivate.
- If somebody wants to do it but doesn't know how to do it—Educate.
- If somebody doesn't want to do it, doesn't know how to do it, and motivation and education haven't worked—Terminate.

FORTY

ESSENTIAL ELEMENTS

Building Your Educational Infrastructure

The employee education equation is Zen-simple: *more input = more output*. Input education and your people will output more productivity. It starts with you. Share what you know. Be a steady conduit of business-building information. If you keep your knowledge to yourself, you'll be a roadblock, perpetually frustrated that nobody else "gets it." The same goes for sharing best practices. If one department or store builds a better mousetrap, make sure it's replicated throughout the company.

Employee education stretches beyond work-related subjects. The best education is multidisciplinary, reaching across all of life's artificial boundaries. Well-rounded employees with mature, sophisticated outlooks are more likely to become (happy) masters of their craft. Imagine fielding a staff of critical, strategic thinkers who can connect the dots between apparently disparate concepts and events. These building blocks will help you get there.

Training. Consuming eight thousand square feet in our suburban Minneapolis headquarters, Tires Plus University included classrooms, an auditorium, and a virtual store complete with showroom and service bays. (In-house universities are expensive, but ours paid for itself countless times over.) We enrolled new employees in a weeklong course with three primary objectives. First, TPU, as we called it, taught standardization—indispensable to an explosive outfit with employees from Milwaukee to Denver. Second, TPU instilled a familiarity with store responsibilities that allowed people to step right in and contribute. Third, TPU taught product knowledge. Nobody in the tire industry knew their "black gold" as well as our staff. Our salespeople provided customers with manufacturer specs—as well as value and safety metrics—for every brand.

TPU also taught old dogs new tricks. The Accelerated Management program put select employees on the fast track, a must for a company in heavy growth mode. "Eventually," said Chris Koepsell, TPU's dean, "we reduced the training timeline from six to twelve months down to three months." The approach was simple—identify an employee's skills, identify the skills necessary for the position, train to the gap.

The formula also applies to bosses, especially entrepreneurial ones. Most people start a business because it allows them to make a living doing something they love. Unlike me, some of my car-loving competitors paid more attention to brakes and oil pans than budgets and operating plans. Every minute they were under the hood was another minute they weren't sharpening their leadership and management skills. (By all means, tinker away if staying comfortably small is your game plan.) The sad truth is, if a restaurateur is more passionate about her dishes than improving her business skills, she'll gradually become overwhelmed by the daily demands of business and wind up running the place by the seat of her pants. And the inevitable frustration that follows may quash the food passion that led her into business in the first place.

It doesn't have to be that way. David Wagner didn't compromise his artistic passion when he bought Horst Rechelbacher's collection of Aveda spas and renamed them Juut Salonspa. David studied the nuts and bolts of management with the same intensity that launched him to global hairstyling superstardom. He and Tom Kuhn, who David brought on as president, see a pendulum resting comfortably between artistry and business. "If the pendulum swings too far toward hairstyling and makeup artistry," said Tom, "it jeopardizes our sustainability. If we emphasize business at the expense of artistry, our promise of quality, uniqueness, and value suffers. Striking just the right balance is the key to our growth and well-being."

Motivational Speakers. Familiarity breeds boredom. A new face in the office complements your in-house experts. Mike Norman, a franchisee for Dale Carnegie Training, lit a fire under a hundred of our regional and store managers during a half-day leadership workshop. "At the time, we needed to reinvent ourselves and quit relying so much on internal leaders to educate and motivate employees," said Chris Koepsell. I always looked to the horizon for fascinating specialists who could speak on anything from business trends to psychology. Our roster of memorable speakers ran the gamut from basketball firebrand Bobby Knight to mind/body author Deepak Chopra. Chalk it up to human nature, but when an outside speaker says something, chances are it's going to be heard and valued more.

But don't just hand over the agenda. Before Mike Norman took the stage, I made sure his message jibed with our mission, vision, and values. I also spoke during Mike's workshop. I couldn't pass up the opportunity to set the stage for Mike—and to pump up a gathering of employees who were in constant contact with customers.

Seminars. Send employees to workshops that fit their positions— and don't neglect yourself. I took notes and collected handouts at numerous classes, conventions, and seminars so I could re-present the content to our management team. It's a waste to keep all that knowledge to yourself. "Our focus on education had a lot to do with our low turnover," said Jim Pascale, our franchise operations veep. "After all, the more educated you are, the more productive and fulfilled you are. Learning new things prepares you to take on more responsibility."

Books. I periodically asked my executive team to read a business or personal growth book. I'd assign each person to summarize a chapter or two at an upcoming meeting. The reaction was predictable—nobody liked doing it but everybody liked having done it. "I have a belated appreciation for Tom's emphasis on downloading information about successful people and companies," said Dave Wilhelmi, vice president of marketing. "I found myself reading more books at Tires Plus than I ever did in school. It was like getting an additional education while going to work every day. With that kind of culture we couldn't help but succeed."

Mentors. Mentoring is a terrific way to leverage one employee's strengths while simultaneously educating another. Mentors and mentees typically trade phone calls and get together for lunch monthly. If the right internal match doesn't exist, go outside the company. Eric Randa, our vice president of loss prevention, trained under Gary Kasper more than twenty years ago at Montgomery Wards. Later, when we hired Eric to start up our loss prevention program, he often called Gary to ask him how he'd handle a particular challenge. "It's always good to talk to somebody who's been there and done that," said Eric, "rather than try to reinvent the wheel every time."

Tuition Assistance. In the early days, Steve Varner was a wholesale rep eager for a fresh challenge. We obliged him with an assignment to the collections department, followed by a bump up to credit manager that required him to squeeze people for money. Figuring there was more to the job, Steve signed up for a credit and financial management course at the University of Minnesota. We were thrilled, and paid half of Steve's tuition for every class in which he earned a B or better. "If I hadn't gone back to school," said Steve, "they would've eventually replaced me with somebody from the outside." He's right. Our rapid growth demanded that Steve know everything from calculating a customer's credit risk to interpreting anti-trust and collection laws. But it was a classic win-win. His bad-debt ratio was well below industry benchmarks, and his stewardship played a key role in our wholesale division's sales growth.

Encourage your people to advance their education however it fits into their busy lives. It's deadly to assume they already have what it takes to play in the big leagues. Night and weekend courses make an immediate impact. And web-based distance learning makes formal education more convenient than ever.

FORTY-ONE
THE CONFUCIUS CHECKLIST
Tell, Show, Involve

"I told him what to do and how to do it—and he still screwed it up!" Whenever I hear this complaint I agree that someone indeed screwed up. The culprit, however, was usually the boss doing the venting. You can't just throw information at people and expect them to process it the same way you do. Nobody shares your precise experiences and frame of reference, so a few links in their chain of understanding may be missing. How do you get them to understand? Stated gastronomically—digesting and assimilating raw information requires that it be chopped into bite-size chunks and sautéed in encouragement by a committed corporate chef.

Teaching is as simple as the Confucius Checklist. But seat-of-the-pantsers usually abandon it after the first step, oblivious that barking orders on the run wastes more time than it saves. Each step takes you a quarter of the way toward becoming a business sensei.

1. Tell him
2. Show him
3. Watch him do it and offer feedback
4. Watch him do it again

Say you're coaching an employee to field calls. Start by reviewing the protocols point by point. Next, take a call yourself and handle it with your usual aplomb. After hanging up, smile and ask him to take a stab. Watch closely. When he finishes his call, critique his performance: "Nice job, Larry. You were polite and friendly, the qualities we look for. A couple minor things. Remember to offer your name before, 'How can I help you?' And try not to hem and haw so much. Project composure and confidence. All right, let's try it again." Watch and listen once more. If he nails it, give him the thumbs up and move on to the next learner.

The Confucius Checklist is grounded in a basic truth—information turns into knowledge when we understand how it applies to us, and knowledge turns into wisdom when we absorb it and act on it. This process has inspired leaders for twenty-five hundred years, ever since Confucius (one of the earliest enlightened executives) said:

> *Tell me and I will forget.*
> *Show me and I might remember.*
> *Involve me and I will understand.*

FORTY-TWO

TRIAL BY FIRE

Developing Via Delegating

Over-delegation is in the eye of the delegator. One of my key execs listed "delegates too much" as a weakness on his annual review. His staff disagreed and then some—70 percent said he didn't delegate enough. My advice on delegating can be summed up in three words: let 'er rip! It develops employees like nothing else can. Hand over anything your people can do

- better than you;
- quicker than you;
- at less cost than you;
- that will add to their development;
- that will free you for more important pursuits.

Under-delegation is rampant. Many seat-of-the-pantsers wear their resistance to parceling out tasks like a badge of honor. Others conceal their reluctance behind a wall of bravado. There are myriad excuses for under-delegating. There's the **I-can-do-it-better-myself Syndrome**, which, even if it's true, doesn't change the fact that your time would be better spent elsewhere. There's the classic **I-can-save-time-doing-it-myself Syndrome.** Sure, it might take awhile to train someone to do a repetitive task, but once it's learned you're home free. Do the math—delegating just one additional assignment each week to seven people who report to you crosses thirty assignments off your to-do list every month. Another malady is the **Somebody-else-might-make-a-mistake Syndrome.**

Mistakes *will* be made, but that's exactly how people develop the experience needed to free you up for more meaningful activities.

Other conditions that cause under-delegation include the **Fear-of-giving-the-wrong-impression Syndrome**, marked by concern that you'll appear to be carrying less than your own weight. In fact, respect deepens when you place your trust in others and focus on big-picture thinking. There's also the **I-feel-threatened Syndrome**—fear of being shown up by a subordinate. That leads to a mediocrity mindset and an idle, cynical staff whose poor performance reflects poorly on you. Last, there's the **I-might-lose-control Syndrome.** Hey, no problem, people love working for a control freak in an office gulag.

That said, good leaders occasionally use overt non-delegation to deliver a message. Take the Monday morning Eric Randa, our loss-prevention czar, and Wayne Shimer stopped by a Wisconsin Tires Plus store. They walked past soda cans and other weekend detritus spotting the lawn on their way inside only to discover the store manager and two associates standing around. Now, understand that we viewed cleanliness as next to godliness, which set us apart in an industry synonymous with "grease monkey" and "industrial waste." Wayne, a vice president and part owner, walked back outside and, for all to see, picked up the trash. "You never saw Wayne have to pick up trash at that store again," recalled Eric.

Nobody ever accused me of under-delegating. "Tom was a dedicated delegator," recalled Wayne. "He forced me to be better by making me do things I didn't think I could do. The downside was that Tom was so strong at it he would over-delegate. His logic was that he never knew how far he could challenge you to find your endpoint, and Tom wanted to find that endpoint. If your optimum capacity was 98, he wanted you at 97.9."

I do tend to overload people. But that's so they learn to unload lesser priorities. Still, there's a fine line. You have to trust that your people will yell "Uncle!" Back in chapter 31, Wayne mentioned the time he had 135 items on his Goals Activity Report. He couldn't get much help because everyone underneath him already had full plates. "I just became adept at figuring out what Tom really wanted done," said Wayne. "What were the $10 items, what were the $5 items, what were the $1 items? I took the $10 items and worked the heck out of 'em. If he hit me on an uncompleted $5 item he'd grill me some, but he never brought up the $1 items. His motto is, 'Be tough, not rough.' I'm convinced he walked out of the building at night smiling and thinking, 'Let's see how he handles this one.'"

Experience has taught me that tough-not-rough delegation benefits everyone. Still, I'm not surprised that many seat-of-the-pantsers refuse to hand off enough work—willy-nilly delegation creates more problems than it solves. Before plopping assignments on desks, do your delegation due diligence.

My top ten delegation directives:

1 **Transfer ownership.** Be clear: "Here you go, this baby's all yours now."

2 **Tell why.** An employee who understands why she's being asked to handle a task is more likely to execute it thoroughly.

3 **Get the wheels turning.** For complex projects, help the delegatee develop an action plan by asking open-ended questions like "How do you see this unfolding?" and "What roadblocks do you anticipate, and how will you overcome them?"

4 **Set deadlines.** Mutually agree on a completion date and time. Otherwise, the task may sink to the bottom of the delegatee's priority list.

5 **Ask for a recap.** It's dangerous to assume the delegatee perfectly understands the assignment. Always double-check: "To make sure I communicated properly, please explain what you're planning to do and why." The answer may surprise you.

6 **Monitor (but don't smother).** The point is liberation, so don't micromanage unless the delegatee is untested or timing is critical. If she starts down the wrong path, say something like, "That might work, but have you considered going in this direction . . . What do you think that could yield and why?" Remember, the weekly one-on-one employee meeting (chapter 31) is your forum for pinpoint advising.

7 **No take-backs.** Don't retract an assignment at the first sign of trouble. That can kill confidence. Setbacks are learning opportunities, so patiently coach the delegatee back on track.

8 **Play to a delegatee's strong suit.** Tailor assignments to people's strengths. Don't saddle a big-picture thinker with a detail-intensive project.

9 **Don't duplicate.** Assign specific duties to specific people, with zero overlap. If there are two people involved, make it clear who's in charge.

10 **Distribute evenly.** Up-and-comers need challenges, too. Avoid the temptation to overload your stars.

FORTY-THREE

ROUNDTABLE REVIEWS

Turning the Annual Review into Something Useful

One day two decades ago, I sat at my desk, flipping through an employee's annual review and growing more frustrated by the minute. I remember thinking, *Man, what a waste of time. There's gotta be a better way to do this.* My compliance-conscious HR people had insisted I use the same tired performance review form that had been around since the dawn of the Industrial Revolution. You ask the same generic questions (repeatedly circling "meets expectations" or "exceeds expectations"), then drop it in the employee's cobweb-covered file.

W. Edwards Deming, the father of Total Quality Management, said the standard review "nourishes short-term performance, annihilates long-term planning, builds fear, demolishes teamwork, nourishes rivalry, and leaves people bitter." No wonder so many leaders are contemptuous of it. Sitting at my desk, I thought, *These multiple-choice questions are pointless. What should I be discovering about employees at review time?* Four themes came to mind:

1. What's he done the past year versus what he said he would do?

2. What's he doing well that I can reinforce and affirm?

3. What could he do better, and how can we help him?

4. Where does he want his career to go, and how can we help him?

I figured the best snapshot would require observations and suggestions from four perspectives—the employee's, his subordinates' (if applicable), his peers', and mine. So I sketched out a

Teammate Review Form (below). The employee being reviewed would fill out a form himself, and ask five to six subordinates and the same number of peers (all of whom I'd select) to do the same. (The employee's version also asks him to list his career goals.) The anonymous forms would then be submitted to HR, which would merge/purge the responses and compile separate results for peers and subordinates. That brand of raw feedback packs a powerful punch. People respect the boss' comments, but nothing sinks in like a written self-appraisal and the straight scoop from colleagues.

TEAMMATE COMMENTS
2005 Roundtable Review

Feedback for _____

I would appreciate feedback on what you perceive I'm doing well. I'd also like suggestions for how I can improve my performance and further my development.

Strengths:

_____
_____
_____
_____
_____
_____

NTIs (Needs-To-Improve areas):

_____
_____
_____
_____
_____
_____

Armed with this no-holds-barred input, I'd then sit down with the employee, his Goals Activity Report, and his individual operating plan (an annual list of goals derived from the company's strategic plan). His triple-decker review looked like this:

1 **Review results.** We'd briefly check the status of his operating plan goals and any other high-priority objectives assigned during the year. This was largely an overview since I'd been monitoring his progress during our weekly one-on-one sessions (chapter 31).

2 **Assess strengths and developmental needs.** First, I'd ask the employee to read me the positive attributes he listed in his self-appraisal. I'd endorse his assessment, then share his subordinates' laudatory observations: "Okay, Joe, here's what your team members had to say. Four of them said you're really caring; three of them say you're running tighter, more effective meetings." Next came favorable feedback from his peers: "Wow, a couple of your peers also noticed you've been more empathetic. You must be putting extra effort into that. Way to go." Then it was my turn. I'd affirm everyone else's positive remarks and compliment him on anything else I noticed over the past year. (Although I have a pretty good memory, I'd also rely on the reminder notes I dropped in his employee file throughout the year.)

Then it was time to move on to NTIs (needs-to-improve areas). I'd say, "Now, let's review everyone's tips, including your own, on how you can become even better." As he read aloud his own suggestions, I'd acknowledge each one with a head nod or brief comment. After reviewing what his subordinates and peers had written, I'd share my critique. We'd then dive into the details and develop action plans to fix what we agreed needed fixing. If he had a temper, he might enroll in an anger-management class. If he regularly exceeded payroll projections, I'd get the CFO to mentor him. For broader NTIs ("Always running late"), we'd add to his Goals Activity Report his desire to be five minutes early to appointments; that way I'd be able to monitor his progress during our weekly one-on-ones. One more check-and-balance mechanism: I'd note the goal in the section of the performance review called Bring Up at Next Annual Review. (I always studied an employee's previous annual reviews in preparation for the upcoming one.)

The best employees were realistic about the review and used it to their advantage. "All that honest feedback taught me a lot about myself," said Hank, a key exec. "But if I had ten or twelve things that needed improving, I was never crazy enough to think I could fix all of them. I'd pick out the top five and work on those for the year." Hank paid particular attention to the multiple complaints and ignored the one-offs. "Maybe you ticked somebody off and it was payback time," he said. "Welcome to the world of management."

After wrapping up the NTIs, I'd recap and affirm what he'd been doing well: "Overall, Joe, you're doing a super job. You've got a great outlook, a superior work ethic, and you interact well with others. I'm impressed with your determination to get on top of the challenges we discussed, like keeping your temper in check, clamping down on payroll expenses, and getting more disciplined."

3 **Look to the future.** I'd ask him to read me the career goals—both two and five years out—listed on his self-appraisal. If his abilities matched his ambitions, I'd help him determine the action steps necessary for him to go from daydreaming to day-doing. If he wanted to nab a promotion, I'd suggest a seminar or mentor, which he'd duly record on his Goals Activity Report. I'd conclude the Roundtable Review by congratulating him and thanking him for his efforts.

Brad Burley credits the Roundtable Review for his promotions. "I was very comfortable expressing to my supervisor what my career goals were," said Brad. "Out of those discussions, I went from being a store manager to being a wholesale sales manager to being a regional manager. That kind of upward mobility was built into the culture."

The Roundtable Review is a potent developmental tool. So I was upset when a sales associate at our Milwaukee store told me he hadn't had a review in two years. I apologized and told the store manager and regional manager who were there with me to make sure his review was completed before the week was out. At the next executive committee meeting, I brought up the incident and said lapses like that were inexcusable. I asked for a monthly listing of every employee whose Roundtable Review was thirty days past due. The company-wide memo that went out the next day said managers violating our review policy could expect to answer not only to their boss, but also in person to the executive committee. End of problem.

FORTY-FOUR
THE APPRENTICE APPROACH
Putting the "Success" in Succession

Business abhors a vacuum. I tossed and turned many a night worrying if people would be ready to step into freshly created vacancies. It's a tricky balancing act, but focusing on both current performance and future potential turns your staff into a major-league team *and* a resource-rich farm club. You'll sleep better at night when you know you'll be ready for the next surprise departure, or when an employee's poor performance forces your hand.

Ten succession strategies:

1 **Don't procrastinate.** Begin planning developmental experiences for tomorrow's leaders *today*. People need a chance to test their wings before you push them out of the nest. Focusing solely on the here and now carries a high cost—frequent turnover, operational interruptions, squandered human capital. As Professor Harold Hill from Broadway's *The Music Man* might put it, "Planning Purely for the Present" starts with a *P*, and that rhymes with *T*, and that stands for "Trouble."

2 **Develop a deep bench.** Routinely prepping people to take on more responsibility minimizes the chaos created by a surprise resignation. "I never knew when I was going to need a new store manager," said regional manager Brad Burley, "so I always had two or three candidates lined up. It was great for morale because people knew there was a plan to help them advance."

3 **Ask, don't assume.** It's easy to think, *Jake's a sales guy; I can't see him as a customer service rep.* Well, maybe *he* can. Don't wait for an annual review to discuss career goals. Take time to chat with people. Ask about their interests and where they see themselves two years and five years down the road.

4 **Cross-train.** Challenge people to learn new skills, especially in unfamiliar areas of the company. Start by asking them to back up colleagues during vacations, illnesses, and so-busy-I-can't-think-straight periods. If they resist, nudge them out of their comfort zone and encourage them to stretch. You won't produce any butterflies if you allow people to stay ensconced in the seductive safety of their cubicle cocoons.

5 **Prevent paranoia.** It's a safe bet people will feel threatened if they're asked to train somebody else to do their job. Assure them their job isn't at risk. Explain that it's critical for the company to build in redundancy in order to run seamlessly when people get ill, or if, God forbid, the proverbial bus hits someone. And toss in this fringe benefit: their desk won't be piled high with projects when they return from vacation.

6 **Move people around.** Don't nail people's feet to the floor. Some companies transfer managers to other departments every few years to keep them fresh and flexible. It also creates a petri dish for innovation, and gives people a better sense of how all the disparate parts of the company fit together. Although it might not be an option for smaller firms, orchestrating an occasional round of managerial musical chairs can be an excellent skill-sharpening strategy.

7 **Use 'em or lose 'em.** There's a tendency to keep a potential all-star right where he is because you don't want to risk replacing him with someone less capable. But burying your head in the sand just makes it easier for life to bite you on the backside when ambitious employees resign. Who knows how many Chris Speakes there are out there. In the course of eight years, Chris climbed from part-time tire tech to full-time sales to service manager to store manager to, finally, store owner. If you don't allow people to explore and express the full range of their God-given abilities, they'll find another employer who will.

8 **Promote from within.** When a job opens up, the first impulse should be to pass the baton to one of your own. Choking off avenues of advancement by regularly plugging outsiders into key positions dashes employees' hopes and cultivates a culture of complacency. Conversely, investing in your people's professional development, and then rewarding them with plum promotions, delivers a powerful message: if you apply yourself, anything is possible. It took years—and plenty of kvetching from frustrated employees—before I wised up to this simple truth.

9 **Avoid ruffled feathers.** Sure, it's sometimes necessary to recruit a heavy hitter with years of specialized training. In that case, let insiders know they, and their feelings, were not ignored. Take the time our less-than-effective CFO resigned. Daily cash crises were poking holes in the suddenly porous wall of our financial stability. Somebody had to step up—fast!—and plug the leaks. Luckily, we were able to counter the wolf at our door with a Wolf of our own—as in Jim Wolf, our treasurer. Jim had briefly served as the CFO of a start-up, but a company our size was a different ballgame. "I basically operated in survival mode and managed the cash on a daily basis to help us limp through the first half of the year," said Jim. "It was a stressful time, but it was also a great opportunity to learn and perform under fire." Six months later we hired Jim Bemis as permanent CFO, but Jim Wolf was strongly considered. "Tom was sensitive about my feelings but I actually felt good about the decision," said Jim. "Jim Bemis came in with better credentials and proved to be a success-ful CFO." Moral of the story? Even though Jim Wolf didn't get the job, he felt valued and appreciated in the end. He continued to play a key role, performing the treasury and planning/analysis functions until we sold the company seven years later.

10 **Collect names.** Keep a short list of all-star outsiders in case a high-level position opens up for which nobody on staff is qualified (or interested in). When I ran across, say, an impressive CFO, I jotted down his contact info. Ditto if a great candidate called about a position that was filled, or if somebody came highly recommended.

KEY POINTS: EMPHASIS ON EDUCATION

Riding Employee Development to the Top

✔ **Invest in education.** Make a healthy PR&D (people research and development) budget a priority. Skills-obsessed employees run laps around rivals. They visualize a brighter future and know how to turn that vision into reality.

✔ **Learn how people learn.** There are four stages of learning and unlearning—conscious incompetent, unconscious competent, conscious competent, unconscious incompetent. Good leaders recognize the signs and guide each person accordingly.

✔ **More input = more output.** Capitalize on the link between increased employee education and increased productivity. Improve their skills through every means, from books and seminars to mentors and tuition assistance.

✔ **Follow the Confucius Checklist.** Tell an employee how to do something and she'll forget. Show her how to do it and she might remember. Involve her and she'll understand.

✔ **Develop via delegation.** Tough-not-rough delegation benefits everyone. Increasing employees' responsibilities develops their confidence and expertise. And that frees you up for more important pursuits.

✔ **Exploit performance reviews.** Transform this annual rite into a real-world educational tool. Toss the generic forms in favor of an interactive process that reinforces success, corrects stumbles, and advances career and personal goals.

✔ **Plan for succession.** Development programs put the "success" in succession. Strike a balance between improving productivity and grooming people for advancement.

VIII.
PEAK PERSONAL PERFORMANCE

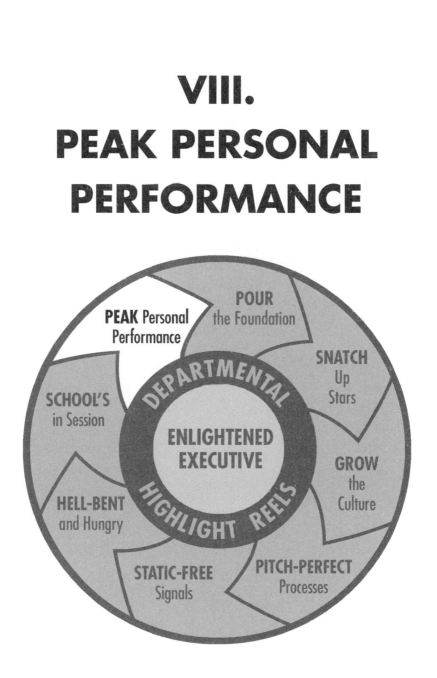

PART I

SELF-MASTERY

Coaching Yourself So You Can Coach Others

You wouldn't believe how many business leaders I see who are oblivious to the thin fabric in the seat of their pants—metaphorically speaking, of course. If you're a few threads short, consider me your personal tailor. This guide gives you all the material you need to patch your business practices, mend important relations, and weave together solid strategies. As you assemble a stronger management methodology, make sure you blend in a swatch of self-mastery strategies. Huh? Self-mastery? What does that have to do with meeting management or marketing?

Good question. Let's start with a definition—self-mastery is a systematic way to become more aware of why you behave the way you do. You then make better choices and reach goals faster. If you're thinking, *There's nothing wrong with me that doubling my profits won't cure*, let me assure you that self-mastery—coupled with enlightened business techniques—*is* key to doubling your profits. Self-mastery strengthens your organizational skills as well as your intellect, body, psyche, and spirit, expanding your capacity to lead. No time for anything but last month's P&L or getting the latest ad out the door? Fair enough, I'll be brief. If you think you can't benefit from self-mastery strategies, chances are you can. It's a Catch-22. You can't change your seat-of-the-pants ways until you recognize you're unenlightened. Yet, you won't realize you're unenlightened until you start down the path of enlightenment.

Confused? Well, simply holding this guide means you're ahead of where I was at forty-one, a year before life went Humpty-Dumpty on me. Had you met me back in 1988, you would've seen the facade of the Classic American Success Story. I had the handsome family, the beautiful home. Every week I had time for church and shooting hoops with pals. I had the growing company and prominence in the community. I would've told you with an ear-to-ear grin and a firm handshake that life was good. Real good.

Next thing I knew, a triple trauma of divorce, cancer, and a business crisis had me flattened on the pavement, surrounded by the shattered pieces of my life. My nerves were twitchy, downed power lines, forcing people to walk on eggshells around me as I tried to glue things back together. I lashed out at anyone who dared suggest I look in the mirror. I remember snapping at a friend not long after my divorce: "Show me anywhere in writing where it says it's healthy to feel my feelings!" One by one, my defenses were splintered by the wicked storm brewing inside me. I pummeled myself for six months: *You really screwed up. You hurt your family. You ruined your business. There's no way out of this one.* I was a dead man walking. Nothing in my life was going right, and it seemed like nothing would ever be right again.

Desperate, I sought a psychologist. I was convinced the pieces of my life would click back into place if I could just get my old self back. I clung to the belief that brainpower and force of will would pull me through. I ignored airy-fairy talk from friends about emotional breakthroughs and deepening my spiritual connection. *Maybe a shrink can tell me what's wrong with everyone else,* I remember thinking. *This mess sure can't be my fault.*

Enter therapist Brenda Schaeffer, one of the smartest calls I ever made. She helped me see that my choices and behaviors were the shovels that had dug the cesspool I was now floundering in. It slowly dawned on me that there just might be a higher purpose behind the sledgehammer that had brought me to my knees. It was then that the writings of philosopher Soren Kierkegaard spoke to me:

> *A man may perform astonishing feats and*
> *comprehend a vast amount of knowledge,*
> *and yet have no understanding of himself.*
> *But suffering directs a man to look within.*
> *If it succeeds, then there, within him, is*
> *the beginning of his learning.*

Humbled, I began exploring healthier lifestyles. I read books and attended seminars on psychological and spiritual wellness. I overhauled my diet. Meditation, massages, tai chi (an ancient Chinese discipline of meditative movements), and individual and group therapy sessions started filling up my calendar. I solicited blunt, objective feedback from friends and colleagues. Without naming it, or knowing where it would lead, I had begun the process of self-mastery. Every step I took toward a healthier life was another small candle in the dark.

I started noticing improvements. Deeper clarity and self-aware-ness enhanced my efficiency and management skills. My strate-gic and operational thinking began firing on all cylinders. To my delight, I was connecting more deeply with teammates. Better still, my healthier frame of mind inspired healthier behavior in employ-ees, who in turn produced a healthier bottom line. I'm actually grateful for that triple trauma. It shook up my priorities and steered me down the road to enlightenment. I hope my screw-ups are sign-posts that will keep you out of ditches.

I could go on and on about the benefits of self-mastery. In fact, I have, in my first book, *Winning in the Game of Life: Self-Coaching Secrets for Success*. In it, you'll find additional insights, info, and strategies to create a positive, productive, and well-balanced life.

KEY POINTS: SELF-MASTERY

Coaching Yourself So You Can Coach Others

✔ ***Commit to an ongoing pursuit of self-mastery.***
It may seem like life is humming along perfectly. Take a closer look. Are you totally satisfied at work and at home? Are you happy with your behavior and state of mind? Are your relationships all they can be? If any of the answers are no, take responsibility and start making changes. If nothing changes, well, nothing changes.

✔ ***Hit the books on healthier lifestyles.*** Go back to school for smart living—research the web, visit bookstores, attend seminars, set aside time for quiet reflection. Methodically improving yourself intellectually, physically, emotionally, and spiritually leads to greater happiness and fulfillment.

FORTY-FIVE

FAST TRACK

Profiting from Your Potential

The ability to coach yourself is a hallmark of an enlightened executive. You can't guide others to greatness until you first clear the brush from your own path. Self-mastery strategies help you:

Fulfill your promise. There isn't much wiggle room in professional sports contracts. It's understood, if not explicitly spelled out, that the athlete will take care of himself so he can perform at optimal levels. Likewise, when you accept a leadership role, you're agreeing to provide your best effort. If you don't take care of yourself physically, emotionally, intellectually, and spiritually, you won't have the stamina or know-how to lead your team to the top of the mountain.

Be a good coach. Leadership demands a passionate sense of purpose, clarity of mind, and stratospheric levels of integrity, energy, and interpersonal skills. You can't get there without a steady focus on self-mastery. As Dee Hock, founder of Visa International, said, "If you look to lead, invest at least 40 percent of your time managing yourself." If you can't manage to manage yourself, you won't be any better than Dilbert's pointy-haired boss at motivating the troops.

Build managerial muscle. The best coaches are also great managers. Always remember: *coach* people, *manage everything else* that keeps an organization running smoothly—like strategic planning, financial analysis, and information technology. A balanced approach to self-care coupled with sound business practices will land you in the Enlightened Executive Hall of Fame.

Improve relationships. It's an aphorism that bears repeating: *people don't care how much you know until they know how much you* *care*. If you haven't worked through your own unhealthy behaviors—if you have more issues than *National Geographic*—you'll be too mired in your own muck to care for the people under your watch. You'll also remain mystified why people don't pay you the respect you think you deserve.

Save time. A focus on self-mastery pays off in spades. First, time management improves because you're focused, organized, and alert. Second, better interpersonal and decision-making skills help you dispatch more issues as they arise, preventing future course-correction headaches. Sure, it's tough to find the time to coach yourself, but avoiding the exercise altogether will make life harder than it has to be.

Keep your antennae up. Get in touch with your emotions, motivations, and feelings, and you'll have a better sense of what makes other people tick. You'll know what to ask and when to ask it to get employees back on track. The ability to approach and comfort a struggling employee is an underrated skill—and difficult to do without going to school on it.

Positively influence others. Think like a parent, even at work. Whether or not you realize it, your attitude and behavior seep through your entire company or department. If you're cheerful and optimistic, your teammates are more likely to be upbeat and positive. If you're moody and negative, you'll have an office full of grouches.

Make work more enjoyable. Office life gets easier the harder you work at self-improvement. You start going with the flow instead of swimming against the current. As you get to know yourself better, you'll interact more authentically with people in all parts of your life. You'll think more clearly. You'll share more smiles and laughter. You'll see more mutual trust and respect. You'll feel more caring and energized, and gain more of a sense that life is unfolding exactly as it should.

Enhance your career. This warp-speed, Who-Moved-My-Cheese business world can be harsh and unforgiving. The most valuable currencies in a meritocracy are superior organizational, management, and people skills. Master them, and you'll respond to crises with the calmness and clarity of Sherlock Holmes.

FORTY-SIX

GOT MISSION?

Crafting Your Personal Mission Statement

A great way to sharpen our life's focus is to put pen to paper—or fingers to keyboard—and craft a personal mission statement. It helps us zero in on why we're here (surely there's more to life than giving pain to our birth mother and consuming natural resources), which gets us thinking big thoughts about what we want to give and get out of life. Think of your mission as your personal lighthouse, a beacon in the darkness that helps you navigate indecision. It prevents dreams from drifting off course and getting dashed on the rocks of inertia. Whether a single paragraph or a full page, your mission statement can mean the difference between living a life of choice and living a life of chance. Transformation expert Werner Erhard said:

> *You can either react to circumstances*
> *or act out of a vision.*

The act of writing out our vision crystallizes our convictions and codifies our moral compass. It reveals the wisdom of the adage, "The purpose of life is a life of purpose." When I'm acting in concert with my mission, big decisions are easier to make. And I'm more aware of opportunities for growth and success.

Stay in touch with your mission, and you'll avoid bolting up in bed some night with the horrible realization that all your dreams have gone unfulfilled, scattered to the wind like so many wisps of smoke. Do the work you need to do, right now. Don't wait until you find yourself on your knees, awash in regrets. I've been there, hated that. Writing my mission statement reconnected my head to my soul. Yet, I don't expect it to shield me from life's vicissitudes. Chaos and calamity may occasionally pay me a visit, especially when I lose focus and drift onto the shoulder. The difference now is that it's easier to regain control and get back on track.

FIRST THINGS FIRST

In the time it takes to see a movie, you can finish the first draft of your mission statement. It's a small price to pay—skipping the latest action flick—for supercharging your life. To set the stage:

Isolate yourself. Find a quiet place, turn off the phones, and, if appropriate, tape a DO NOT DISTURB sign on the door.

Get in the zone. Close your eyes. Take slow, deep breaths, and go to a calm, peaceful place—a river valley, a mountain glade. Experience it with all your senses and let the tension melt away.

Sequester the judge. Give your inner critic the day off and let ideas gush freely. Otherwise, the process will be as slow and dry as a crawl through the Sahara.

Be patient. This isn't *Jeopardy!* Take your hand off the buzzer and your eyes off the clock. Take as much time as you need to tap into your longings.

Open wide. To the extent you can, temporarily suspend your analytical mind and material desires. Open yourself to a deeper source of wisdom. Sure, seats on powerful boards and accumulating reinvested dividends are goals worth pursuing. But you don't stand a chance of fulfilling your destiny if your mission is grounded purely in egotism and worldly wants. Carl Jung, a founder of modern psychology, wrote:

> *Your vision will become clear only when you can look into your own heart. Who looks outside, dreams; who looks inside, awakens.*

ASK THE RIGHT QUESTIONS

Take a deep breath, Clark Kent. You're about to duck into a phone booth. First, ask, *What was I sent here to do?* To be sure, it's a broad question, one often obscured by daily stressors. Narrow your focus by applying the question to each key area of your life. *What were you sent here to do for*

your spouse?	your children?
your parents?	your extended family?
your friends?	society at large?
your career?	your colleagues?
your community?	your country?
the planet?	your spirit?

The only mission you can trust springs from your heart, mind, and soul. Strip away everything that's limited you—money, age, health, family, geography, and the mother of all bugaboos, people's expectations. Forget all that. Concentrate solely on your destiny. Now, jot down your thoughts. Remember, your mission is a collection of simple guideposts, like *Maintain physical health through proper diet, exercise, and self-care.* Don't worry about measurable goals—*Lose ten pounds by next birthday*—quite yet. To spur your thinking, ask, *What can I do every day to fulfill my purpose?* Here's what I came up with:

- Nourish myself with more spirituality
- Build my communication skills
- Ignore distractions that tend to impede growth
- Be caring and loving
- Guide people one-on-one and in groups
- Model health and well-being for others
- Tap my Higher Source for wisdom and discipline
- Make my mission a high priority

Now, imagine that one of the cool things you discover when you die is that you get to be a fly on the casket and eavesdrop at your funeral. What will your friends and loved ones reminisce about? What do you *hope* they'll reminisce about? (Are the answers different?) What parts of your personality would you like to stand out? What deeds would you like to define you? Here's what I jotted down after pondering, *How would I like to be remembered when I die?*

- He was a loving son, brother, and mate.

- He was the best father he knew how to be—a friend and mentor to his sons.

- He shared wisdom that helped his friends get what they wanted from life.

- He tried to find the goodness in everyone and to bring people together.

- He shared his blessings.

- He had a sense of humor, lightened the load of people around him, and had fun.

- He was caring, loving, and gentle with himself.

- He stood up for his beliefs and challenged power in the name of community.

- He supported organizations that shared his values.

PUTTING IT ALL TOGETHER

After harvesting all these ideas, I sifted them around and mixed in a few more I plucked from my suddenly fertile imagination. Voilá! My mission practically wrote itself from there. It's a living document, but here's my latest:

1. To evolve toward an enlightened and loving state.

2. To strengthen connections to my Higher Power, friends, and family.

3. To support my evolution through education that integrates body, intellect, psyche, and spirit.

4. To develop habits that build my knowledge and communication skills.

5. To build nurturing environments that contribute to the growth of family and friends.

6. To contribute to the growth of colleagues by helping them optimize their talents and productivity.

7. To teach leadership skills to organizations that improve the world.

8. To tread lightly on the Earth and ensure that future generations inherit a healthy planet.

9. To help people determine and achieve their missions.

With a working draft in hand, set aside ten minutes here and there over the next few weeks for revisions. Keep turning ideas in your mind as you garden, golf, or rock on the porch. If you can, get quiet and ask yourself whether there's any more information. Be still, listen. And keep a notepad ready. When ideas are brewing, you never know when they'll percolate.

When you think you've nailed it, repeat your mission statement out loud a few times to burn it into your consciousness. But don't just say it. Display it. Frame it and hang it on your office wall, or put it on your desk next to the family snapshots. Make a wallet-size copy so it's always within reach. But remember, just as you can't live in a house that only exists in blueprints, your mission can't produce anything until you grab a hammer and nails and start pounding away.

KEY POINTS: GOT MISSION?

Crafting Your Personal Mission Statement

✔ **A mission statement deepens your sense of purpose.** Recording your heartfelt desires—what you hope to give and get in life—adds focus and meaning to every day. It's the difference between living a life of choice and living a life of chance.

✔ **Don't rush.** Find a quiet place to think and write. Relax. Be patient and positive. Look beyond your analytical mind and material desires to a deeper source of wisdom. Take time for revision and rethinking.

✔ **Drill down to your deepest longings.** Pan over every part of your life and ponder what you were sent here to do in each one. Project into the future—what will people say about you at your funeral? Are you dictating a regrettable obituary?

✔ **Assemble the picture, refer to it often.** Make your mission statement visible in your daily life. Hang it on your office wall. Keep a copy in your purse or wallet. Make it into a screensaver. Keep it front and center to remind yourself why you're taking up space on the planet.

FORTY-SEVEN

READY, SET, GOALS

Turning Dreams into Destiny

It's pretty darn hard to get from here to there without a roadmap. Laying out your goals bridges the gap between who you are today and the person you sketched out in your mission statement. Yet, when I ask people all over the country whether they write up their goals each year, barely one in ten say they have. But that 10 percent gushes over how spelling out their goals transformed their lives.

So why the disconnect? Lots of reasons. Chronically impatient people think goal-setting is a waste of time. They wonder why they should spend hours writing down what they want to do when they could be out there actually doing it. These are the same people who prefer driving around lost for an hour over stopping for directions. Others are wary of introspection, a prerequisite for pinpointing what they want from life.

Some folks actually fear success because living the dream might turn their lives upside down. Personal demons trap others into thinking they don't deserve happiness and financial security. And then there's fear of failure, a particularly acute malady for fragile egos whose self-esteem just can't take the blow of another disappointment. Any of this sound familiar? Then read and re-read the self-mastery section. It'll help clear away the obstacles in your path.

Rustling and herding your goals into one place—a digital file, a legal pad, a planner—is deeply satisfying and clarifying. The simple act of writing down a goal and resolving to achieve it is deceptively powerful. In his 1951 book, *The Scottish Himalayan Expedition*, W. H. Murray explained:

> *There is one elementary truth, the ignorance*
> *of which kills countless ideas and splendid plans:*
> *that the moment one definitely commits oneself,*
> *then Providence moves too. All sorts of things*
> *occur to help one that would never otherwise*
> *have occurred. A whole stream of events issues*
> *from the decision, raising in one's favor all*
> *manner of unforeseen incidents and meetings*
> *and material assistance, which no man could*
> *have dreamed would have come his way."*

GETTING STARTED

With the framework of your personal mission statement in one hand, writing down your goals with the other is as easy as filling out a job application. (Who better than you to apply for the job of improving your life?) The five steps you used to craft your mission statement also apply here—find a quiet place, relax, don't judge, be patient, and open yourself to a deeper wisdom. Once grounded, take a minute to review your mission. Let it sink into your consciousness. Next, jot down what you'd like to accomplish in the next twelve months in each category of life:

Family	Romance
Career	Finances
Friends	Physical fitness
Social life	Spiritual fitness
Intellectual fitness	Recreation
Emotional fitness	Community service

Want to trim two inches off your waistline? File under *physical fitness*. Want to get your temper under control? File under *emotional fitness*. Intend to nab that promotion you're eyeing? File under *career*. Ready to start working Wednesday evenings at the soup kitchen? File under *community service*. Before you start filing, however, check out my top ten goal-setting guidelines:

1 **Have fun.** Choosing what you want from life shouldn't feel like homework. For me, it's like picking out flowers, fruits, and vegetables at the farmer's market. Or, think back to the childhood excitement of paging through holiday catalogs and making out a wish list. Only now, *you* decide which goodies you'll get.

2 **Make it user-friendly.** Arrange your goals in an easy-to-read, easy-to-modify format—perhaps a bulleted list of items or research paper outline.

3 **Be specific.** Clarity and precision make goals measurable, whereas vague, moving targets are difficult to hit and easy to abandon. Where possible, add a measurable metric (the percentage of a raise, the number of sit-ups) and a time element (vacation departure date, weekly visits to the gym). The more details the better. Which goal do you think is most likely to spur action: "Lose weight"? "Lose ten pounds"? or "Lose ten pounds by May 15"?

4 **Shoot for the stars—or not.** Goal-setters fall into two camps. The dreamer likes to hang a humdinger of a target—make a million bucks, date a supermodel, play polo in the Hamptons—knowing he'll fall short but looking forward to the adventure. The pragmatist, on the other hand, is motivated by challenging, yet accessible, objectives. She's disappointed if she can't put a line through everything on her to-do list. Which camp are you in?

5 **Examine your motives.** Don't just identify *what* you want but *why* you want it. I discovered I wanted to build a successful tire company in order to brighten our customers' day and provide opportunities for teammates to grow in a healthy work environment. Had I wanted to grow my company purely for ego gratification—which, I admit, was my primary driver early on—the results would've been markedly different. Our company didn't shift into higher gear until I did.

6 **Walk the tightrope.** Life is a daily balancing act. A lot of people zero in on their career and tune everything else out. I can relate. All the late nights and weekends I worked exacted a toll (cancer, divorce). The world is full of hardworking moms and dads who would gladly return the extra money they earned if they could turn back the clock and cheer at a couple more Little League games or boost their kids up a few more jungle gyms. The ultimate gift of time is the moments when you're fully present, without the faintest thought of work. Yet, success is impossible without hard work. Indeed, sometimes circumstances legitimately demand an obsessive focus on work over an extended stretch. (Operating out of balance occasionally may even help you achieve a better balance in the long run.) Trouble is, lingering too long in workaholic mode leads to burnout, health problems, and relationship crises. Or, at the very least, a vague feeling of emptiness and a life that just doesn't work very well.

7 **Mix it up.** Blend together short-term goals that can be nailed in a few weeks, medium-termers you can reach in a few months, and long-term goals that may take a year or more. Spacing out goals produces a sense of ongoing accomplishment and keeps you motivated. Also, find a nice mix of difficult goals and chip shots. Envelope-pushing projects can test your abilities, but an agenda top-heavy with them may be a setup for failure.

8 **Make it your own.** It's unavoidable that some goals will find their way onto your list out of a sense of obligation. Just make sure the majority spring from your wants and desires rather than somebody else's.

9 **Be gracious in defeat.** No matter how massive your effort, uncontrollable circumstances may prevent you from reaching a goal. That's okay. Look at what you accomplished—knowledge, relationships, confidence—during the pursuit. (If at least part of the goal is still doable, put it back in the mix for next year's list.)

10 **Stay flexible.** Keep your eyes on the prize, but don't ignore the rest of the midway. If priorities shift, shift with them rather than blindly plowing ahead. Stay grounded in your mission and receptive to new information, and your goals will evolve as naturally as winter gives way to spring.

FINISHING TOUCHES

Once you're satisfied with your list, sign and date it. Treat it like the important document it is—a compact with yourself that you will honor. But it's not chiseled in stone. There's room for amendments (and they shouldn't require an act of Congress). Review and revise your goals every few months so they're up to speed with life's twists and turns. For instance, you may need to adjust your exercise routine in the wake of a promotion that demands more time or travel—a development that could also impact financial, social, and relationship objectives. If you've slowed down to a trot, tweaking your goals sparks a renewed dedication to dig in your spurs and start galloping again.

Your list of goals is a companion document to your mission statement. Keep them both conspicuous, at work and at home. Don't lose sight of why you get out of bed every morning. Carry an easily accessible copy in your BlackBerry, planner, or wallet. A quick glance now and then helps me keep my goals top-of-mind. Sure, you can skip all this. None of it is convenient. But then you'll be a human ping-pong ball—always in the middle of the action and moving at breakneck speed, but getting smacked in so many different directions you'll be lucky to wind up where you started the year. If that's not appealing, don't let another day slip by without giving serious thought to what you want to give and get in life. As former General Electric CEO Jack Welch bluntly put it, "Control your own destiny, or someone else will."

KEY POINTS: READY, SET, GOALS

Turning Dreams into Destiny

✔ ***Goal-setting leads you to your destiny.*** Articulating your goals crystallizes your dreams and desires. It shifts your focus from the here and now to a big-picture view of a happier, more successful future.

✔ ***Reap the power of writing down goals.*** The moment you commit to a goal, circumstances start conspiring in your favor. Goethe recognized this basic universal law: "Whatever you can do or dream you can, begin it. Boldness has genius, power, and magic in it."

✔ ***Customize goals for each slice of life.*** Target what you want in each area of your life—from career, romance, and friendships to finances, recreation, and emotional fitness.

✔ ***Keep your goals top-of-mind.*** Display your goals at home and at work. Refer to them often. Tweak them regularly to keep them relevant. With every glance, you're one step closer to controlling your own destiny.

FORTY-EIGHT

WORKING THE PLAN

Linking Goals to Action Steps and Schedules

Jim Pascale was just twenty-seven when we hopped in my car and took off for Iowa. It was our first market outside Minnesota and I'd just promoted Jim to regional manager there. Speeding out of Minneapolis and down I-35, I asked to see his schedule. Gripping the wheel with one hand, Jim grabbed his planner from the back seat and handed it over. I was not pleased with what I saw. "Do you have a copy of your goals with you?" I asked. Jim froze and shot me a deer-in-the-headlights look. "Pull over," I said. "I'm going to drive." Back on the interstate, I told Jim to write down everything he wanted to accomplish for the year, from career and financial goals to travel, health, and relationships. He listed the categories and wrote things like, "Hit my bonus target," "Pay off personal debt," and "Visit my parents in Chicago." Then I told him to list the action steps his goals required. Finally, I asked him to establish deadlines.

When Jim finished, I congratulated him, but cautioned that it was only the first step. I told him to rewrite his monthly schedule by first finding homes on his calendar for what was personally important. Next, he added mandatory work meetings. Finally, he added other high-priority tasks and appointments. "As I entered each item," said Jim, "I began connecting the dots between my goals and my daily activities. In order to hit my personal financial goals, I had to hit my bonus targets. To hit my bonus, I had to fix up my stores and hire good people. It was obvious those things were related but I hadn't been working toward specific, measurable goals in such a step-by-step way." By the time we hit Iowa, I sensed that something in Jim had shifted. In the months that followed, he was clearly more purposeful and disciplined. Two years later, he was named vice president of franchise operations, at double the salary.

Expecting to hit the better-life jackpot without investing in disciplined, efficient habits makes as much sense as hoping to win the lottery without buying a ticket. Do what you've always done and you'll get what you've always gotten. You can conquer the summit of any mountain you choose—if you set your mission in motion by creating and executing action plans. Eloquent mission statements and lofty goals are a good start. But without deliberate deeds, they fade like yesterday's paper. The last trace is a vague sense that you'd once been at the doorstep of greatness. As Will Rogers said, "Even if you're on the right track you'll get run over if you just sit there."

First Create, Then Integrate

An action plan is just what it sounds like—a list of what must be done to change a goal's status from "To do" to "Ta-daaa." For example, six years ago I decided to deepen my relationship with my parents, who are divorced and live far from my Minneapolis home. My mother, Elizabeth, now eighty-six, lives in southern Indiana, and my father, Bill, now eighty-two, put down stakes in southern California. Here's how I linked that goal—and its action steps—to my mission. (The same drill works for business goals.)

PERSONAL MISSION STATEMENT *(relevant portion)*:
To build nurturing environments that contribute to the growth of family and friends.

GOAL CATEGORY: Family.

GOAL: To enhance my relationship with my mother (I created a separate plan for my relationship with my father).

ACTION PLAN:

1. Call Mom three times weekly.

2. Take a weeklong vacation with her wherever she'd like to go.

3. Spend six long weekends annually at her Indiana home.

4. Host her in our Minneapolis home from Christmas to New Year's Day.

5. Send cards on her birthday, Mother's Day, and other holidays.

6. Financially assist her to ensure she lives a comfortable, active life.

7. Consistently check in on her feelings and her life, and leave nothing unsaid. Regularly express that I love her and appreciate all the love she's given me.

Building action plans is invigorating but, like your mission and goals, they're still just words on paper. Transferring your action plans onto your schedule and to-do list is the critical link between your goals and day-to-day life. Just be sure to mind your priorities—schedule your personal life first, then plan business around it. Personal goals pave the way to a healthy, balanced life, which makes you more effective at work. Lay important family dates on your calendar like coats of paint—birthdays, Little League, family outings, vacations, and so on. Sure, something will come up at work, and you may have to miss a game or two. The point is, if you *don't* schedule them you'll miss a lot more.

It's easier than you think to integrate your action plans into daily life. After calling my mother to discuss what dates worked for her, I typed everything—the weeklong vacation, long weekends, Christmastime, annual financial review—into my Microsoft Outlook calendar. I also added send-a-card reminders three days ahead of each birthday and holiday. As always, "Call Mom" anchors the top of my Outlook Task list. It's a joy to lace my action plans—

business objectives, financial planning, physical exercise, spiritual growth—into my daily life. I know it dramatically improves the chances that I'll do what it takes to achieve my goals.

SCHEDULING BREEDS SPONTANEITY

I can already hear the critics calling for my head: *Whoa, does this guy's calendar tell him when to brush his teeth? If I wanted that much structure I'd join the military! Where's the flexibility? Where's the spontaneity?* Look, I'm not suggesting you become a lean, mean scheduling machine. Block out plenty of breather breaks on your calendar and be spontaneous within the boundaries of your schedule. It's foolish to pass on serendipitous opportunities simply because you've got an appointment, especially one that could easily be rescheduled. Enjoy the freedom to improvise—as long as you don't put off high-priority issues.

You ratchet up productivity by connecting the dots between your mission, goals, action plans, and schedule. You're also more relaxed and spontaneous because the parts of your life that really matter are (generally) on track and accounted for. For me, that means I'm free to live more fully in the present moment. And with everything in sync, my mind isn't cluttered with the debris of a million to-do's: *Oh, no! I was supposed to meet George for lunch two hours ago! Shoot, Mom's birthday is tomorrow and I forgot to send her flowers.* That kind of spontaneity I can do without.

Think of action plans as suggestions and reminders. They aren't commandments chiseled in stone, a lesson I learned the hard way. Time was when my days were wound so tightly I made every meeting only if my schedule worked like a Swiss watch and nothing unexpected came up—like an ill-timed red light. No matter how much I rushed for the next meeting or the next flight, I felt like Wile E. Coyote chasing the Roadrunner. I finally wised up and built some cushion between appointments. That gave me time for a few deep breaths and let me catch up on minor tasks. I still find myself in an occasional tight spot, but now it's an exception rather than the rule. Bottom line: schedule your time or it will schedule you.

Keep in mind Professor Cyril Northcote Parkinson's tried-and-truism: "Work expands so as to fill the time available for its completion." That is, the more air you build into your schedule, the more you court inefficiency and waste. If you're among the discipline-challenged, you're going to find yourself accomplishing little and watching your goals drift away. Eventually, you'll feel like a helpless bystander watching your life pass by with nothing to show for it but gray hair and regret. The solution? A middle ground where scheduling is less an obligation than an art. It takes practice to find just the right blend of flexibility and structure. But once you're in the zone, you'll be able to sense when you can cancel or postpone activities and appointments without causing too many ripples in the lake of your daily life.

TAKE YOUR EYES OFF THE PRIZE

As I work toward a goal, I occasionally visualize what achieving it will look and feel like. But to actually get there, I need to focus on a series of short-range, easily attainable steps. As poet M. C. Richards wrote:

> *A knowledge of the path cannot be substituted*
> *for putting one foot in front of the other.*

Let's say you want to land the Acme account. Sure, it's fun and inspirational to visualize nailing it in Technicolor detail—whooping it up at signing, pumping up team morale, adding it to your portfolio and watching it snowball. But the lion's share of focus must shift to the steps required to accomplish the goal. That calls for an action plan. Ask yourself, *What's the smallest step I can take right now toward my goal?* Then ask yourself what the next smallest step is. And then the one after that. Keep going until you've written down every step you can imagine. Perhaps your list will look like this:

GOAL: Land the Acme account.

ACTION PLAN:

1. Research the company.

2. Hone sales skills by reviewing my last refresher course and scanning sales books for inspiration and tips.

3. Ask colleagues why previous efforts to land the account fizzled.

4. Prepare for upcoming sales call by analyzing the fizzle's cause and detailing in writing our company's enhanced pricing package and ability to service the account.

5. Introduce myself via a letter to the decision maker at the parent company.

6. Follow up a week later with a phone call to secure an appointment.

Now, weave the steps through your schedule and to-do list, and start crossing them off one by one. Take five minutes each morning and fifteen minutes at week's end to review progress and priorities—with market conditions in constant flux, a goal that seemed essential six weeks ago might be ready for the scrap heap today. If you think of another step you can take, update your action plan, schedule, and to-do list accordingly. Then dig in again, and keep shoveling until you hit pay dirt.

KEY POINTS: WORKING THE PLAN

Linking Goals to Action Steps and Schedules

✔ *Scheduling is an art.* Make time to find the right blend of flexibility and structure. Once you've established a rhythm and you're more purposeful with your time, you'll have a better sense of when you can cancel or postpone activities.

✔ *Scheduling breeds spontaneity.* You're more relaxed and spontaneous within the boundaries of your schedule when important parts of your life are on track and accounted for. Schedule in blocks of breathing room, build some cushion between appointments, and reschedule low-priority appointments when high-priority opportunities come along.

✔ *Take your eyes off the prize.* Visualizing the completion of a goal can be a big motivator in and of itself. That said, it's necessary to shift your focus from the goal itself to the steps required to reach it. Integrate these action steps into your schedule and to-do list, then methodically execute them.

FORTY-NINE

TRANSCENDING TIME

Embracing Enlightened Efficiency

So many leaders have the equation half right. Take the executive who's enlightened but inefficient. He's like the absent-minded preacher, late to the pulpit with lines of a great sermon running through his head—some written on scraps of paper in his pocket, the rest scattered around his cluttered office. His heartfelt attempts to inspire confuse the flock instead. Then there's the unenlightened, but efficient, boss man. He's like a world-class surgeon with arctic bedside manners. His skill would save more lives if he wasn't undermining his patients' will to live by describing the progression of their disease like it was a mutual fund chart.

An executive who's both enlightened *and* efficient is like a trusted family friend. She deeply cares about the well-being of people under her watch, tirelessly coaching and challenging them to be passionate and productive, disciplined and daring. To her fans, she's like a double shot of espresso.

Enlightened efficiency isn't an end in and of itself. Without it, however, you stand little chance of achieving your goals and ultimately living out your mission. Steadily ratcheting up your efficiency lays the groundwork for handling future challenges. It's the tipping point that can take you from frustration to fulfillment. As one of my favorite aphorisms goes:

> *The will to prepare to succeed is more*
> *important than the will to succeed.*

I Can't Believe It's Not Clutter

Working in a blur of disorganization is like driving in a blizzard—inevitably, you lose track of the road. Shooting for efficiency without first getting organized is like trying to break the speed limit on a highway under construction. Potholes and roadblocks would send you into a ditch before you get out of first gear.

Organization paves the way to enlightened efficiency and goal achievement. Can you be productive with a messy desk and chaotic files? Sure, anything's possible. But it's easier to get it done without the clutter. Especially when you add a personal digital assistant (PDA)—BlackBerry, Palm Pilot, Clio, Treo—to the mix to keep mission-critical data at your fingertips. The idea is to conserve both time and adrenaline. You'll be calmer, better focused, and more effective.

I'd be lost without my BlackBerry. Before I leave the office, I sync it with the address book, to-do list, and calendar on my PC. On the road, I update and revise on the fly; I stay connected in an airport or doctor's office through phone, web access, and wireless e-mail. Then I upload everything back into my PC once home. I prefer a PDA to paper planners because it's compact and reduces redundancy (plus, it's a wireless wonder—when I update my calendar on my BlackBerry or PC, the other device is automatically updated). But there are as many planning systems—digital and manual—as there are personalities. PDAs also help capture those fleeting, firefly thoughts. A micro-cassette recorder or good old pen and paper also do the trick. Even if you're driving, don't let a good idea flutter away. In the car, paper and pencil are impractical (if not lethal), so I leave voicemail for myself with hands-free cell-phone calls. "Tom? This is Tom," I say, amusing whoever's riding shotgun. "Got an idea ..."

Cleaning up the clutter begins from the inside out. Internal clarity naturally stirs desire for external clarity, and makes your personal and business life flow more smoothly. Changes unfold subtly, but the day will come when you stop in your tracks and marvel at how such a heady concept as enlightened efficiency has become as natural to you as breathing.

ALL THE TIME IN THE WORLD

A few years ago, after a keynote address to Students in Free Enterprise, I judged a national student business competition. Later that day, I chatted with a supplier manning a convention booth. By coincidence, his daughter had given one of the forty-five-minute presentations I judged. I asked how he'd enjoyed it. "Oh, I had to stay at my booth," he said. "There's business to get, you know." My heart sank. *You poor soul and your poor daughter*, I thought. Here his daughter was competing in a national contest and he couldn't spare forty-five minutes? Imagine the message that sent her. What clouded his judgment and twisted his priorities so badly?

Sorry to say it, but I know the answer—fear. In my lean early years, I was so scared about making payroll I couldn't slow down. Every meeting, every resignation, every sales dip—everything was a red-hot priority. Even when business clicked into place, I couldn't part with the mindset. Any problem could whisk me back to the bad old days, and I'd be off to the races again.

If twenty-four hours in a day seems to shortchange you, you're not alone. A *Wall Street Journal*/NBC News poll showed that 80 percent of us describe our lives as busy or busy to the point of discomfort. More telling: surveyors had to call 31,407 phone numbers to find 2,001 Americans with enough time to answer their questions. The I-don't-have-enough-time mantra becomes a self-fulfilling prophecy—you don't have enough time because you never believed you would. Enlightened efficiency demands that you consciously choose to experience time differently. You replace the old mantra with a new one: *I have all the time I need to do everything I need to do*.

Something magical happens when you add purpose to your life by identifying your goals, breaking them into action plans, and building your schedule and to-do list around them. Time. Slows. Down. It's easy to explain. The smarter you are with your time, the more of it you have. Still, no matter how sharp your focus, you'll likely get snared by the time-wasting traps lurking in every office. The Meeting, which can rank among the deepest black holes, is covered in chapter 22. A few other traps to avoid:

Trim the talk. Imagine. If you have thirty conversations daily, each running four minutes longer than necessary, you lose two hours a day. Zeroing in on the matter at hand and cutting just a little fat goes a long way toward reclaiming control of your schedule. Saving ten minutes here and fifteen minutes there ultimately frees you up for those times when people need you most. Three trimming tips:

✔ *Push your purpose.* Be cordial, of course, but minimize the small talk. Prior to longer conversations, I list the questions I want to ask and the points I want to make. Just one minute of preparation makes for a more productive and punctual exchange.

✔ *Bottom-line it.* Our people had a gentle way of cutting off ramblers. We'd respectfully interject a phrase I learned from efficiency guru Edwin Bliss: "What's the bottom line?" Without fail, the rambler cut to the quick, if a little sheepishly, and made his point. A softer variation sounds like this: "I'd love to hear more but I've got an appointment. Can you bottom-line it? Or we can talk later." Remember that bottom-lining is a business move that works only if it's caring rather than demanding. It's not a shortcut for handling personal matters.

✔ *Do it digitally.* Whenever possible, handle the matter via e-mail. I send and receive dozens of messages a day—many of which instantly go to multiple parties—to inquire, inform, and build consensus at lightning speed. Thanks to e-mail, actually talking to another person simply to exchange information sounds positively archaic.

Get dialed in. The telephone is either your greatest ally (an alternative to writing letters and memos) or your worst enemy (a font of interruptions). Making cell-phone calls during away-from-the-office downtime (if not at the expense of family time) is a good first step. Here are two more ways to avoid getting hung up in the phone zone.

✔ *Appoint an auxiliary gatekeeper.* My outgoing voice-mail message was a trusted sentry at Tires Plus, unfail-ingly repeating: "Hi, this is Tom Gegax. Please leave a message detailing your needs and desires so either I or the appropriate person can get back to you in a more helpful way. Thanks for calling, and make it a great day." The upbeat message worked because it prompted callers to say *exactly* what they needed. It stopped them from simply leaving their contact info, the first serve in a maddening game of telephone tennis. Plus, it saved Dorie, my executive assistant, a ton of time.

✔ *Leave precise instructions.* When your contact is unreach-able, leave a thorough message and ask him to respond on *your* voicemail. Voilá! You've eliminated phone tag and done some business. It's the same concept that made e-mail a business revolution. We don't always need two-way conversation. When you do, say as much in your voicemail message, detailing when and where you can be reached. Of course, when reaching out to a valued customer, be willing to be more high-touch and less high-tech.

Be upfront, not uptight. For longer conversations, presenta-tions, and informal meetings, be clear about how much time you've got. Nothing forces people to condense their points better. A saleswoman once told me she needed an hour. I told her I could afford only fifteen minutes and suggested she pack her points into three five-minute stages: sales pitch, questions, decision discussion. Recognizing that fifteen minutes was better than zero, she talked fast, hit the high notes, and wrapped it up at minute fifteen—with an occasional gentle nudge when she drifted off course. I was polite and friendly, but firm. Value your time and others will, too. Sound too tough? Would you rather miss your kid's soccer game because you didn't have time to complete that day's priorities? I don't think so. It's easy to get consumed by whatever's in front of you at the moment. Keep reminding yourself to be mindful of who you're with, why you're with them, and how the encounter fits into the larger picture of your day, your career, and your life.

BATTLING BRUSHFIRES: THE SIX D'S

When's the last day you *didn't* have a high-priority phone call, an urgent e-mail, or a stressed-out colleague begging for attention? Getting pulled off course is in every leader's job description. That's why enlightened executives have a strategy for dealing with daily interruptions. I call mine the "Six D's." When something pops up, rather than robotically just doing it, I start with the first option. If that doesn't apply, I move to the second. I keep cruising down the list until I reach the appropriate action.

1 **Don't do it.** Seriously, some things will simply go away if you ignore them. As you become more focused and purposeful, you'll be less likely to let unimportant tasks pull you off the path to your goals.

2 **Delay it.** Some interruptions disappear if you simply delay them. Think of all those urgent voicemails, e-mails, and memos you returned to after vacation. You never knew about them, yet they invariably cooled.

3 **Deflect it.** Some flare-ups only get hotter when they're delayed. If something belongs outside your work group, don't let it clutter up your desk. Pass it on.

4 **Delegate it.** Enlightened executives don't do things other people are paid to do. You're not hiring the right people if you're thinking, *If I want it done right, I have to do it myself.* Delegate whatever you can. Otherwise, mindless minutiae will slam the brakes on your professional development and career growth. (Delegation is so crucial that chapter 42 is devoted to it.)

5 Do it imperfectly. Don't automatically shift into perfection-ist mode when a task turns out to be something only you can do. You'll burn huge chunks of your schedule and brainpower that could have been devoted to worthier enterprises. A large number of my projects could hardly be described as perfect, yet were successful nevertheless.

6 Do it. Some brushfires demand your full, immediate atten-tion. But it's a lot easier to find the time and energy for big challenges when other flare-ups have been doused with the first five D's.

KEY POINTS: TRANSCENDING TIME

Embracing Enlightened Efficiency

✔ **Enlightenment + efficiency = success.** Enlightenment without efficiency (and vice versa) is like a three-wheeled car. Sooner or later, you'll roll over on a curve.

✔ **Clean the clutter.** Organization lays the groundwork for enlightened efficiency—and for achieving your goals. Stop rationalizing that a messy desk and sloppy files (digital and physical) aren't holding you back. A clean environment, leveraged with organizational technologies, brings calm and focus to your day.

✔ **Get time on your side.** Everything magically slows down when you're organized and wired. The better use you make of time, the more of it there seems to be. Substitute e-mail and phone calls for time-chomping, in-person meetings. Learn talk-trimming techniques to cut out coversational fat.

✔ **Douse brushfires with the Six D's.** When interruptions inevitably arise, walk through these six choices: don't do it, delay it, deflect it, delegate it, do it imperfectly, or do it.

FIFTY

LIFE LESSONS

Introducing Enlightened Self-Care

Would you sit back and twiddle your thumbs until a competitor finished poaching your customers and employees? Would you blow off network security until a vicious virus crashed your computer system and destroyed critical data? Doubt it, and doubt it. When it's business, some of us are laudably proactive. When it comes to personal issues, however, too many of us have upside-down priorities. We wait until a crisis bodyslams us before contemplating the possibility of making better choices.

Case in point: the triple trauma that steamrolled me when I was forty-two years old flattened my assumptions about health and wellness. Divorce and a business cash-flow crisis crumbled my psychological and spiritual foundations. Then cancer came along and forced me to rethink physical fitness. Those ordeals poked gaping holes in my theory that a shrewd and calculated intellectual approach was the only arrow I needed in my workplace quiver. Six painful months of self-analysis revealed the barriers I had erected between life's four essential elements—body, intellect, psyche, and spirit:

INTELLECT
- "smarts" or thinking
- a non-physical part of our being
- sometimes referred to as "left brain"

PSYCHE
- sensing, feeling, our source of emotions
- a non-physical part of our being
- sometimes referred to as "right brain"

BODY
- our vehicle for experiencing the world
- the physical part of our being
- can be measured and quantified

SPIRIT
- sense of connection to a Universal Source
- a metaphysical part of our being
- cannot be measured or quantified

Not only were the four players on my "inner team" incommunicado, they never had been formally introduced. My intellect was calling all the shots, my body never looked beyond its next run, and my psyche and spirit were neglected stepchildren. For years I had been in constant motion and felt healthy. But a lack of inner harmony had blocked my path toward true wellness and peace of mind. When that realization washed over me, I was embarrassed to admit that I had sidelined much of my inner team. In business, I would never have wasted over half my workforce. My life looked like this at triple trauma time:

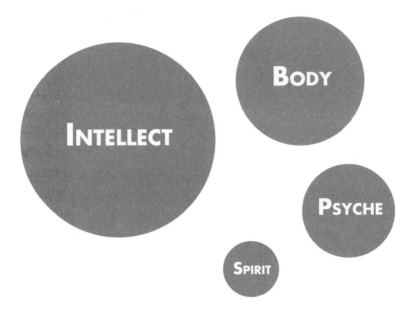

What's it mean to get all four players on the same page? Imagine if John, Paul, George, and Ringo had all pursued solo careers. They may have each scored a hit now and then. But they never would have defined pop music for generations without combining their talents and transcending the sum of their parts. As I began developing wellness strategies for each player in my life, here's what began to happen:

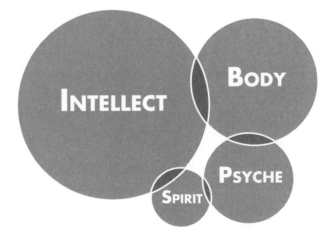

This integration produced clearer thinking, sharper instincts, and more energy. I started feeling the quantum leap in wellness that occurs when our inner elements align. Ideally, it looks like this:

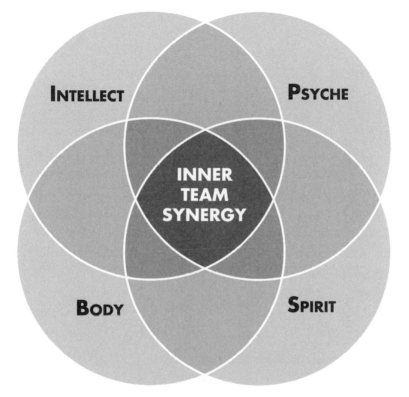

Not a minute passes when every part of our being isn't enhancing or sabotaging our decisions and actions. When coaching a team member on a sensitive issue, for instance, your reasoning is influenced by the state of your physical, emotional, and spiritual well-being. That new business plan that needs analyzing tests more than your intellect—your body, psyche, and spirit are in on the action, too. And they're all affected by how you slept the night before and whether you hit the treadmill or the doughnut shop over lunch hour.

Of course, inner synergy is always in flux. Self-mastery strategies aren't about perfection but about balancing the care we give the members of our inner team. When that balance is struck, all will benefit each time one is strengthened.

FROM EXHAUSTING TO EXHILARATING

The more I balanced the scales of my inner life, the more my thinking shifted. Like a gosling tailing a mother goose, my behavior followed suit. I started to realize I deserved better for—and from—myself. That simple self-care epiphany inspired me to give myself more fully to the people I worked with, lived with, and cared about.

I came to view wellness as a holistic bank account, a metaphor established by stress-research trailblazer Hans Selye. Withdrawals are poor food choices, sleep deprivation, emotional tension, and other life stressors. You make deposits with exercise, healthy meals, meditation, and supportive relationships. When withdrawals exceed deposits, you're grouchy, stressed out, foggy-minded, and weak-willed. When deposits exceed withdrawals, you're blessed with supercharged energy, crystal-clear thinking, and deep serenity. Not only that, you'll have enough fuel in the tank to shift into fifth gear when crises strike.

The wellness track doesn't demand huge chunks of time. You can immediately reduce stress, for instance, simply by reminding yourself to breathe deeply whenever you're nervous or rushed. Take the time I brought my friend Deepak Chopra, the well-known mind-body author, to dinner at the home of a high-profile consulting client of mine. As we were waiting in the entryway, Deepak began breathing very slowly and deeply. The next day, our host asked me if Deepak had asthma. "No," I laughed. "He was just doing his breath work. He calls it his Vader (as in Darth) breath. It clears his mind and helps him stay calm and centered." Deepak taught me the "Vader breath" and I can vouch that it works.

Better choices lead to a better life. Rather than watch a sitcom tonight, for instance, read a chapter in a personal growth book. Or, before going to bed, take a brisk twenty-minute walk. Better still, next time you're in a restaurant, choose vegetable soup, a spinach salad, and bottled water over a burger, fries, and beer. Rather than react defensively to a comment from your spouse, open your mind and try to understand her feelings. It may not be easy, but neither is getting what you want out of life. Fortunately, the life-affirming consequences of making healthier choices are often so immediate and profound that you'll have all the motivation you need to continue making them. I was thrilled to discover a newfound vibrancy I never believed possible. It was like I'd tapped into an extra fuel tank.

Be prepared for unsupportive responses. Over the years, most of my executive team poked fun at me for the way I ate, exercised, meditated, and focused on psychological growth. Yet, one by one the teasers inevitably knocked on my door. They'd blurt out a frightening diagnosis or test result and beg me to spill everything I knew about nutrition and wellness. It was as if a switch had been flicked on and they were suddenly flooded in the light of understanding.

Find that switch, now. The body is an amazing work of art; its hard-wired intelligence is constantly striving toward optimal health. If disease hasn't taken root, your odds of reclaiming vibrant physical health are excellent. If your body is already under siege, slamming on the brakes and hanging a right on Synergy Street may add more years to your life and more life to your years.

It All Adds Up

My cancer was a blessing in disguise. It jolted me into recognizing the consequences of diet and lifestyle choices. My attitude had been, *As long as I'm not sick, I must be healthy.* But that kind of reasoning can lead to disaster quicker than you can say, *Gimme a bacon double-cheeseburger.*

Defining wellness as the absence of disease is a start, I guess. But it's like saying you won a tennis match because your opponent never showed up. Not losing isn't the same as winning—it's not even close. Just as your opponent forfeited the match, if you don't show up as your own wellness advocate, you may be forfeiting your health. Wellness can be boiled down to two words: cumulative effect. As nutrition author Adele Davis cautioned, "Every day you do one of two things—build health or produce disease in yourself."

Health problems, whether physical, emotional, psychological, or even spiritual, don't "break" overnight. The seeds are often planted early in life in the form of poor nutrition, lack of exercise, and a negative attitude. Watered by steady neglect, they can germinate undetected for years, even decades. Then, boom, they sprout, take over, and overwhelm everything in their path—just as a car can be driven for months or years without an oil change before "suddenly" burning up and shutting down. Until that day of reckoning, the repercussions of our lifestyle choices are bubbling away inside us, growing more toxic by the day.

Until my early forties, I often felt sluggish and mentally foggy. In those bleary-eyed days, I knew I wasn't giving my personal best. I sensed I was missing something but didn't bother giving it much thought. I certainly had no intention of changing my behavior— not until a malignant tumor grabbed me by the throat and nearly squeezed the life out of me. Lemme tell ya, when the grim reaper pulls over and offers you a ride, hitchhiking your way into Introspection City becomes much more appealing.

Bottom line: the choices you make today determine the quality of your relationships, health, and effectiveness at work in all your tomorrows. It isn't about living longer, it's about living better. Right now, today, with greater vitality, mental clarity, and energy to burn. As harsh and unforgiving as it sounds, life stares each one of us in the eye and demands, *Pay me now or pay me later*. Why wait?

KEY POINTS: **LIFE LESSONS**

Introducing Enlightened Self-Care

✔ ***Be proactive, not reactive.*** Don't wait till a crisis bodyslams you to consider making better choices. Monitor and balance the four members of your inner team—your physical, intellectual, psychological, and spiritual selves.

✔ ***Manage your wellness bank account.*** Poor food choices, sleep deprivation, tension, and other stressors are withdrawals. Exercise, healthy meals, and supportive relationships are deposits. When deposits exceed withdrawals, you have more energy, crystal-clear thinking, and greater serenity.

✔ ***Start with small steps.*** Subtle changes in diet, attitude, and behavior are self-perpetuating. Their consequences— vitality, clarity, renewed zest for life—are all the motivation you need to continue pursuing healthier habits.

✔ ***Choose health today, not tomorrow.*** Health problems rarely develop overnight. They grow undetected for years, becoming more toxic by the day. The choices you make today can impact your effectiveness at work for years to come.

FIFTY-ONE
BODY BEAUTIFUL
Pursuing Physical Fitness

Browsing a bookstore years ago, a title caught my eye—*Please, Doctor, Do Something!* I read it in two sittings. Dr. Joe Nichols, then president of the Natural Food Associates, argued that the high-fat, artificial-everything American diet was lethal. I closed the book, sat back, and saw myself in the pages. I was twenty-five pounds over-weight and frequently exhausted. I figured I had two choices. I could deny Nichols' scientific conclusions or I could experiment. If nothing changed, well, I'd go back to "normal." Following Nichols' advice, I eliminated sugar, red meat, white bread, and fried anything. In a few months, I shed twenty-five pounds and noticed a conspicuous surge in energy. Wow, this "good health" stuff really packed a wallop!

A decade later, a cancerous lump on my neck sharpened my urgency. Was there something more I could do? I stumbled across the answer at a tai chi retreat. Initially, the meditation exercise felt odd, and the organic vegetarian meals were bland. I missed my chicken and milk. But as the week unfolded, my taste buds woke up—and so did I. The link between food, mood, and health was stronger than I thought. After all, if a single pill can alter our physical and mental states, imagine how our bodies react to the hundreds of pounds of food we consume each year. Poor dietary choices may leave us too foggy-headed to think on our feet, too out of sorts to treat employees well, and too depleted for evening projects. By retreat's end, I was sold. When I got home, I emptied my refrigerator and christened it an animal-free zone (although an occasional salmon still drops by for a visit).

Ultimately, I found the best information in two groundbreaking books—*Diet for a New America* by John Robbins and *Dr. Dean Ornish's Program for Reversing Heart Disease*. Their work impressed me so much that I struck up friendships with both men and began supporting their global-health work. Ornish's nonprofit research, for instance, proved heart disease could be reversed through nonsurgical methods. Now, Ornish is examining whether the same regimen can halt or reverse diabetes and cancer.

Keep in mind that cleaning up your diet isn't an all-or-nothing proposition. Think it's more likely you'll be crowned Emperor of Earth than become a vegetarian? Then just try to work in more fruits, vegetables, whole grains (brown rice, spinach pasta, whole-wheat bread), and legumes (beans and soy products) in place of processed, packaged foods. Substitute fish or poultry for beef and pork. Lower portion sizes by sharing entrees. Even a few minor tweaks—popping a daily multivitamin, switching to soy milk, substituting herbal tea for coffee—can deliver noticeable results. Eating more natural foods boosted my energy, sharpened my thinking, and helped me feel more grounded.

Revamping your diet isn't easy. Most of us are literally addicted to the foods we love. Some find it easier to go cold turkey on certain foods; others prefer slowly cutting back. But take heart—as your taste buds adjust, your craving for unhealthy foods is sure to diminish. If you're determined to make changes, be kind to yourself and don't get discouraged when you slip off course. Keep telling yourself, *If there is no change, then there is no change.*

Disclaimer time: consult a health professional before changing your diet and exercise habits. That said, here are four suggestions that made a big difference in my life:

1 **Easy on the animals.** Animals are the only things we eat that contain cholesterol—they clog up our body. On the other hand, high-fiber foods like fruits, vegetables, and legumes are free of cholesterol—they clean up our body. If we're clogged up, decaying food and toxins can wreak havoc and cause disease. High-fiber foods, even when combined with animal products, can reduce the risk of colon cancer—not only does fiber help lower cholesterol, it shortens the digestion of animal products, decreasing our colon's exposure to carcinogens. There are countless tasty alternatives to meat and dairy. Some are at your neighborhood grocery. Most, like meatless hamburgers, soy milk, cheese-free pizza, and non-dairy ice cream, are at the nearest food co-op or Whole Foods Market.

2 **Drink to your health.** Water flushes the body. It cleanses the cellular waste and toxins produced by the food we eat and the air we breathe. Turning water into your beverage of choice greases the gears of your digestive system. It's also the foundation for vibrant health and smooth, youthful skin.

3 **Decaffeinate your day.** A cup of coffee may be your first thought of the day for a reason. It's a jump-starter. Truth is, it only takes out an energy loan on the future. How? Caffeine stimulates your sympathetic nervous system, which artificially elevates your levels of adrenaline and other stress hormones. Later in the day, as your body tries to reestablish its equilibrium, your energy level actually drops lower than it was before your first morning hit of joe. Now, of course, you need that afternoon cup. Highs get higher, lows get lower. Giving up caffeine may seem unthinkable, but eliminating stimulants will even out your energy level *and* your mood. Try switching to decaf coffee or herbal tea.

4 **Tame your sweet tooth.** Atkins at least got this right. Refined sugar sets off a heck of a domino effect. It causes your blood sugar level to shoot through the roof. Your pancreas reacts by churning out insulin. That causes your blood sugar level to fall rapidly, which in turn causes your pancreas to stop secreting insulin. But, because the brakes aren't slammed on quite fast enough, your blood sugar level often dips even lower than its starting point. That's why you hit a wall after eating sugar—and why you reach for another Snickers to get back up. Yep, the sugar cycle is like the stimulant cycle. Another problem with sugar is the company it keeps—foods high in saturated fat. Sure, they may give you a quick burst, but you won't feel quite so jerked around if you eat less sugar. I get natural boosts out of 100 percent fruit juice, apple butter, and raw fruit.

RUN FOR YOUR LIFE

Born and bred in Indiana, I emerged from the womb dribbling a basketball. Two years ago, knee surgery forced me into early retirement and pushed me to find other exercise options. Fortunately, there are countless ways to raise the heart rate, even for a fifty-eight-year-old ex-round-baller. Three times a week, I do twenty minutes of running on an elliptical machine and thirty minutes of weight training. Add in a healthy diet, daily stretching, and yoga, and I've got energy—and patience, generally—to burn.

Regularly working up a sweat helps in other ways, too. As Mr. Science might explain it, vigorous exercise increases blood flow and floods the body with endorphins (those fantastic little brain chemicals whose pleasure-inducing properties are similar to opium). In other words, exercise sparks a natural high that can keep you pumped up for hours. An active lifestyle helps you stay limber, increases and maintains bone mass, and extends heart and lung efficiency. It also keeps you chemically balanced and shores up your immune system. Yet, scientific principles aren't what inspire me. I run, practice yoga, and lift weights because it clears my mind, reduces stress, and recharges my batteries.

The terminal-time-crunch syndrome can permanently bury exercise at the bottom of the priority list. Believe me, it's worth reworking your list. Spending just four hours a week sweating—a mere 3 percent of waking hours—can deliver a big return on invested time. Not only will you sleep better, you'll recoup the time spent exercising in newfound energy and mental clarity. Plus, you'll strengthen your physiological systems (immune, cardiovascular, nervous, and muscular), which can save tons of time—and heartache—down the road. Vigorous exercise can also reframe perspective; problems that seem monumental before a workout can look minuscule afterward.

Years ago, I experimented to see if I could squeeze a few more hours out of the week. When I eliminated exercise, I suddenly felt trapped on the Titanic, taking on water (stress) and sinking fast. Serenity, physical energy, mental clarity—all of it was compromised. Worse, I wasn't as caring or tolerant of others—reason enough to hit the gym again. The kicker: I figure my attempts to save time actually cost me an hour or more per day in lost productivity.

How to begin? First, don't wait until you have the energy; the energy doesn't come until you start exercising. Start by choosing an activity you think you'll enjoy and that, if need be, you can do alone. Simply walking twenty minutes, three times a week, is one of the best ways to ease into shape. Ready to take the next step? Finding someone to help you train is a piece of cake—er, tofu—now that there are as many health clubs as Starbucks. Either sign up for a fitness membership—many clubs offer at least one free session with a personal trainer—or visit a fitness or discount store, lug a few dumbbells home, and you've got a home gym. But there's no need to wait till you're home or at the club to exercise. Look around. You're surrounded with opportunities to power up, even at the office:

- ✔ Take a brisk **ten-minute walk** during your lunch break. A rejuvenating noontime workout ups your chances of doing quality work the rest of the day. Enlist a colleague to join you to make the time more enjoyable—and to provide motivation on low-energy days.

- ✔ **Take the stairs** instead of the elevator. You'll be surprised how quickly your stamina improves.

- ✔ Make a **chart of simple exercises** you can do at your desk. Set aside five minutes in the morning or afternoon to zip through them. (Hint: Google "desk exercises.") Take your regimen along when you travel, and arrive at your destination refreshed and good to go.

✔ **Stretch, stretch, stretch.** Stand up at least once an hour and walk around your workspace, especially if you toil at a computer. Move your arms, wrists, neck, and shoulders. Your lower back will be grateful. Retaining range of motion as we age is a key fitness goal.

✔ More and more organizations offer an **onsite workout facility**. It's a crime to ignore it. Ask your company to sponsor a class in yoga, aerobics, or stretching.

Whatever you enjoy, make exercise a lifelong habit. Upgrading your nutrition and physical fitness is like sticking your finger in a cosmic light socket. The potent pairing of high-octane meals and high-energy workouts will reinvigorate your tired muscles, recharge your life, and revitalize every cell in your body. Proceed at the pace that's right for you and you'll be amply rewarded with a powerful new life.

KEY POINTS: BODY BEAUTIFUL

Pursuing Physical Fitness

✔ ***Open yourself to nutrition.*** Food determines your mood, which influences your feelings and actions. Watch that newsmagazine segment about healthy eating. Pick up the occasional nutrition book. Gradually, you'll begin connecting the dots between what you eat and how you feel.

✔ ***Proceed at your own pace.*** Most people can't imagine overhauling the way they eat. Go with what works for you—cold turkey or slow and steady. You can get positive results by committing to even a few minor changes. Gradually eat more fruits, vegetables, whole grains, and legumes. Take all the time you need to transition into healthier habits.

✔ ***Prioritize exercise.*** Don't put off exercising until you find the energy; the energy doesn't come until you start exercising. Make time in your schedule to regularly walk, stretch, lift, or hit the treadmill. Just a few hours a week of vigorous activity sharpens your mind and improves your productivity. When you exercise regularly, you're saving time, not spending it.

FIFTY-TWO
MENTAL MASTERY
Making Conscious Choices

It was at a company picnic, a few years after my triple trauma of a midlife crisis, when I first became aware that I had stepped from the shadows of self-absorption into the sunlight of genuine human connection. Between helpings of potato salad, I found myself chatting with Gwen Heimer, wife of Eric, one of our regional sales managers. As she explained her family's summer plans, I realized that I actually cared. For ten minutes I was engaged and present. And it felt good. As our conversation drew to a close, I told Gwen I had enjoyed it. She gave me a puzzled look, smiled, and said, "I'm sensing some real differences in you, Tom."

True enough. Company picnics had been strictly perfunctory affairs—dutifully talk to employee's wife, nod head, move on, repeat. Odd how an ordinary conversation at an ordinary picnic on an ordinary day could signal an extraordinary sea change. My awakening, of course, wasn't a random, isolated event—I didn't snap out of my stupor thanks to exceptional potato salad. Over the last few years, I had been steadily recovering from simultaneous relationship, health, and financial crises. The combined power of books, seminars, healthier eating, meditation, therapy, and tai chi had reached critical mass on four fronts:

Emotionally. I dropped my armor and interacted with people empathetically.

Psychologically. My interactions were inspired by authenticity rather than hidden agendas.

Spiritually. My connection to a universal force was deepening.

Intellectually. I looked beyond absolute logic and into non-linear thought.

As much as I value exercise and working out, I came to realize that introspection—"working in"—is even more valuable. As Oliver Wendell Holmes said, "What lies behind us and what lies before us are tiny matters compared to what lies within us." Nurturing your intellect, spirit, and psyche (the vessel of psychological wellness) is to an enlightened executive what water is to our survival. It's impossible to cover such a vast topic in one short chapter. But perhaps these executive summaries of key concepts will encourage you to explore your own inner landscape.

LOGIC + CREATIVITY = WHOLE-BRAIN THINKING

Of all the members of our inner team, intellect is valued highest by our meritocratic, information-saturated times. Indeed, intellectual passion—the longing to manifest internal vision through external invention—has helped shape the world throughout history. Striving to expand your intellectual capacity is important. But you can end up shortchanging yourself, as I did in spectacular fashion, if you try to get by on raw wattage alone.

For years, I tried. After all, left-brain thinking was essential for meeting the challenges of my budding business. Still, it felt like every time I lifted my head above water, another wave would pound me under the surf. Sputtering, I'd push myself to upgrade management skills like strategic planning, problem solving, and delegation. I also raised the bar for goal-setting, organization, and time competency. That brand of intellectual know-how is certainly indispensable. But success requires the alchemy of creative thinking to transmute information from knowledge into wisdom.

Like many businesspeople, I felt long on straight-ahead thinking and short on creativity. Heck, creativity was the province of painters, musicians, and designers, not pin-striped, results-oriented executives. Then one day I was telling a friend about an organizational chart I'd drawn up. Instead of the hierarchical flowchart of rectangles that represents traditional top-down thinking, I drew a series of concentric circles. Floating out from a central source like ripples in a pond, it suggested an inside-out approach to communication and customer service. "Wow, what a creative idea," he said. "How did you think of that?"

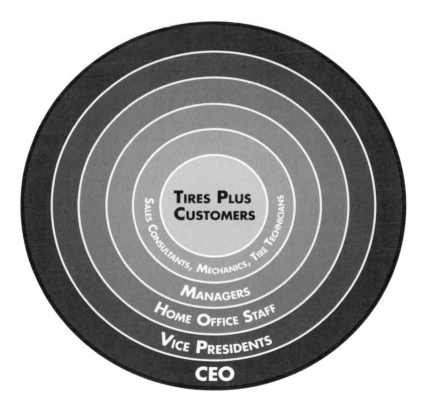

I had intuitively tapped the creative part of my intellect. This right-brain thinking allowed me to transcend the eminently logical practice of combining two known quantities in order to produce a third. Anyone can access logic (which too often narrows our options) and creative thinking (which infinitely expands our possibilities). Trouble is, these complementary sides of our intellect often fall out of balance. Finding parity revitalizes your intellectual passion and launches you into an exciting new realm where you're unencumbered by limitations. Artist Mason Cooley said it succinctly: "Intelligence complicates; wisdom simplifies."

Revving up our intellect can help us keep pace with the speed of business. But the daily grind of familiar habits can deepen our mental ruts and make us stale. Refresh your mind by exposing yourself to new subjects and ways of thinking. Some ways to do that: take courses on subjects you've always wanted to learn about; tackle fun mental aerobics like crossword puzzles and board games; change your surroundings—hang up a new picture, rearrange furniture—to subtly shift your perspective; move (temporarily) from a mindset of solve, solve, solve to think, think, think; break out of your comfort zone by doing something you're not good at.

A WELL-MANICURED MIND

An enlightened executive must have a healthy psyche, yet psychology is routinely brushed aside at the office. That's dangerous. Your psyche is an air-traffic controller overseeing all your psychological and emotional flights: *Thought #364, you're cleared for landing on runway three. Emotion #42, prepare for takeoff.* Pay scant attention to your psyche, and chances are you're in for a crash landing.

Psychological wellness is a firm handshake between healthy thoughts on the inside and positive habits on the outside. After all, how you feel about yourself influences your conclusions and actions, and ultimately your well-being. If you allow every single setback to pummel your self-esteem, for instance, both you and the quality of your business decisions will suffer. Bearing down and logging seventy-hour weeks won't fix things. You can't outpace your self-image.

I used to be a brawling, take-no-prisoners corporate honcho. Back then, my intellect muscled me through the emotional hurt of unhealthy relationships, ruthless self-criticism, and the disconnect between who I was and how I was being perceived. I pretty much shut down my emotional life to avoid painful feelings. I remember my wife saying once, "Is anybody in there?" I had to go through a world of hurt before I discovered that ignoring a wounded psyche is shortsighted; sooner or later, emotional deluges will rip out the moorings of your life as if they were made of papier-maché.

For years I managed to avert my eyes every time life thrust me a mirror. Looking back, I can see why. My intellect side was as familiar as my childhood neighborhood. But my feelings and emotions were ominous, like an unexplored cave. My psyche contained the very essence of who I am, yet it was foreign terrain. The first time I ventured into a psychologist's office, I felt like I was stepping off onto another planet. Thankfully, the therapist I had carefully selected helped me connect the dots between my thoughts, feelings, and behaviors.

One of the first steps toward vanquishing bad behavior is sleuthing its source. It shouldn't be a revelation, but the seeds of psychological challenges—moodiness, hair-trigger temper, low self-esteem, debilitating guilt, inflated ego—are planted early in childhood. Regardless of whether we're conscious of those formative impressions—and whether they sprang from flawed role models or the demands of a harsh environment—they cling to the psyche and become prisms through which each new moment is evaluated. By adulthood, however, our childhood defenses usually lose relevance. As a kid I developed the smiling defense—"everything's peachy"—to shield myself from issues too large to comprehend. As I grew older and more resourceful, I still confronted conflicts with that same stupid grin pasted on my face.

I learned that if a behavior no longer served me, regardless of its origin, it was my choice—and my responsibility—to change it. Yet, so many people spin their wheels in the ruts of unhealthy habits and poisonous patterns. A damaged car won't fix itself, a mentor of mine always says. A car with a dented fender remains a car with a dented fender, until the dent is pounded out. Trouble is, if you ignore the dent long enough you wind up forgetting it's even there. It becomes part of the car, like it rolled off the assembly line that way. Likewise, we become so used to, and even attached to, our dents that we no longer can distinguish them from who we really are.

You have two choices. You can wait for a head-on collision and risk being scraped off the highway like I was. Or, you can start taking steps toward living an introspective life. The more consciously you live, the less you're weighted down by guilt from the past, fear of the future, and anger in the present. Resolving issues that have hampered your growth frees you to be creative, to act boldly, and to connect deeply. The more you get to know yourself, the more you'll greet change with calmness and confidence. And the better you'll be able to spot and confront dysfunctional work behavior in others. A few ways to get started: read self-improvement books; practice self-policing your interfering behaviors; ask a loved one to regularly give you gentle, but candid, feedback; deepen emotional intimacy with friends by sharing more of your thoughts and feelings; engage in individual and group therapy.

That's the Spirit

Once upon a millennium, a bunch of angels hid the secret of direct experience of God. (Stick with me for a second.) One angel suggested concealing it on a mountaintop. "Humans are always reaching higher," another angel said. "They'd find it some day." A third angel suggested burying it in a deep valley. "Nope," another angel replied. "Humans are always digging for answers. They'd find it there, too." Yet another angel suggested, "Let's launch it into outer space." "Can't," said a doubting angel. "Humans are never satisfied with staying on the ground. They'll learn how to fly and track it down." Finally, one small angel piped up. "Let's put it inside them," she snickered. "They'll never find it there!"

Touché. In our search for God, we typically look outside ourselves. By far, the most profound and rewarding gift I received during my quest to become an enlightened executive was reconnecting with the divine source from which I'd been estranged. Part of the mystery and majesty of deepening this relationship is that not every question you ask can be unequivocally answered. It's a point of frustration for logic-oriented execs, one that author Kent Nerburn describes well: "When we try to understand God, we are like children trying to hold sunlight in our hands."

For me, being spirit-filled is all about feeling connected—with myself, my Higher Power, my mission, and other people. The connections are indefinable, but when I'm plugged in I know it. My step is lighter, a warm energy buzz radiates through me, and I feel surrounded by a protective glow. In those moments, I'm more inclined to reach out and be considerate of others. One evening in a restaurant, for instance, Mary and I were waiting for a table. The couple in front of us reluctantly agreed to be seated at a small table inches from a crying baby rather than wait fifteen minutes for the booth they had requested. A minute later, a booth opened up and the hostess guided us right by the first couple. I had two competing thoughts: *Boy, did we luck out,* followed by, *No, this doesn't feel right.* I knew if I didn't act on that feeling I wouldn't be able to enjoy my meal. Mary, of course, agreed when I suggested we offer to switch. The other couple gladly accepted. The warmth and connection we all felt was, as the commercial goes, priceless. Our food not only tasted better, that crying baby sounded like sweet music.

When I feel spirit-filled, I know that I'm an integral part of an intelligent universal plan, that everyone has a unique and valuable mission. I trust that everything is unfolding as it should—and I'm more inclined to look for and recognize the blessing in whatever occurs. Instead of just living life, I'm *loving* life. Unfortunately, such moments of feeling calm, centered, and connected can be fleeting. Especially when your CFO abruptly resigns, a focus group just trashed your new product, and employees are squabbling just outside your office.

That's why it's important for me to start each day with a spiritual practice that brings some measure of peace. Perhaps a few minutes of quiet reflection and deep breathing. A few pages from an inspirational book. A guided meditation. Yoga. There are hundreds of ways to strike a calming chord. The office may not know you spent thirty minutes practicing tai chi before you came in. But it shows up in how you behave once you get there—in your encouragement of teammates, in how you respect others even while disagreeing with them, in how you make a fresh pot of coffee (decaf!) whenever you take the last cup.

My stress builds—and connectedness wanes—when I skip my meditation, yoga routine, or four-step daily prayer. Wobbly days are a reminder that the cornerstone of any spiritual wellness program is daily ritual. Don't expect the sublime without putting in the time.

KEY POINTS: **MENTAL MASTERY**

Making Conscious Choices

✔ ***Relying on intellect alone limits your potential.***
Logic is indispensable. But only the alchemy of creative thinking can transmute information from knowledge into wisdom. Developing the creative side of your intellect opens new worlds of insight. Take a night course; adjust your surroundings; shift from solve, solve, solve to think, think, think; tackle something you're not good at.

✔ ***Monitor your psychological and emotional well-being.*** How you think and feel about yourself impacts your decisions and actions. You can't outpace your self-image. Take responsibility for changing the thoughts and behaviors that no longer serve you. Read books; self-police your bad habits; ask your significant other to give you candid feedback; share more of who you are with friends and loved ones.

✔ ***Get into the spirit.*** Feeling connected—with yourself, your Higher Power, your mission, other people—starts with being spirit-filled. Beginning each day with a ritual— an inspirational book; a guided meditation; a daily prayer; yoga—can bring some measure of peace. A regular spiritual practice can help us stay calmer and more centered when crises arise.

IX.
DEPARTMENTAL
HIGHLIGHT REELS

PART I

INNER SANCTUM SECRETS

Key Concepts and Killer Tips

Deep in the bowels of my workplace laboratory, I regularly tinkered with the ingredients of our "secret sauce," that proprietary blend of personality, philosophy, and protocols that differentiated us from every other business on the planet. Intentionally or not, every business creates its own unique corporate footprint by virtue of its culture, people, and processes.

Yet, every company, whether run by a seat-of-the-pantser or an enlightened executive, contends with supply management, marketing, sales, customer service, finance and accounting, information technology, legal issues, and outside advisors. (Human resource functions are woven throughout earlier chapters.) A working knowledge of every department is mandatory. Get careless with just one and your company will be like a car with a malfunctioning cylinder. You'll be sputtering along, trying to figure out how your can't-miss strategy misfired so badly.

If you've got the time, bushels of books have been written about each of these subjects. If, however, you're a bottom-liner, permit me to rip back the curtain and reveal the department-specific secrets every business leader ought to know.

FIFTY-THREE

SUPPLY MANAGEMENT

Strengthening Every Link

Almost from day one, we called on Jack McClard for all our equipment—wheel balancers, alignment machines, hydraulic lifts. I loved Jack like a brother. But after ten years, big national vendors started taking notice of our growth. One of Jack's rivals offered us a package of product lines that would save us $100,000 annually, without sacrificing service or quality. Now, I've always had a rule of thumb for doing business with friends—all things being relatively equal, go with friends; if the price or quality gap is significant, go with the better bid. I called Jack and asked if he could match the offer. He tried but came up well short. "I hate to do this, Jack," I said, "but one of our principles is to give the best value to our customers and shareholders. So I've gotta go with the other guy's offer."

It was painful for both of us. But there was more at stake than dollars. I felt the eyes of my people on me, watching to see if I would walk my talk. Afterward, Jack and I maintained a friendship but it was never the same. I still felt guilty a few years later when he died. And yet, I'd have to make the same decision again. Doing otherwise would've compromised our principles, and that would've burdened me with a whole lot more guilt for a whole lot longer.

Since those early days, supply management has evolved into a complex discipline. The ultimate goal used to be the lowest price. Now, every link in the supply chain is ferociously scrutinized for both economy and efficiency. It's what the big boys do best. It's also a competitive necessity. You can have the right plan, product, and people, and still end up spinning your wheels. To gain traction, you'll have to out-negotiate, out-cost-cut, and out-purchase the rest of the field.

MANAGING THE SUPPLIER RELATIONSHIP

Make sure your supply chief is skilled at complexity management. She has to grasp how all the internal and external links in the chain impact each other—and how to coordinate them all to land the best deals. For starters, that means forging strong supplier alliances. It's vital to:

Maintain clear channels. On day one, establish expectations, responsibilities, accountabilities, and an objective measuring stick to track results. To minimize back orders, for instance, stipulate penalties for incomplete shipments. Sustain this clarity via regular check-ins (refer to the Ask/Tell Technique in chapter 25).

Cooperate and collaborate. Your suppliers are trusted teammates who want to help you achieve your goals. That, at least, is how the relationship should work. Smart companies practice "strategic sourcing"—factoring in a vendor's ability to identify new business opportunities, develop new or deeper markets, provide technological improvements, or add input to strategic decision making. Involving suppliers in brainstorming sessions—at the strategic level and when product-related problems flare up—deepens mutual understanding of objectives, strengthens bonds, and creates win-win outcomes. Look for suppliers who are positioned to grow along with you, who have more capacity today than you think you'll ever need. (Collaboration works both ways. I visited Michelin, Pirelli, and other important vendors to give management seminars to employees. When your suppliers' operations improve, guess who benefits.)

Widen the loop. Broaden contact with your suppliers throughout your organization. Regularly put your top execs in the same room as the senior management of valued suppliers. Consistent contact—beyond purely transactional moments—builds rapport and trust, key ingredients in any valued relationship.

Share your vision. If your volume doesn't justify preferred rates, bust out the PowerPoint and show your plan to vendors and suppliers. Convince them you're the horse to bet on. The depth and breadth of our business plan—plus the passion of our presentation—made believers of our partners. They got excited by the extra dollars waiting for them—win, place, or show. In return, we won better pricing than our volume warranted. Caveat: guarantee confidentiality in both directions. Your suppliers may also be working with your competitors.

Get the straight scoop. Comparing one vendor's apples to another's oranges can be difficult. When I'm unable to sort out conflicting information by going back and forth between two vendors, I initiate a conference call for a quick point/counterpoint. Once, I had to choose between two automotive-product manufacturers. One refuted the claims of the other, who stuck by his story. So, right then and there, I got them both on the line and listened while each made claims and counter-claims. It was like a mini-debate. Tone of voice, confidence, and quality of argument told me who had his facts straight, and who I wanted to do business with.

Track price increases. Keep a running spreadsheet on vendors, detailing the date, amount, and reason for each price increase. A pattern may emerge once you've culled enough data. For instance, if a supplier's been upping prices every July for the last five years, you may be able to fend her off this time around: "You've asked for a price increase every July, and each time you've had a different reason. What's going on?" When suppliers know they're under a microscope, they tend to be more upfront. Cluelessness will cost you.

Watch out for the friendship trap. Vendors are great schmoozers. They know flattery will get them everywhere. They'll shower your purchaser with tickets and gifts, take her out to dinner, and treat her like royalty. In time, your purchaser can't help but feel disloyal for even looking at another vendor's bids. No matter how careful you are, buddy-buddy relationships can cloud a purchaser's vision.

Coach your purchasing reps on the perils of getting too chummy. Also, implement a "no gifts" policy. Make no mistake—gifts, while given partially in appreciation for past business, are primarily a subtle bribe intended to influence ongoing purchasing decisions.

Hold your buyer accountable for supplier performance. Don't measure buyer performance on cost savings alone. End-user satisfaction is just as important. Are you getting customer complaints? Are they reconcilable? Supplier performance will improve if your buyer has a personal incentive—bonus targets for customer satisfaction, say—to make it happen.

Keep them honest. I value loyal, long-term partnerships. Yet, habitually doing business with one vendor can cost you. Suppliers are more likely to jack up prices when they think you're in their hip pocket. Bidding out business—when there are multiple competent suppliers—keeps everyone sharp. They know their competitors may slash prices just to get in the door. We told transactional vendors right upfront they had to earn our business every year and that we'd periodically solicit bids from their competitors to compare cost, quality, and service packages. Just don't overlook the soft costs of changing suppliers. Acclimating to one another (culturally and technically) takes time. Of course, your leverage options dwindle with suppliers who dominate an industry (like commercial airline manufacturers and aluminum suppliers) or who provide new technology (like dealers of hybrid vehicles for your company's fleet).

Be careful, especially when comparing strategic vendors, that you don't throw the bidder out with the bathwater. You can weaken the supply chain by swapping out links all the time. That lesson isn't lost on the director of a large purchasing firm near my home turf. One of his suppliers provides engineers who design new products for his company. He won't be bidding out that business anytime soon. "What incentive does a supplier have to invest time, effort, and capital in serving my needs," he said, "if he knows I'll hand over the account to the lowest bidder at the end of the contract period?" Yes, all suppliers should be kept on their toes and negotiated with. But the more strategic the relationship, the more non-price factors there are to consider.

PURCHASING POINTERS AND NEGOTIATION NECESSITIES

Handshakes and small talk done, I took a deep breath and headed to the whiteboard. Arrayed around the conference table, top execs from one of the world's best-known companies had canceled their evening plans to hear me out. The president had asked me to fly out after I informed him we were putting our account in play. I was frank. Their pricing was a drag on our ability to compete, I told them, and only a significant cost cut could salvage the relationship. Marker in hand, I detailed what we needed and why. We wanted to do business. But at the end of the day (literally, in this case) we would do what was right for our company, understanding that they would do the same.

Their response was immediate. "If we agree to your terms," the president said, "will you commit to a five-year contract?" Inside, I was jumping up and down: *You bet! Where do I sign?* On the outside, I paused and turned to our purchasing veep. "Larry," I said, "are you willing to commit to that?" He thought for a minute (or at least pretended to), and nodded. I turned to the president and paused for thirty seconds. "If we agree," I finally said, "will you draw up an agreement-in-principle for all of our signatures right now?" An hour later we were shaking hands again, cementing the deal. Larry and I saved our high-fives for the airport. Thanks to exhaustive prep work and playing the right cards, we had lowered our annual costs by two million bucks.

Enlightened executives don't negotiate by the seat of their pants. They prepare a list of what they're willing to give up and what's non-negotiable. Then, they stick to it. Don't take a seat at the table until you've studied these bargaining benchmarks. (They're targeted at suppliers, but most also apply to negotiations with customers, employees, and strategic alliances.)

Get good intel. Going into our conference room showdown, we knew our supplier was desperate for volume because a major account had just bailed. Get your corporate intel specialist to chat up industry insiders to find the latest dirt. Is the other guy running anywhere close to full capacity? What's his share of your market? Look for suppliers who are underperforming. They'll deal. The window needs only to be cracked open just so wide for you to grab a sweetheart deal.

Find common ground. One-sided arguments lead to lopsided results. Turn win-lose into win-win by telling the other party exactly what you need and seeking to understand what they need. For instance, in hopes of lowering costs, we asked a major tire manufacturer how we could help lower *their* costs. They suggested we improve our forecasting accuracy by digitally linking our inventory to their HQ, triggering automated ordering. They also recommended shipping some orders directly from their factory to our retail stores, bypassing warehouse expenses on both sides. Caveat: if netting a win-win is a priority, you're working for both your company and the supplier. That's noble. And when it works, it's a beautiful thing. Trouble is, the supplier may not hold your best interests in the same high regard. By all means, give it a shot, but don't assume responsibility for your supplier's wins. If he's not happy, trust me, he'll let you know.

Wear good walking shoes. Pinpoint the number that nets you the best possible package, yet provides the other side enough incentive to do business with you. You'll know you've overshot their number when they start to walk. If they're still at the table, but refuse to come within spitting distance of your number, it's your turn to walk. If they call you back to the table, you've got 'em. If they don't, and you can't afford to lose the relationship, don't panic. Call them a day or two later and say you've re-crunched the numbers and would like to reopen negotiations.

Turn all the cards face up. Take nothing for granted. Before signing off, reach accord on every micro-issue, not just price, terms, and freight. These things are going to come up sooner or later. Sooner is better. For instance, inventory issues—what are the costs, how fast is turnaround, what happens if it doesn't move, what happens to volume discounts if supply runs out? Smart companies also add contractual clauses that mandate continuous improvement—essentially brainstorming sessions between you and your supplier that aim to reduce costs and improve efficiencies for both parties.

Be friendly. Smile. Make small talk. Share a laugh or two. In other words, lighten up. Suppliers are more willing to cut deals with people they like and enjoy working with.

Timing is everything. Working with a mat maker? You better know that sales of big, heavy entry mats are off the charts in peak slush and mud season—but fall off the radar during summer months. Use that to your advantage. Arrange your contract to expire in July; the slow season's sting will loosen the supplier's hand. In general, you'll improve your horse-trading odds by hitting vendors up for deals at the end of the month, when they're scrambling to nail monthly targets.

Have another dance partner in the wings. The morning of our two-million-dollar meeting, we told our big-time supplier we had an offer from their competitor. That gave us more confidence going in. It also created more urgency on our supplier's part, especially when we told them—truthfully—that an agreement had to be inked that day because their competitor's offer expired the next afternoon. (We were literally racing against the clock. After poor weather scrubbed our afternoon flight, Larry and I dashed to the only other airline with an impending flight. Only one ticket was available—until we sprinted to the gate and I shouted to a cluster of passengers that I'd pay someone double for their ticket.) The best deals are struck when there's competition in the hunt. Suppliers who think they're the only name on your dance card leave zero wiggle room.

Get in the driver's seat. A rule of commerce: never let the seller dictate the transaction. Manufacturers often called with one-time offers that would expire by day's end (the old "standing room only" close). They hoped we'd get excited about the diamonds in the deal and not notice the coal buried beneath. Occasionally, time-sensitive offers are valid and you need to go with the flow. Typically, however, there's room to maneuver. Our purchasers were trained to snap up good-quality products at bargain-basement prices. But when we said no thanks to marginal deals, the drop-dead expiration date—and details—were suddenly negotiable.

Dissect the details. Our uniform company was taking us to the cleaners. Literally. Once a week, they laundered uniforms for our shop employees. If a shirt was stained with oil, the company pulled it from rotation and charged us for a new one. And whenever somebody quit, his shirt and pants disappeared into the Bermuda Triangle of uniforms. Once we realized what was going on, our purchasing point man, Mel Donnelly, sat down with the uniform contractor. "Look," Mel said, "if a guy changes oil for a living, chances are good he's going to spill oil on himself more than once. Showroom salespeople need unstained shirts; mechanics don't. Second, when an employee quits after a few weeks, his uniform's in great shape. We want to reuse those shirts and pants for new hires with the same measurements." "Sorry," the uniform rep said, "that's not the way we do things." "Well," Mel shot back, "you better change the way you do things if you want to keep our business." They saw the light and we saved the green.

Assemble the whole puzzle. Let's say you're an industrial launderer shopping for a washroom chemical. Supplier A's solution will cost you ten cents per hundredweight of white shirts. Supplier B breezes in at eight cents. Ah, but what Supplier B didn't mention is that his chemical requires a hotter water temperature, which drives up energy costs. Further, water that hot demands another chemical to balance acidity. Plus, Supplier B's chemical also extends the rinse cycle, which extends your production time. You get the picture. Doing some old-fashioned due diligence to ferret out hidden expenses lets you calculate the total cost of ownership. Whenever possible, contractually bind the supplier to a total-cost solution. Apply the same logic when comparing services. Hotel Y will charge your sales force a no-frills $85 per night. Hotel Z's rooms are $100 per night, but include breakfast and Internet access. Run the numbers on what your people spend per diem on breakfast and the Net before inking the contract.

Sweeten the pot. Don't be shy about asking for value-added extras. We always tried to improve what we got for what we bought. If standard terms are two months, ask for three. Request geographical or product-related exclusivity. Get 'em to throw in additional training. If an ambitious ad campaign promises additional sales, ask the vendor to pitch in. Incentive trips are a fun add-on (and, unlike individual employee gifts, are earned). A vendor once offered a Caribbean vacation to our senior execs. We asked for, and got, more seats on the plane. It was a cost-free, and greatly appreciated, way to reward deserving employees.

Curb your enthusiasm. Careful about blurting YES too soon. Zeal to seal the deal is good. But overeagerness makes the other party think they left too much on the table. They may even try to pocket a few more chips before the final card is dealt. Wear a poker face. Let them think they're drawing blood. Ask for more than you actually need. When they balk, feel the pain. Then agree, reluctantly, to the number you wanted all along. Or, play the *If I do this, would you do that* card. For instance, when our big-time supplier said, *If we agree, will you commit?*, I doubled down by hesitating and slowly replying, *If we agree, will you make it official?* Everyone left thinking they made all the right moves.

Contract your contract. Locked into a contract for another eight months? No worries. Solicit and analyze other proposals—the better to stay abreast of market conditions. If circumstances shift in your favor, ask your vendor to tear up the contract and write a new one. If he resists, play hardball. Tell him you'll honor the existing contract if he forces you to, but that he shouldn't count on your future business after it expires.

Team up. To increase our purchasing clout, I cofounded a consortium of the country's six strongest regional tire dealers (none were direct competitors). Our high-wattage buying power gave us pricing leverage on everything from tires to insurance to office supplies. Caveat: successful purchasing cooperatives can become mini-empires, complete with deluxe offices and big salaries, which gobble up cost savings.

DISTRIBUTION SOLUTIONS

Want to keep or move distribution in-house? Be ready to invest in space, equipment, software, and people as you grow. And keep these factors in mind.

Number of distribution centers. How many do you need now and how many will you need down the road? The low number always wins. Sure, you'll have to travel a greater distance to reach the average customer. But your higher outbound transportation costs will be more than offset by lower facility, equipment, inventory, and management expenses. Do the math. If your options are using one to six distribution centers, put your outbound transportation costs on one axis of a graph and your non-transportation costs on the other—wherever they meet is your optimum number of distribution centers.

Location of distribution centers. Generally, the closer to the East Coast, the lower the cost of transportation. That's because the East is considered the consumer coast, while the West is the producer coast. Shipping to consumer cities is usually a dead-end shot for transportation companies. Sending a hundred trucks in and getting back eighty empties jacks up costs.

Energy costs. Many companies with in-house distribution take it on the chin. When employees go home at four o'clock they plug their electric equipment—pallet jacks, forklifts—into chargers. The overhead lights are still on and conveyors are still running. Boom. The juice spike triggers a demand charge from the power company. Avoid the power penalty by adding a simple timer that throws on the recharging switch later in the evening. Stagger usage on each timer and drive costs even lower. Likewise, a "disconnect" installed between overhead lights and chargers ensures that chargers stay off when the lights are on. Overall annual savings in a large building can reach fifty grand.

Deployment of product. Got ten thousand SKUs (stock-keeping units) and three distribution centers? Stock all three with the top five thousand sellers and house the slow-moving stuff in just one center. Delivery time on the five thousand slow sellers will indeed suffer. But you'll require substantially less inventory and have more space for high-demand items. Productivity goes up because most warehouse employees are dealing with half as many products. Costs go down because you need fewer storage racks, pallet jacks, and forklifts.

Employee management. Labor management software establishes quantity and speed goals for each warehouse staffer, and monitors their performance in real time. Too "Big Brother"? Think again. Research shows morale improves when employees are monitored, given fixed expectations (a.k.a. engineered standards), and provided with ongoing on-the-spot training. Contrast that with the traditional "shepherd" method of management—walking through the warehouse, making sure everyone's working, leaping on 'em when they're not. With labor management software, employees get immediate feedback when they log each order into an RF (radio-frequency) handheld device. Constant positive feedback, even from a gadget, keeps people motivated.

Inventory management. Back in the day, warehouses closed down once or twice a year for physical inventory. The advent of "cycle counting"—sampling a number of items each day—improved inventory accuracy. Now, we've got "real-time checkpoint" systems. The technology senses—and asks for verification—when an order-filler picks the last item from a bin. Voilá! Your cycle counting is done, minus the manpower hours.

Order taking. Thanks to RF technology, when inventory is removed from a bin, the system knows how many items are left, how many orders are queued for those items, and how to prioritize customers accordingly. That means customers can see your entire inventory when placing an online order—if you want them to. The downside of inventory transparency is that customers may go elsewhere if their item is temporarily out of stock.

Traffic coordination. Used to be, when a forklift operator pulled a pallet of product off the shipping dock and moved it three hundred feet into the warehouse, he'd return to the dock empty-handed. No more. Today's software guides him to pick up an outgoing product on his way back to the dock. There's no easier way to nearly double productivity.

OPTIMIZE YOUR OUTSOURCING

To outsource or not to outsource, that is the question. (William Shakespeare, who, according to some academics, had no discernible talent as a playwright, may have been an early outsourcer.) Smart companies undertake the discipline of process uncoupling. They size up, based on core competencies, which supply functions should be kept in-house and which should be handed to outside experts. In the end, every process gets performed by whoever does it best. But signing an outsourcing contract doesn't mean your work is over. To squeeze the most value from your outsourcing strategy:

Keep current. New processes and technologies may influence your outsourcing decisions. Supply management specialists can keep pace with industry advances by enrolling in local and national professional organizations. The Institute for Supply Management (www.ism.ws) is the world's largest association of its kind. Its website details how to obtain a CPM (Certified Purchasing Manager) designation. Also check out the Association of Purchasing and Inventory Control Specialists (www.apics.org). This international organization offers educational and professional certification programs. Your people can sign up online for APICS webinars (web-based seminars).

Get your own house in order. Internal chaos and external order can't coexist. Don't expect seamless outsourcing relationships until your interdepartmental relationships are smooth, efficient, and aligned with company objectives.

Get specific. The devil is in the details—the ones you leave out, that is. Forget to mention during the bid process that holidays are your busiest time? Hello, triple-overtime. Likewise, don't estimate your average monthly volume and neglect to mention that 90 percent of your orders stream in during the final week. If the contractor's people sit on their hands for three weeks only to work overtime the fourth, you may get dinged a little extra.

Include a contractual exit strategy. If a contractor's bid works out to 1.8 percent of sales and you've determined your costs can't exceed 2 percent, structure the contract to leave you with ironclad options. For instance, when the 2 percent threshold is crossed, the contract is automatically voided.

Make sure it's love at first site. If you decide to outsource distribution, invest the time upfront to do a thorough contractor search. Changing distributors at the end of a contract is expensive. Setup costs may prohibit a move even if other bidders offer more attractive rates and services. What happens if you change your mind and try to bring distribution back in-house? You might wind up in the outhouse. It's hard to reconstitute a function once its space has been repurposed and its personnel have been let go.

GLOBAL GUIDELINES

Technology has flung open the gate to new, worldwide markets. But proceed with caution—the road to international profits is littered with hurdles that can trip up even the most experienced pros. When dealing with overseas customers:

Know the hard costs. What's the best way to get goods from A to B? Is it cheaper by sea or by air? Truck or train? What size containers will you use, and how much do they cost? Find out. Next, make arrangements at the other end—from port to warehouse. Tap the Internet for info on foreign freight "forwarders." Duty rates vary by country—a 10 percent duty hikes the customer's price by the same amount at the other end. A hefty value-added tax (what Americans call sales tax) may be added on top. And don't forget to tack on tariffs (at both ends) if you transfer a shipment from, say, Canada to Mexico.

Play by their rules. Countries have their own commercial regulations. Maybe disposable diapers require a higher absorbency rate. Maybe a speedometer must display kilometers more prominently than miles. Perhaps officials stop dated products at the border. You may have to tussle with a country's equivalent of the Food and Drug Administration. Bottom line: the product—diapers, cars, pajamas—is useless if it doesn't meet regs. Worse, it may be confiscated, forever.

Get insured. Whether importing or exporting, there's no guarantee the goods won't be tampered with, stolen, or destroyed in transit. Ask your commercial insurance agent how to protect your investment. Or, check out www.exim.gov for insurance coverage through the Export-Import Bank of the United States, the official export credit agency of the U.S. government. Ex-Im programs insure the receivable from 90 to 100 percent of the total invoice. Without insurance, special circumstances can create major heartburn. One fellow I know of imported a shipment of cheese to his McDonald's franchise in Sweden. The gauge in the refrigerated container indicated that, for fifteen minutes, the temperature was two degrees too high. The shipment was rejected, and the franchisee's cheeseburger-loving customers settled for chicken sandwiches.

FIFTY-FOUR

MARKETING

Increasing Brand Equity

Marketing is like parenting. Everyone who does it thinks they're an expert—and takes offense when told otherwise. We all form opinions on what works and what doesn't based on our tastes and experiences. And most of us think our own sensibilities float right in the middle of the mainstream. Everyone thinks they can write a clever radio spot or design the perfect showroom. To paraphrase a truism from the legal profession, businesspeople that do their own marketing have a fool for a client. Don't get me wrong. Leaders should help market the company's image, message, and offerings. But hire pros with solid track records to do the heavy lifting.

Increasing market share is an ongoing battle. Some of our locations captured a third of their market—triple the volume of our closest competitor. A huge lead, sure. But sometimes our people acted like we had cornered the market. That's when they needed a splash of cold water. "Do you realize," I'd say, "that two out of every three people who could be buying from you are going to somebody else?" I was pleased, but never satisfied, every time our numbers climbed higher. If you don't have the market share you think you deserve (who does?)—and if sales and customer service are hitting their marks—then put your marketing under a microscope. It will close the gap between where you are and where you want to be.

Marketing is the only way to pull potential customers toward you. From there, it's like a relay team. You have the opportunity to pass them to sales and, after the purchase, to customer service. Careful, though. Even the most brilliant strategy can collapse if you ignore the first law of marketing—"Know thy customer." In other words, hold off on casting until you get a feel for who's likely to bite on your lure. Don't spend a penny on advertising or merchandising until you're intimately familiar with the psycho-demographics of your target market. Then calculate the most efficient ways to reach their eyes and ears. (Be sure to keep in touch with your customers through regular surveys and focus groups so you can grow with them.)

This chapter focuses on six primary marketing elements. After identifying or shoring up your (1) differentiating factors, (2) identity, and (3) offering, beef up your (4) promotional efforts, deepen your understanding of (5) evolving tastes and trends, and strengthen your (6) merchandising. They're all linked, to each other and to every customer touch point. It's this synergy which gives rise to a successful brand. Six steps create big-league recognition and market share:

1 **Differentiate.** Don't listen to the naysayers. Remember Charles Lindbergh's solo transatlantic flight? Roger Bannister's four-minute mile? Creative Carton's perfect record for same-day orders? Missed that last one? It may be the most impressive—to manufacturers of corrugated packaging and displays. Minneapolis-based Creative Carton had already carved out its market position as the go-to guys for quick turnarounds. Then a desperate customer shouted four words: "I need it today!" After lots of hits and a few misses, CEO Mike Sime had the people and processes to go for same-day gold. Five years later, Creative Carton's perfect-delivery winning streak is still unbroken. Same-day service is a differentiator even though it accounts for just a portion of total monthly orders. "Is it a big deal?" asked Mike. "Well, it is to a customer sitting at his desk with white knuckles and a supervisor breathing down his neck. It's like the old Federal Express commercial—when you absolutely, positively have to have it delivered the same day, what's it worth?" Plenty, especially in an industry notorious for fickle customers. When you offer customers something they can't get anywhere else, they can't not order from you. Today's need-it-yesterday business environment is good news for companies like Mike's, whose core competency is compressing time. "It's great when the world moves faster and faster because that plays right into our business model," he said.

Most differentiation decisions focus on where you want to land on the price-quality-service continuum. One isn't necessarily better than the others, but a choice has to be made. The low-price, bag-your-own-groceries niche has been staked out by the likes of Wal-Mart, Southwest Airlines, Home Depot, and Motel 6. Plant your flag in the middle of the spectrum and value-conscious customers will pay a little more to get a little more—think Banana Republic, Applebee's, Holiday Inn, Crate and Barrel. Customers of premium-positioned companies—Mercedes, Nordstrom, Neiman Marcus, Ritz-Carlton—will shell out top dollar for top-quality products and white-glove service.

A hybrid position is "low-price, nicer experience." Look at Best Buy, IKEA, JetBlue, and Kohl's. Early on at Tires Plus, this is how we differentiated ourselves to compete with the big boys. Some competitors could match our prices. But nobody else was offering upscale stores with clean-cut sales consultants in dress shirts and ties, cappuccino machines, framed art, VCR movies, and children's play areas. Target Corp.'s strategy to neutralize other discounters' low prices was much the same. "We tapped into a large consumer segment that wants low prices and a pleasant shopping experience," said John Griffith, a senior vice president for Target. This position is being staked out by more and more companies. Check your industry. Is there a void?

Beyond price, quality, and service? Look at sub-categories. Creative Carton was already known for speed; same-day delivery added one more point of separation from the pack. It helped the company create a "nested niche"—a niche within a niche. Likewise, FedEx is synonymous with "overnight shipping." But the company knew the only way it could maintain market share was by creating sub-niches—various pricing and delivery options, extended hours, and convenient drop-off locations. Enterprise Rent-A-Car has become the largest car rental company in North America, thanks to its differentiator—"We'll pick you up." Geek Squad, a Best Buy-owned "computer support task force," filled a neglected niche by offering personalized security, repair, and technical support to both business folks and "civilians." Further distinguishing itself, Geek Squad "agents" in white dress shirts and skinny ties make house calls—they'll race to your home in colorful, logo-laden Volkswagen bugs as fast as a pizza delivery man.

2 **Put your identity on the couch.** When I challenged Charles Lukens to rename his company, he resisted. "The name Planet Salvage was like my kid's name to me," said Charles. "Plus, I was hung up on our cool little icon, a planet with a tire around it." The logo was striking, I said, but neither it nor the cartoonish name Planet Salvage fit the company's mission and offering. To his credit, Charles agreed to cut his emotional ties. At a staff brainstorming session to noodle a new name, I suggested zeroing in on the company's offering. We boiled it down to: *We harness the Internet to help companies manage and increase alternative parts utilization* (auto-insurance and body-shop industry jargon). Given that the acronym APU was constantly on the lips of industry execs throughout the business day, the perfect name was a no-brainer—APU Solutions.

I wasn't as disciplined with my own company. Back in 1982, when I decided to shift our focus from wholesale to retail, our three stores were called (City Name) Tire & Auto. Catchy, huh? I knew I needed something better. At a party one evening, I leaned over to my neighbor and said, "Hey, Bob, I'm starting a chain of tire stores. Gotta tell you the name—Guarantee Tire." Bob scowled as soon as it left my lips. He was ten years my senior, a street-wise ad man from Philly. "Tom," he said, "that's the most screwed-up name I've ever heard" (PG-13 version). Flying dollar signs raced through my head—we already had our logo designed and had given the green light to a sign company. Bob noticed how deflated I was and offered to brainstorm names with me. The next day, I was telling Bob my new company would offer tires plus other services. He cut in. "Tires Plus," Bob said. "I like that. Add it to the list." I liked it, too. It conveyed optimism, promised that we had more to offer than our competitors, and left open the door for endless brand extension. Every seat-of-the-pantser should have a neighbor like Bob Bechir. (Bob died a few months before I sold Tires Plus in 2000. We invited his two kids to a company party and presented them with a plaque and remuneration to recognize their dad's contribution.)

Satisfied with your name? Look next to your tag line. Does it holler why you're different? After Charles Lukens settled on the APU Solutions name, I sat in on a meeting with a prospective client, a Farmers Insurance Group v.p. He wanted a guarantee that the parts he purchased would be in stock and shipped the same day at locked-in prices. "Look," he said, "I need real steel, real time." The minute we left the building, I said to Charles, "Did you hear that? 'Real steel. Real time.' Isn't that what sets you apart?" He nodded. "There's your tag line. It sums up your business model in four words. It's perfect." So is Best Buy's ("Thousands of Possibilities. Get Yours."), Target's ("Expect More. Pay Less."), and Wal-Mart's ("Always Low Prices. Always.").

Each and every exposure to a strong brand—a succinct, powerful name; a memorable tag line; a bold logo (think Nike swoosh)—cements your market position and produces free advertising. The name Tires Plus told people exactly what we did. Our tag line—"Warehouse Prices. World-Class Service."—told them exactly what to expect. Any time people heard either, our brand message sank deeper into their consciousness. To be sure, a lot of Fortune 500 companies have nondescript names. But odds are it took one heckuva big marketing budget to educate the public. If your name doesn't describe what you do, your tag line better. Bottom line: if after hearing your name and tag line, people on the street can't say what your company does—and why it does it better than anyone else—it may be time for a change.

3 Tie your offering to your point of differentiation. Good companies never stop trying to make their offering more appealing. But that doesn't mean they stray from their differentiating factors. Ryanair, the Dublin, Ireland-based no-frills airline that raised the low-airfare bar, continues to find ways to drive prices even lower. Freebies? Forget about it. Weary passengers "rent" pillows and blankets. They even pay extra for air-sickness bags. Instead of installing seat-back TVs, Ryanair will be renting hand-held mini-entertainment centers.

Continually scrutinize your offering. Studying your competitors' offerings provides perspective on how to optimize your strengths and neutralize theirs. To the extent you can, shed your passion for your industry and look at your products and services through your customers' eyes. It was easy for me because, like most of our customers, I wasn't a car-loving gearhead. Ask yourself, *If I was happy doing business with one of my competitors, what would it take to get me to switch? Price? Speed? Service? Warranty? All of the above?* I liked that customers would come to our stores armed with detailed competitive analyses. It gave us opportunities to gain further insight into our guests' needs and desires.

Pricing is a key element of any offer. We were able to occupy the "low prices with niceties" niche by offering how-low-can-you-go pricing on commodity-like products and making a bit more on out-of-the-mainstream items, exclusive product lines, and premium products and services. Positioning aside, every company has to raise and lower prices periodically to meet marketing and margin pressures.

Some pricing factors to consider:

✔ When commodity markets are rising, it's easier to raise prices in a B2B (business-to-business) environment than in a B2C (business-to-consumer). Corporate customers are more sophisticated and aware of rising material and energy costs. And competitors throughout the industry will also be raising prices.

✔ Price hikes are sometimes unavoidable. In a B2B market, everybody shares the pain. Still, you need to finesse it by balancing two factors—how much to raise prices and how often? Let's say you're a supplier whose input costs have gone up 3 percent. You've got to raise prices by that much just to break even. Best bet: bump prices up 10 to 20 percent over your break-even point. You'll stay competitive, and that extra little oomph will buy some breathing room.

✔ Raising consumer prices is touchier. Retail customers aren't nearly as likely to appreciate the competitive pressures you're under. Plus, it's easier for them to walk next door. Whether you sell to retailers or directly to consumers, presenting a price hike as a surcharge may work. When public awareness of market pressures (rising costs of gasoline, freight, steel) is high, a pass-through charge is generally accepted—as long as it's tied to a promise to revert to old prices when the crisis ends.

✔ Lowering prices, on the other hand, is generally a matter of competition. It's done either defensively to match competitors' prices, or offensively to win market share. In a B2B environment, the key to lowering prices while maintaining profit margins is introducing new products. (This works for raising prices, too.) Here's an example. Let's call your flagship product Widget X. It's priced at $1,000. Rather than drop it to $800, create a new product, Widget Y, with a different value proposition—a few less features and a lower price point. Now, you're differentiating yourself instead of devaluing your brand. This is how you sell to the big boys. Otherwise, staying with one product sticks you with an inevitable pricing arc—essentially a scheduled sunset of your margin structure (40 percent in the first year, 30 percent in the second, 20 percent in the third). Why?

Big retailers relentlessly drive down prices. If you don't play by their rules, they'll find someone who will.

New products keep the sun from going down. Back to our example—Widget Y has different features, benefits, and price point. But it's structured to have a gross margin of 40 percent. See where this is going? In year two, Widget X drops to 30 percent but Widget Y starts out at 40 percent. In year three, Widget X falls to 20 percent and Widget Y slides to 30 percent. But then, out of nowhere, Widget Z charges out of the gate with a 40 percent margin. That's managing your margins (if not your alphabet). Most companies see their margins squeezed because they don't change their product set. Do the same thing over and over with the same negative result, and you'll either go crazy or out of business. Bottom line: innovate or die.

4 **Promote, promote, promote.** One thought bounced around my brain as I walked into our brand-new Burnsville, Minnesota, store: *Where the heck are all the people?* It was years ago, when we were still the new kid on the block. But we had great people, competitive prices, better hours, and a perfect location. We just had to get our message out—I knew there'd be no stopping us if we got people in the door. But we were caught in a budget bind. Our advertising and public relations resources were slim. Yet, if we didn't juice up our promotional wattage, we couldn't bring in enough revenue to cover costs. I started to appreciate the old marketing line, *Cutting back on advertising to save money is like stopping a watch to save time.* The only way to drive revenues up was to achieve top-of-mind awareness in the marketplace. That called for a promotional blitz.

Not long afterward, we had an opportunity to plaster our logo on the largest sign at the Hubert H. Humphrey Metrodome, home to the Minnesota Twins and Vikings. The package also included sixty seconds of big-screen ad time for our tire mascot races at all

Twins games. My executive team thought I was crazy to commit $1 million over ten years, particularly since the cost equaled our annual profits. They said we couldn't afford it. "Guys," I said, "we can't afford not to." I pointed out that the contract would give us the exposure and credibility our young company needed. I swung the bat and didn't look back. It was a grand slam.

More than great advertising, the Metrodome contract turned into great public relations. What's the difference? As Dave Mona, founder of Weber Shandwick Minneapolis, the Midwest's largest p.r. firm, explains it, "If I tell you I'm a great lover, that's advertising. If someone else tells you I'm a great lover, that's public relations." The operative words are "someone else." A positive magazine article or news feature is more credible than an ad because it's essentially a third-party endorsement. Sure, advertising has its advantages—an ad will be exactly where you want it and say exactly what you want it to say. But there are times when a creative p.r. campaign trumps anything the ad wizards can offer.

Take the time Dave sat down with reps for the annual Minneapolis Home and Garden Show. The lengthy list of features for the new show was sleepy at best. There was no gee-whiz hook to build a public relations campaign around. A show rep ticked off the last item and turned to Dave. "Well," he said, "what do you think?" Dave scanned the list again, stopped at number eighteen, and smiled. "Tell me about the carnivorous plant display," he said. Not much to tell, said the client. It was just a bunch of Venus flytraps and other plants some guy kept in his van while traveling from show to show. "What are they going to eat?" Dave said to the puzzled client. "That's not our problem," said the client. "What if it were our problem?" countered Dave. "What if these plants need insects to live on? We don't have a whole lot of insects around here in February. What if we had a crisis and we had to import some insects—for instance, mosquitoes—to feed to these plants?" Everyone grinned.

Thus was born the infamous carnivorous plant display crisis of 1984. There was just one catch—hard as it is to believe, there aren't many mosquito retailers. Dave's team finally tracked down a Florida medical lab that experimented on mosquitoes. The lab manager laughed when Dave's people asked if they'd be willing to sell a few hundred mosquitoes. "If you come down here," said the lab guy, "we'll *give* you the mosquitoes." A staff member was dispatched to Florida—but not until Dave alerted the local media. "Everyone recognized it for what it was, a blatant publicity ploy," said Dave. "But it was a slow news day, and when the plane landed we had two newspapers, two radio stations, and four TV cameras waiting for our person to get off the plane. It was reported that it was the first time in history that anybody had imported mosquitoes—'the state bird'—into Minnesota." Talk about buzz. It was classic look-for-the-hook promoting. "You always try to think, *What is there in this that would make people smile and be irresistible to the news media?*" said Dave. By the time the home and garden show opened, people waited in line thirty minutes to see the (well-fed) carnivorous plants.

Some advertising and p.r. promotion pointers:

Clarify your objective. Imagine sitting down with all your customers at once. What would you tell them? Something about your company (an image ad)? Something about a specific offer (a direct response ad)? The former is good when you aren't well known; the latter is good when you are. Helping your customers get to know you is as crucial as getting to know your customer. People want to know and like you before they'll part with their money. If you're focusing on your image but the offer is also important, include both by way of an offer "tag"—a five-second spot within a thirty-second image ad.

Preach to the choir. Aim a big chunk of your ad budget at current customers. Retention campaign response rates are typically ten times that of bring-in-new-customer efforts. Moreover, attracting a new customer (according to one of my industry's trade organizations) costs six times more than bringing back an existing customer. Plus, repeat customers are 38 percent more profitable.

Track the metrics. Three of the most important measurements for TV and radio ads are:

- ✔ **Reach**—the percentage of your target market you're reaching.

- ✔ **Frequency**—the number of times your targets see or hear your message in a given period. The term "3+ reach"—often referred to as "effective reach"—refers to the percentage of your audience that will see or hear your spot at least three times. Generally, it takes three or more exposures to a message to prompt an individual to act on it.

- ✔ **Cost per point**—the cost to reach 1 percent of your target market. Calculate it by dividing your total cost by your reach.

Television is the most obvious medium for max reach (larger audience, broader demographics, fewer and more expensive spots). Radio is effective for building frequency (narrowed demographics, more spots). Reach and frequency numbers will vary according to your offer and objectives. For instance, are you trying to drive traffic to your stores, or focusing on branding? Are you launching a new product, or advancing a long-term campaign? Is your message time-sensitive? How are you divvying up your promotion budget? How competitive is your industry?

Promote early and often. Breaking into a new area? Launching a new service? Open up the floodgates and saturate the market. Upfront expenses can be amortized over time, and offset by extra revenue from both the initial campaign and its carryover effect. For first-year markets, we upped our advertising and p.r. budget from 4 percent to 8 percent of sales—that included our over-the-top grand openings. We scaled back to 6 percent in the second year before settling back to 4 percent in year three.

Match the new kid's noise level. Brand loyalty ain't what it used to be. Don't let a new competitor—or your current foe, touting a new product—out-gun you. Not even for a brief spurt. Pump up the volume before, during, and after the competition's campaign. Try a customer appreciation promotion to remind your customers why they've always found you attractive—and why the new guy is just a pig in a wig.

Dare to be different. Global insurance giants and talking ducks go together like peanut butter and mustard. That is, until AFLAC took a quack at it in a hugely successful ad campaign. The company's agents thought management was crazy—until new business started pouring in. It takes guts to veer out of the mainstream. Until Michael O'Leary, Ryanair's chief exec, did it, I doubt that any business leader had driven a tank to a competitor's headquarters to call attention to his company's war on their high fares. The free media coverage O'Leary got was worth hundreds of thousands of dollars. Caveat: *different* grabs attention; *obnoxious* (O'Leary was on the line) drives people away.

Send a news release to media outlets. TV and radio news producers, magazine publishers, and newspaper editors are always scouting for good story ideas. Make your news release stand out by keeping these tips in mind:

- ✔ **Create a wish list.** These are the publications and shows your customers read, watch, and listen to.

- ✔ **Do your homework.** Check out a publication's editorial calendar to find out if your product or service dovetails with upcoming themes.

- ✔ **Cultivate a relationship.** Call the producer or editor (the Internet is a great source for names and contact info) and introduce yourself. Tell her why your business is a good fit for her show or publication and ask if she's open to receiving story ideas.

- ✔ **Put on your editor's hat.** Brainstorm with your staff to come up with a hook that readers or viewers would find interesting. You may be as excited as a kid on Christmas morning about your plant's new jumbo press—but an editor will just yawn and toss your release into the circular file. She may, however, find it unique that you deliver flowers and candy with every order. How to begin? Ask, *What are we doing differently from anyone else?* Then build on it.

✔ **Write a straightforward headline.** Convey the thrust of your release in a handful of words—*Customers get flowers and candy with every print order.*

✔ **Write in "inverted pyramid" style.** In other words, lead with the most important information (the broad base of the pyramid). The first paragraph should tell the whole story—who you are, what you're doing, and when, where, and why you're doing it. Each successive paragraph provides additional info in order of descending importance.

✔ **Stick to the facts.** A news release is just that—news. If you even start going down the *Here's why our company is so wonderful* road, you blow your credibility out of the water.

✔ **Focus on people, not things.** If possible, add a human face to your story. If your news is product-related, what will your customers' perspectives be? Including photos may help.

✔ **Don't go it alone.** Sprinkling in quotes and facts from industry authorities adds credibility.

✔ **Customize it.** Tailor your news release to each publication or show. If your story isn't in sync with a magazine's or newscast's personality, you're wasting everyone's time and inadvertently burning bridges.

✔ **Anticipate the final product.** When you release information, you lose control over placement and perspective. Have your team comb over the release in search of positive and negative spins. Make edits to increase the odds of getting the coverage you want.

✔ **Build news releases into your strategic efforts.** An article or news segment relating to your business can be leveraged in multiple ways. For instance, you can send reprints to customers and prospects, and reference or excerpt it in your advertising.

Do it yourself. A founder or chief exec is sometimes the best person to sell the company's story. Lee Iacocca pioneered it at Chrysler. He paved the way for Victor Kiam of Remington ("I liked the shaver so much, I bought the company"), Steve Jobs of Apple, and Richard Branson of Virgin Group. I took the publicity plunge at my company and did our TV and radio ads for five years. I figured if I could talk to prospects on air as effectively as I did one-on-one, I could persuade them to give us a chance. It worked—our same-store sales trended due north. Caveat: for every leader who makes a successful spokesperson, there are ten who are god-awful. Don't try it unless you have a pleasant appearance, some natural charisma, and are able to express yourself powerfully before a camera or microphone.

Communicate internally. You have to create internal excitement before you generate buzz out there in the real world. Whether you're launching a new service, rekindling your brand, or changing your product, get your employees revved up about it. Hang posters. Hold a pep rally. Throw a launch party. Customers expect to hear the same enthusiasm from your people as they hear in your promotions. The more you involve employees, the better. Get your sales staff and others to kick in ideas for promotion design (management and sales may have completely different ideas about your product). When a promotion's set, brief your sales team and support staff on every last detail—what, why, where, when—through meetings and e-mail blasts. You don't want anyone to drop the ball when it's thrown their way.

Find the right media mix. Do you know who and where your customer is? Until you do, you're wasting your money. You gotta know whether to rifle (narrow market) or shotgun (broad market). Ad agencies and p.r. firms hike up the quality of your promotions; just make sure their loyalty is to you and not the media they purchase. Your promo options:

- ✔ **Television.** Anecdotal evidence suggests that TiVo and channel surfing are blunting the power of commercials. Plus, younger generations are spending more time with a computer than a TV, and baby boomers are diversifying their entertainment options. Still, nothing beats TV for searing your brand into the consciousness of the market. Thanks to the proliferation of cable channels, lasering in on your customer has never been more doable—or more complicated. Channel fragmentation may have lowered ad rates, for instance, but are they cheaper from an efficiency standpoint? Does a thirty-second spot on The Dry Cleaning Channel really garner an efficient cost per point? Find a freelance media buyer who can navigate through the numbers, find deals, and negotiate for you.

- ✔ **Radio.** An economical sixty-second radio spot offers more ear time—compared to a pricy thirty-second TV ad—to sell your brand *and* your offering. Radio offers more flexibility than TV. You can swap out creative content in minutes and digitally send spots to a station at the eleventh hour. Radio also delivers a captive audience—listeners are typically sitting in their vehicle or office, and they channel surf less than TV couch potatoes.

- ✔ **Newspaper.** Personally, I'll always prefer turning the pages of my morning paper to clicking through it online (could be a generational thing). Papers work best for direct response, not image building. Place ads where your target market will see them (our customers were sports fans; twenty-somethings may read only the arts and entertainment section). Page three of any section—above the fold—catches readers' eyes first. The next best are other right-hand pages. Ask an ad rep what sections and days of the week make sense for your offer. Whatever the plan, grab 'em with big headlines—otherwise, you'll lose 'em to the funny pages. Roughly 80 percent of your headline words should be five letters or less for quick reading and retention.

✔ **Yellow Pages.** Still a must, even with online directories and multiple books to choose from. Make sure your ad is larger than your competitors'. Figure out where users may look for you and place smaller ads in those categories that direct them to your primary ad—you know, the one with the screaming headline.

✔ **Direct mail.** Best way to hit a bull's-eye? Zero in on targeted criteria like ZIP codes, household income, age, or gender. Tap an experienced list broker for high-quality addresses for just pennies per name. Done right, direct mail delivers big time—perpetually rising mailing costs be damned. Make sure your creative content delivers a quality brand message—clip art on a postcard isn't going to sell a lot of new homes. Test price points, headlines, envelope copy, and anything else you can think of; track results and keep refining. The newspaper headline rule (80 percent of words are five letters or less) applies here. And don't forget the call to action—ask customers to act in a way that nets them something. It could be calling for a free brochure or video, or stopping by your store for a free gift or tax-free purchase. Print overruns of your mailing and leave them wherever potential customers cluster—grocery stores, malls, coffeehouses.

✔ **Trade publications.** Decision makers count on these industry rags for news and trends. Best bet: submit an article with your byline. A published article delivers more credibility than an ad and you'll position yourself as an industry expert. Writing the article yourself (use a first-rate ghostwriter) also gives you more control of the content and saves the editor time, especially if the magazine has suffered staff cutbacks.

✔ **Consumer magazines.** Whether local, regional, or national, match the demographic of the readers—age, lifestyle, income—to your customers. Who else is advertising? Call them and ask if their ads are working.

✔ **Sports marketing.** Our ads and promotions with the Twins, Vikings, Green Bay Packers, and Kansas City Chiefs were big winners. We also generated word of mouth with JumboTron tire mascot races at NBA games. (Our mascots—Sporty, Tuffy, and Classy—were also hits at parades and other community events.) Fans can't help but associate your name with their warm feelings for the home team.

✔ **Out-of-home marketing.** Brand loyalty has been waning for each successive generation since WWII. People, especially the under-forty set, don't watch as much TV (when they do, they're more likely to TiVo out the commercials). They listen to satellite radio, and they don't read the paper. The best way to deliver your message to the elusive twenty-five-to-forty demo is to hunt them down and get creative. That could mean slapping ads in restaurants, theaters, bathroom stalls, or on bus stop benches. Consider turning your truck into a mobile billboard, or use the traditional, stationary variety. But for heaven's sake, limit the copy to a handful of words that are large enough to communicate in a quick glance.

Build an online colossus. Your digital presence has to be more than "brochureware." It's often your website that introduces your company to prospects. Every aspect should reflect your brand—the look, the feel, the text, the forms. Best bet: install a professional web designer on your team of external partners. Here are some ways to stand out:

- ✔ **Connect marketing partners.** Collect your web and marketing experts in the same room to ensure your promotional efforts are consistent and interdependent.

- ✔ **Design a "sticky" site.** Regularly update resources, offers, news, or data to give users a reason to come back. That holds regardless of your site's purpose—retail, lead generation, information hub.

- ✔ **Drive traffic via all channels.** Feature your website address on all marketing materials—direct mail, TV, print ads. Create collateral pieces solely to announce your online presence, or to flag people to your site for special offers or info.

- ✔ **Maximize e-visibility.** This isn't a do-it-yourself job. Partner with a specialist in search engine optimization. You can have the greatest site in the world, but it's chattering in a vacuum if your target audience never sees it.

- ✔ **Be brief.** Users will read concise paragraphs and bullets, but aren't likely to scroll through pages of text. Enlist a professional web-copywriter to shape and spice the content.

- ✔ **Get specific.** Design your site with your target audience in mind. You have multiple audiences—consumers, wholesalers, investors? Either develop separate URLs (uniform resource locators—geek-speak for website addresses) or cleanly split your site into sub-sites.

- ✔ **Sync with sales.** If your site is sales-focused, link a primary offer from your homepage to an opportunity to buy. You also need an easy-to-use shopping section that takes advantage of opportunities to value-sell (a.k.a. up-sell) and cross-sell, particularly at the "shopping cart" step.

✔ **Highlight the fresh stuff.** The "What's New" section on any homepage is like catnip (especially if you add video). It keeps visitors up-to-speed on the latest products, sales, news releases, and events.

✔ **Lights, camera, action.** Audio and video touches get visitors to linger awhile. The operative word is "relevant," however. Posting extraneous clips just to add multimedia flavor can backfire.

✔ **Harvest qualified e-mail addresses.** Direct visitors to sign up for periodic newsletters, updates, and offers, and soon you'll have a golden address book. Install a sign-up button on your homepage, at checkout, or both. For best results, consult with programming and list-management experts. Lists need regular pruning and sorting into appropriate categories based on customers' needs and preferences.

✔ **Leverage the power of e-mail.** Make a habit of mailing offers and updates to customers and prospects (auto-responders triggered by database settings can do this automatically). But exercise restraint—sending messages too frequently may annoy your audience. Important: post an opt-out link at the bottom of your e-mails so people can unsubscribe. (Anti-spam laws require opt-out links on e-mail blasts.)

✔ **Secure affiliate programs.** Give affiliate partners unique URLs that link back to your site. Featuring these URLs on their sites and e-mails can generate qualified web traffic and improve your conversion rates. If you're offering commissions, it's easy to chart the traffic and sales each affiliate generates.

✔ **Get in the feedback loop.** Web reporting, typically from your site host but also available from subcontractors, produces all kinds of valuable metrics. Stay on top of traffic, visitors' origin (sites, affiliates), purchase patterns (conversion rates, frequencies), and other usage indicators. Another option: use product discounts or free information to encourage visitors to fill out surveys.

5 **Make trends your friends.** Volvo's plan to design a car for Gen-X was stuck in neutral. The Scandinavian car company knew there were forty-four million consumers born between 1965 and 1977—but that's about all they knew. Enter Iconoculture, a Minneapolis-based leader in consumer trend research and advisory services. "In order for Volvo's brand to appeal to Gen-X, its car designs need to connect with the innate core values of the Gen-X consumer," said Vickie Abrahamson, Iconoculture's cofounder and executive vice president of cultural analysis. Vickie's team put Gen-X's cultural DNA under their "Macrotrend" microscope. They read their books, listened to their music, ate where they ate, shopped where they shopped. Iconoculture's observations led them to identify five key Gen-X Macrotrends—Artisan (one of a kind, personal style), Carpe Diem (passion, adventure), Torquing (style + high performance), Neo-Puritanism (traditional family values), and Great Expectations (luxury). The Volvo team translated those trends into concepts and designs relevant to Gen-X lifestyle values. The upshot? Five new interior prototypes and a stockpile of fresh promotional angles.

Seat-of-the-pantsers may try to pummel the competition, but if they don't leverage trends they're like a boxer with a glass jaw. One good punch, and it's lights out. Maybe you have a sense of how customers relate to your product. But do you know how they live their lives? What are they passionate about? How do they view family, relationships, environmentalism? What defining events helped form their belief system and values? (For Gen-Xers, it's the first Gulf War, the fall of the Iron Curtain, and the Challenger explosion.) What contemporary people, places, and cultural dynamics are influencing your customers? Enlightened executives understand what makes each generation tick, from Boomers and Gen-Xers to Matures (older than Boomers) and Millennials (younger than

Xers). Use that knowledge to create opportunities all across your business, from product development, brand equity, and positioning to sales, promotions, package design, and customer care.

Trend trackers think of themselves as immigrants trying to dial in to the language and lifestyle of a new culture. After all, trends are signposts for underlying consumer values. Understand those values—by getting in the heads and hearts of your customers—and you understand what drives their pocketbooks. Iconoculture's Lifestyle Trend Tracker Checklist translates your customers' needs, desires, and values into a healthier bottom line:

Open your media maw. Read every magazine and newsletter that touches your industry or is read by your customers. Get a feel for where the two markets intersect. Don't worry about language barriers—it doesn't matter if you can't *read* Italian, you can still *see* Italian.

Look up. Customers in every economic class dream of reaching higher. Take it from someone in the tire biz, you don't always have to reinvent the wheel. Consider carrying luxury products and services to the mainstream by reconfiguring and repositioning them to make them more affordable.

Look outside. Befriend your customers. Move beyond statistics and get to the point where you can finish their sentences. If possible, spend some time walking in their moccasins. Visit their stores, communities, and sporting events. You've gotta understand them where they live. Also, track trends outside your industry and expertise. You'll be surprised at how quickly you connect the dots.

Open your ears. Ask customers—in one-on-ones, focus groups, surveys—about their passions. Are they newshounds or sports buffs? Do their hobbies land them in the kitchen, the music room, the greenhouse? What brings their family and friends together, why, and how often? Great input leads to great insights.

Factor kids into the equation. Today's kids aren't shy about speaking up, whether the topic is wall colors or their first big-girl bed. Doesn't matter if it's a frozen pizza, a backyard playhouse, or the latest iPod—you're fooling yourself if you don't think kids are a major influencer in purchasing decisions. What Junior wants, Junior usually gets.

6 **A word to the wise—merchandise.** The first Brunswick billiard table was built in a small Cincinnati wood shop in 1845. One hundred fifty-five years later, the company's selling channel seemed just as antiquated. Most Brunswick tables were sold in mom-and-pop dealerships that cared little about the prestige of the brand. Many stores commingled brands and stacked tables on top of one another like cheap chairs. No surprise then that merchandising master Sandy Stein was summoned to Brunswick's headquarters in Bristol, Wisconsin. His assignment? Create a customer experience that would yield higher perceived brand value, create excitement, and separate Brunswick from all the commoditized, low-end tables.

The solution? Sandy, founder of Minneapolis-based Stein Trending Branding Design, came up with the Brunswick Pavilion, a store-within-a-store concept that the company rolled out nationally. In a typical store, a dozen or more tables are positioned for optimal viewing, a processional-like entrance features history panels extolling the company's heritage, and backlit floor-to-ceiling fabric scrims display photos of additional table styles in various home environments. The result? A brand appreciation that transcends price and, more importantly, appeals to the "female factor." "The Brunswick Pavilion concept," said Sandy, "makes an emotional connection to women, typically the gatekeepers on large purchases. The showroom spurs the reaction, 'That's the way I want our room to look.'"

Sandy had racked up a big success but now he wanted to run the table. Brunswick, however, passed on his idea to develop its own national prototype retail store. Convinced that the concept would change the face of billiard retailing, Sandy joined forces with a retailing colleague and invested twelve months' worth of spare time in writing up a business plan. Impressed, the company gave Sandy the green light, and the first Brunswick Home & Billiard store opened in

Wilmette, Illinois, in September 2003. A consistently high revenue producer, it's the first billiard store to leverage cross-marketing. The Wilmette store also serves as a laboratory that schools Brunswick dealers across the country in the art of merchandising.

More merchandising tips:

Provide a feel-good experience. Whether in-store or online, comfort is important. Emotions and feelings often drive purchases. Our store personnel were trained to treat guests like gold. And our stores appealed to all of our customers' senses—sight (beautiful showroom, ability to watch cars being worked on), sound (upbeat music), smell (pleasing scents to offset the not-so-pleasant rubber smell), taste (great coffee and, in select stores, cappuccino), and touch (handshake greeting when entering and hands-on product displays).

Make shopping intuitive. Presentation is everything. Target Corp. knows this. Its well-organized, visually appealing displays prompt customers to understand their options—good, better, best—and move smoothly from one category to the next. An intuitive shopping experience through merchandising clarity is a huge differentiator. Target's customers not only enjoy the brand, they *join* the brand.

Anticipate questions. Brunswick's lean, clean, in-store graphic imagery answers top-of-mind questions—"How big does my game room have to be for this table?" "What's the difference in height between a bar stool and a kitchen stool?" At Tires Plus, guests browsed displays that laid out our products and services alongside features, benefits, and prices. These quick-glance visual answers to frequently asked questions (put them online, too) empower customers to move further along in the sales process without feeling any hard-sell pressure from salespeople.

Edit offerings. Too many choices can overwhelm the buyer. Some independent bar stool retailers, for instance, offer up to two hundred styles. That's confusing enough, but they're poorly displayed, too. Can you say "unshoppable"? By contrast, Brunswick's Wilmette store sports a well-lit "chair wall" featuring forty top styles and brands. Customers can stand in one area and leisurely select an ideal combination of style and finish.

Leverage the web. The Internet fundamentally changed the way we shop. Customers are more savvy and more likely to shop unassisted. Smart retailers offer intuitive online shopping experiences that seamlessly sync with in-store visits. But that's not the half of it. The web is an avenue for building and reinforcing customer connections. Remember, relationships, not transactions, are the building blocks for long-term wallet share. Link your customers' core values (you've already done your trend research) to value-added propositions that appeal to a virtual community. This online community is a home where customers can exchange thoughts and information about your offering—and exchange instantaneous feedback with you. That puts you in touch with customers' thoughts about your products and services, and tells you how effective you are at solving their problems.

Going Global

Thanks to the Internet, companies of any size can become global players (97 percent of U.S. exporters are small and midsized firms). It's as easy for shoppers in Bangladesh to browse your website as it is for people in Baton Rouge. Perhaps you're already exchanging virtual handshakes with overseas partners. No? Just wait. Chances are you'll eventually be selling and shipping products overseas, purchasing materials from overseas, setting up an office overseas, or exporting jobs overseas (only as a last resort to stay competitive, of course). The world market is vast. Ninety-five percent of the earth's population—and two-thirds of its purchasing power—resides outside the U.S.

When doing business abroad:

Stay current. Even seasoned vets need to keep abreast of shifting geopolitical and global-financial dynamics. Start with your state trade promotion agency—most states have a small office within their Commerce or Economic Development departments. It's a clearinghouse for federal, state, and local initiatives. Many offer export promotion assistance through workshops, seminars, and one-on-one counseling. Or, check out these websites to see what the latest hoops are and how to jump through them:

✔ **Federation of International Trade Associations** (*www.fita.org*). FITA lists more than 450 independent national associations and provides links to seven thousand international trade websites. Sign up for *Really Useful Sites for International Trade Professionals*, a free e-letter.

✔ **The U.S. Government Export Portal** (*www.export.gov*). This site gives you the skinny on international-trade logistics and requirements. More importantly, it provides access to the U.S. Commercial Service, the global business solutions unit of the Department of Commerce. Through its 108 domestic offices and nearly 150 posts in seventy-six countries, the U.S. Commercial Service offers customized solutions to help small and midsized companies compete in the global marketplace.

✔ **International Chamber of Commerce** (*www.iccwbo.org*). ICC, the voice of world business, champions the global economy as a force for economic growth. Here you'll find the home page for Incoterms 2000, thirteen international rules accepted by governments, legal authorities, and practitioners worldwide. Incoterms 2000 rules bridge communication gaps by spelling out buyer and seller responsibilities.

Set your strategy. Selling your product overseas? Bringing that function in-house could overtax people and processes dedicated to domestic sales—you may have to reallocate and add resources. Plus, plan for complex travel arrangements, warranty repairs, and after-sales support. If you go with distributors to represent your product and manage post-sales issues, will you train them on their turf or fly them to your office for annual sessions? Other options: open an office in the foreign market, appoint an intermediary to find deals, or sign over your international development rights to a management company that will develop your sales in exchange for a cut. (Whatever the strategy, make sure you integrate step-by-step processes for overseas trading into your order taking infrastructure.) Next, establish profiles of your ideal business partners. Perhaps you need someone who stocks warranty replacement parts and does onsite repairs. Another firm may offer twenty-four-hour tech support. Or, is it more important to have engineers on staff to do installs?

Appreciate cultural differences. There's always more to learn about countries you do business with. Go to school on their cultures, from business protocol to entertaining etiquette. Americans and Europeans, for instance, rely on meticulously detailed contracts, while the Japanese favor oral agreements or brief written summaries. In Japan, take a small gift if you're invited to someone's home. But don't wrap it in white paper—it's a symbol of death. Elsewhere, if you dive into a French or Saudi company's customer data before building the proper rapport, you'll get the cold shoulder. Standing too close to a Spaniard or too far from a Saudi suggests indifference. In some Asian countries—Hong Kong, Korea, Taiwan—triangular shapes are interpreted negatively. Germans and Japanese tend to be punctual, while time is more flexible in Latin American countries.

Habla Español. It certainly helps to have employees who are fluent in foreign languages. But many growing firms can't afford the luxury. English, of course, is the lingua franca of business in most industrialized, non-Spanish-speaking countries. If you plan to do business in Latin America, learn Spanish. Or, hire someone who's fluent. South America might be a good market for factory seconds, but if consumers can't decipher labels and packaging you may be forced to give steep discounts. Then there are advertising's linguistic landmines. Take Parker Pen. When it marketed a ballpoint in Mexico, its ads were supposed to read, *It won't leak in your pocket and embarrass you.* Trouble was, the firm thought the Spanish word "embarazar" meant "to embarrass." Mexican consumers were amused when they heard Parker Pen's claim, *It won't leak in your pocket and make you pregnant.*

FIFTY-FIVE

SALES

Increasing Market Share

Jeff Thull had four weeks to prepare for a million-dollar sales call. The CEO of Prime Resource Group, a Minneapolis-based performance consulting and sales training firm, didn't waste a minute. He set up hour-long phone interviews with thirteen of the prospect's key execs. One by one, Jeff and his staff asked them to identify their company's greatest challenges. What symptoms were they experiencing, and how would these things impact the future? When the big day arrived, Jeff's team recapped the critical issues and invited discussion to clarify and prioritize them. They concluded by explaining precisely how Prime could resolve each and every issue. Jeff's firm won the business.

Later, Jeff learned that his new client had been so impressed with Prime's thorough prep work that they had asked the competing consultants if they would also like to arrange informational interviews. The competitor declined. No surprise there—few companies go the extra mile like Jeff's does. That's why, at crunch time, it's no contest. "Doing the discovery gives you credibility," said Jeff. "Instead of generic questions and the standard dog-and-pony show, your presentation demonstrates a thorough understanding of your customer's business and the issues they face." It doesn't matter if you're selling office supplies, software, or industrial equipment. Understanding your customer's performance requirements and offering tailor-made solutions will have your company opening accounts and closing sales like clockwork.

It's worth mentioning that the word "sales" needs a good slander lawyer. If Sales were a person, the image many would conjure is a chatty, slick salesman wearing a plaid sport coat and preying on helpless naifs. My perspective was shaped by the wisdom of my dad, a lifelong salesman who taught me the value of ethical, win-win selling. To him, sales was a philosophy, an honorable relationship between buyer and seller in which value is exchanged. It's what bartering looked like in the grain-for-gunpowder days.

Managing the Sales Function

There's a lot riding on how well a sales team is coached. Its performance determines whether your non-sales employees get bonus checks or pink slips. These rules helped us lead high-flying sales teams in our wholesale, retail, and commercial divisions.

Spend a bundle on a sales manager. Many a CEO studies sub-par sales figures, scratches his head, and wonders, *What am I missing?* A field general, that's what. A creative sales manager sniffs out the right slice of the market, trains and inspires rookies and veterans, and herds volatile personalities. Volatile? Salespeople tend to be mavericks. They're more impulsive than cube dwellers. On top of that, physically and digitally pounding the pavement armed only with traditional, unenlightened sales techniques can exact one heck of an emotional toll. Unfortunately, the way many sales departments operate is negatively self-reinforcing—a lot of leaders simply promote their best salesperson to sales manager. Good luck with that. There may be some overlap in expertise—people skills, for instance, and all the aspects of sales success. But management is a different animal. If your sales wiz doesn't have noteworthy leadership experience, his supervising stint may be a short one.

Track down the best salespeople. You won't make the big leagues without an all-star sales force. The best are probably already employed—but don't let that stop you. Many are treading water, plying under adverse conditions—a mediocre product, poor merchandising, scant inventory, shoddy support. Those roadblocks are curbing their earnings and steering them toward greener pastures. Fling that window of opportunity wide open. Besides checking out the star-catcher methods in chapter 4, ask yourself, your people, and everyone in your Rolodex: *Has anyone knocked your socks off lately?* It's a fishing expedition, but it often nets great leads.

Be your own search firm. Ask yourself, *If I was a great salesperson, where would I work?* Then start dialing. Express interest in the company's offerings: "I want the complete picture, so have your best salesperson give me a call." When you get the star on the phone, tell her you heard she was a great rep and you figured she could refer you to other talented salespeople who might be interested in a great new opportunity. If she gives you leads, great. If she asks for details, she's on the hook. Does she sound intelligent and experienced? Would you buy something from her? One more proactive move: ask the firms you do business with for permission to pick their best reps' brains. To each one you get on the line, say, "Your boss says you're the best. I need a top gun, too. Where can I find somebody like you?" If he expresses interest, take the high road ("Thanks, but I can't do that") and be satisfied with a good referral.

Go deep with your hiring M.O. Salespeople are a unique breed. They need thick skin and a Kevlar ego to survive the battering ram of rejection. During the hiring process, ramp up your personality probing and role-playing exercises (chapters 5 and 6). Make sales aptitude and psychological testing mandatory (assuming legal issues aren't a roadblock). Look beyond numbers when reviewing applicants' accomplishments. Did they build a territory from scratch or inherit it? Remember, you've gotta sell them, too—on your mission and vision for the company and the rewards that follow.

Offer seductive incentives. Dangle a fat carrot in front of salespeople, and you'll find them racing around the track long after the nine-to-fivers have gone home. Big hitters prefer a generous commission arrangement with a get-the-bills-paid base. That's fine. Higher commission rates equal lower impact on your fixed costs. I always told salespeople I wanted nothing more than for them to make a lot of money because that meant the company was making money, too. (In the retail world—Best Buy comes to mind—fair-market compensation without commissions can work just fine.) Commission caveat: hire only ethical, caring people who would never sell anything wrong for the customer. Preach incessantly that financial rewards flow naturally when they have the customer's best interests at heart.

Set performance goals. Settle on reachable, yet challenging, goals. Sit down together and analyze current sales, historical cycles, and the rep's track record. Benchmark her versus her peers. Make sure she walks away with goals she can call her own. There's not a lot of life in arbitrary numbers handed down from on high. Be patient with newbies—but not too patient. Build an exit strategy into your agreement ("If you fail to reach 70 percent of goal after four months, we'll shake hands and go our separate ways"). That helps you cut your losses early and prevents uncomfortable terminations.

Train your force. Don't give up on your current players quite yet. With the right system (my favorite, the Sandler Selling System^{SM}, is outlined ahead), even chumps can flower into champs. Invest in your salespeople by enrolling them in a great sales course. The cost is a pittance compared to the extra revenue it's sure to produce.

Build authority. Turn your sales team into doctoral candidates in their target industries. Demand that they understand everything from lingo to probable pains, so they can put together the value propositions, price points, and solutions that work best. Every pain that arises should prompt a sales rep to tap three case studies— "Let's look at how I solved that problem in the past and go from there." Mastering product knowledge is just as crucial. Our retail, wholesale, and commercial personnel earned Ph.D.'s in Tireology at our in-house university. They pored over product and marketing literature until they could write the textbooks themselves, reciting nuances, features, and benefits for every brand. They knew how each product could cure customer pain. That's how you add value to every customer contact. The higher you rise above the pack, the more valuable you, and your brand, become.

Measure results. Where there's measurement, there's motivation. Our weekly e-mail reports ranked the entire sales force by various metrics. Sales folks are fierce competitors who aren't satisfied being an Avis when a few more deals can land them in Hertz territory. Healthy—repeat: healthy—competition within the ranks leads to healthier profits for everybody.

Demand input from salespeople. As Dad used to tell me, "Appreciate and listen to your salespeople—they bring in the bucks that pay everybody else." Think about it. Your sales force is a direct pipeline to customers. They're the first to know when your customers' needs and desires morph—and they're an early-warning system for what your competitors are doing about it. Require your sales manager to tap that rich source of intel via regular sales team meetings and one-on-ones—and then work with other departments to incorporate adjustments on the fly. For example, I own a stake in a technology concern that hired two battle-tested salespeople with broad industry experience. Their former employer had completely tuned them out. So they were shocked when we treated their input like sage advice, adjusting our product offering, training, and customer service just as they recommended.

Embrace Big Brother. Weekly one-on-ones have limitations. The only way to ensure a salesperson is following protocol is to monitor her on a prospect call. Compliment her on what she's doing right and address her NTIs (needs-to-improve areas) with the four-step Confucius Checklist (chapter 41)—tell her, show her, watch her do it and offer feedback, watch her do it again.

Advocate for your sales team. Drum up support for your sales staff via employee communication channels—e-mail blasts, executive meetings, employee meetings, one-on-ones. If it arouses resentment from the cubicles, nip it in the bud by encouraging empathy for the sales force: *Hey, it ain't easy hitting the bricks every morning and getting doors slammed in your face every hour.* Make sure your sales manager stays on top of technology trends so his team has all the hardware, software, and tracking reports it needs to stay dialed in and a step ahead of competitors.

Create material support. To present a first-class image, you've gotta have first-class business collateral. That's everything from business cards, stationery, and brochures to website, newsletters, and trade show booths. Make sure they all deliver the same brand message. They're your silent sales force, at it 24/7.

MANAGING THE FUNNEL

Think of your sales funnel as a place to pour all your prospects, everyone from current customers to people unfamiliar with your offering. Our sales funnel report listed current and prospective accounts along with current or potential sales levels, goals, follow-ups, roadblocks, and solutions. Performance reports, filled with individual stats like the back of a baseball card, were e-mailed to everyone on the team daily, weekly, and monthly. The sales manager used weekly one-on-ones with each salesperson to stay on top of things.

Constantly sift your sales funnel to separate hot leads from dead-enders. A good way to keep costs—and your sales team's frustration—down is to bring in savvy assistants to qualify the leads. Efficient above-the-funnel management keeps your rock-star sales reps happy and productive. Expecting sales pros to do their own cold-calling and lead qualifying is like asking Shaquille O'Neal to launder the team's uniforms. (Cold-call caveat: mine isn't a one-size-fits-all strategy. It may indeed be worth sales reps' time to cold-call. Much depends on things like the size and maturity of the territory, the universe of available leads, the average account value, and the difficulty of reaching decision-influencers.)

That sales assistant? He qualifies leads by getting prospects on the line—perhaps even arranging a face-to-face—and asking lots of questions: "Would you like to lower your monthly widget bill by 30 percent?" "What are your company's biggest roadblocks?" "Gosh, how long has that been happening?" "How are you personally affected?" "How much is that costing you?" "What are you doing to fix the problem?" "How well is that solution working?" You'd be surprised at how prospects open up. Still, most leads won't pan out. That's okay. It's quality, not quantity, that counts—80 percent of your business comes from 20 percent of your prospects. They're the ones that get top billing on your sales funnel report. Stay on their radar with regular contact (e-mail updates work beautifully) and value-added offers.

SNIFFING OUT SUCCESSFUL SELLERS

The nature of the work demands that salespeople embody certain characteristics. Fine-tune your hiring and training processes to spot and develop these eight qualities:

1 **Goal-oriented.** Show me a five-star salesperson and I'll show you a go-getter with a track record of setting goals and achieving them. Real-world experience is the No. 1 predictor of sales success. Look for take-charge people who can rattle off case histories of how they set a goal, formulated an action plan, overcame obstacles, executed the plan, and got what they wanted.

2 **Self-acceptance.** Self-esteem is the best form of rejection protection. The greats don't take losses personally. They stay confident in their abilities and recognize that circumstances beyond their control sometimes influence outcomes. Take every opportunity to remind your reps they're great people, regardless of what the week's numbers look like.

3 **Empathy.** Great salespeople are great listeners. Customers sense the difference when a rep tosses aside the plaid sport coat and slips into the role of caring consultant. You can't fake it—the greater the suspicion, the lower the commission. Come to think of it, the term "sales force" is something of an oxymoron because a sale will fail if you force it. Bottom line: if your salesperson does right by his customer, he'll do right by himself.

4 **Zeal.** If your sales reps don't believe your offering is the greatest thing since e-mail, forget about revved-up customers. You got a guy missing passion for what he's selling? Help him connect the dots between what he's providing and how he's helping people. If he can't access his passion—and express it genuinely through verbal and nonverbal cues—he's dead in the water. Counterfeit enthusiasm kills off more sales careers than tacky menswear ever will.

5 **Education-obsessed.** The best salespeople settle for nothing less than complete mastery of their offerings. They consume every scrap of literature like it's a map to buried treasure. No nuance is lost on them. They know that customers are drawn to the magnetic pull of expertise.

6 **Friendliness.** It's human nature. People do business with people they like. Never underestimate the likeability factor.

7 **Doggedness.** The "yes" a salesperson yearns to hear may be waiting patiently in line behind thirty-six door-slamming "no's." Slogging through that cold-shoulder quagmire has broken the spirit of countless Willy Lomans. Top salespeople apply their batting average—for both number of sales and dollars per sale—to their goals. It's how they calculate how many at-bats they need to hit a home run.

8 **Hunger.** The best salespeople thrive on the thrill of the hunt. They're never complacent or satisfied. Oh, they celebrate when they score big, but only briefly. Then it's on to the next quest. There are always more prospects to find, more appointments to make, more people to help. Great hunters require only cursory supervision—just throw plenty of red meat their way and watch 'em run.

THE SANDLER SELLING SYSTEM

You've developed the mother of all widgets. Your can't-miss marketing strategy is locked and loaded. You've built a principled, outgoing sales force. But the cash registers won't start singing until you've plugged in the right sales process. I've seen and experimented with countless techniques. Hands down, the best is the Sandler Selling System (www.sandler.com), which has notched countless win-wins for me the past twenty years. No-nonsense and digni-fied, Sandler was founded on mutual respect between salespeople and clients. Sandler wins because it recognizes the two dynamics at work in the buyer-seller dance—the prospect's system and the salesperson's system.

Sales reps won't blossom until they catch on to the prospect's system. Over the years, through exposure to countless sales pitches, prospects have learned enough about the traditional selling process to thoroughly undermine it. Why? Because they feel they have something to lose—their money.

The four pillars of the prospect's system:

1 **Prospects don't always tell you the truth.** Otherwise honest folks have no problem withholding information from, and even misleading, salespeople. They fudge the facts and hold their cards close, all out of self-preservation. Why? Prospects believe that while they're busy managing their daily affairs, salespeople are sharpening their talons. So they stay on their toes lest you finesse them into, heaven forbid, buying something. Precious little indication is forthcoming on how much they actually need your product or service because, well, that would play right into your hands.

2 **The prospect wants to know what you know—for free.** Your prospect assumes you possess a secret for, say, improving productivity, or lowering costs. Why else would your firm invest in the marketplace? She knows your first goal is to generate interest in your offering, so she'll feign interest to pump you for information. She'll also try to secure your best price, but only to use as leverage against her current supplier. Unfortunately, unsuspecting salespeople often give insincere prospects all the free info and price quotes they want. That ultimately corrupts the marketplace, turning valued goods into cutthroat commodities.

3 **The prospect commits to nothing.** Information in hand, she may imply she's close to committing. She'll dangle just enough hope to string you along as an unpaid consultant. You hang on, confident you've notched another win, when in reality you've got nothing. You may even get a gushing thank you note. Might as well keep it, because it's the only signature you'll ever see from her.

4 **The prospect disappears.** Overnight, it seems like she's skipped town. Voicemail and e-mail barriers spring up—salesman kryptonite. The relationship was terminated without your knowledge. Yet, you continue following through because you've invested too much in chasing a phantom sale to admit you've been had. When reality sinks in, well, let's just say it's a bad day.

Now, let's look at why the traditional selling system doesn't work. Whatever brand it goes by, its underlying structure is predictable. The salesperson must

- sell features and benefits;
- withhold price and terms until value is established;
- rely on presentation skills to gain agreement;
- anticipate and handle objections;
- employ an array of manipulative closing techniques.

Sure, this system has survived longer than snake oil. But it's so widely used that savvy buyers see it coming a mile away—which considerably waters down its effectiveness. Worse, the manipulation it advocates contributes to today's adversarial sales environment in which the prospect's system of defense flourishes. To top it off, each step is flawed:

- People don't want features and benefits, they want solutions.
- Delaying vital information wastes valuable time on dead-end pursuits.
- Presenting to blasé prospects wastes everyone's time.
- Focusing on objections gets the buyer's back up and makes the sale even harder.
- Your best pitches work about as well as one-liners at a singles bar.

In contrast, the Sandler Selling System frames the call as a business meeting among equals. The salesperson assumes the role of a highly paid consultant, offering an honest exchange of information.

The seven-step Sandler Selling System:

1 **Establish rapport.** Stop acting like a salesperson. Shift your mindset from *What can I get?* to *How can I help?* Be warm and genuine. That is, smile, maintain eye contact, use first names. Mention a tidbit you learned from your pre-meeting research. Forging a bond breaks down barriers that prevent you from understanding what she needs—and prevent her from appreciating what she has to gain. Continue building empathy and trust throughout the sales relationship.

2 **Establish an upfront contract.** Be clear on a few important ground rules. Establish the purpose of the visit, the prospect's agenda, your agenda, the length of the visit, and the options going forward. For instance, cover all five bases by saying, "Hi, Jill, I've set aside an hour. Is that good? Great. What do you need to cover to make the best use of your time? Would it be okay if I ask a few questions first so I'll be in a better position to answer your questions? If it makes sense to go forward from there, terrific. And if it doesn't look like a good fit, we'll know upfront. Sound good?"

3 **Uncover and probe the prospect's "pain."** People buy emotionally and justify intellectually. A prospect who doesn't have the tools she needs to do her job experiences emotional pain. Ask questions until you discover the issues causing that pain—and just how painful each one is. To move closer to a sale, the old adage is true—no pain, no gain. If the prospect is pain-free in your area of expertise, congratulate her and tell her she's good to go.

4 **Put money issues on the table.** Clearly deliver this message: the most important cost is not the price of the goods but what the prospect stands to lose if she does nothing. That said, determine the financial impact of the issues (the pain) you've uncovered. Then make sure the prospect's budget allows her to heal that pain with your cure.

5 **Learn the prospect's decision-making process.** Can the prospect make the final call? If not, ask for an appointment with the decision maker. If you first need to sell the gatekeeper, do it with the same respect you afford her superior. Before moving on, get clarity on all decision-related matters—*Who else has to sign off? To whose attention should you send additional information? What's a decision's typical timeline?*

6 **Present a solution that cures the prospect's pain.** Again, people don't buy features and benefits. They buy ways to avoid and overcome pain. Describe how you can fix her problem and heal her pain. Then measure her temperature using the "thermometer close." For instance: "Jill, you seem interested. Is that fair to say?" Follow up with, "Where are you on a scale of one to ten, with zero being 'no interest' and ten being 'sold?'" If the answer is five or less, you've got a problem. Retrace your steps. Probe deeper into her pain. If she answers between six and nine, say, "What do you have to see to get to ten?" After clearing each roadblock, repeat, "Where are you now?" until she gets to ten. Once there, say, "Great, what's the next step?" This erases pressure and places responsibility for the decision where it belongs—squarely on the prospect. Let her close the sale.

7 **Reinforce the sale with a post-sell strategy.** When a competitor realizes he's been cast aside, he may fight back with a low-ball price or some trash talk. Shore up your sale before you leave by anticipating buyer's remorse and unearthing hidden objections. Thank her for taking your meeting, say you look forward to working with her, and add: "But could I ask, is there anything we haven't covered that may pop up and throw a wrench in the deal?" After addressing any issues that come up, ask what her next step is and what you need to do to keep things moving. Finally, thank her for trusting your solution and your company, and leave on an upbeat note.

Remember, business is won or lost on the sales dance floor as rapport is established. It's the moment of truth, when you determine whose selling system will prevail, yours or your prospect's. Without a strong system, you default to a passive role. Don't let that happen. The best dancers lead gracefully, always staying a step ahead of their partner.

FIFTY-SIX

CUSTOMER SERVICE

Making Your Guests Feel at Home

One day I walked into one of our suburban Minneapolis stores to find a young salesman in a heated argument with a middle-aged customer. I intervened and offered the older guy a cup of coffee. We sat down and I asked what I could do. He told me his car was late, and also confided he had just been diagnosed with terminal cancer. I told him how sorry I was, that I understood why he had been upset by the delay. Fifteen minutes later his car was good to go and he left satisfied.

No matter how customers behaved, our people were prohibited from acting disrespectfully. No exceptions—the salesman mentioned above never battled another guest. If I found an employee fuming over a testy customer, I'd ask, "Ever have a day when everything went wrong and a minor incident set you off? Maybe the customer's child is sick or he's going through a divorce. If you're calm and caring and ask how you can help, he'll probably apologize when he snaps out of it. So don't take it personally and return fire."

Tires Plus' customer service was legendary. I asked our people to add a touch of volunteerism to the job, to be the sort of beneficial presence that made the customer's day a little brighter. If we concentrated first on kindness and empathy, I told them, healthy profits would naturally follow. That is, as long as we had competitive prices and our costs were in line. Some of my proudest moments were getting notes from grateful customers who said they had come to Tires Plus thinking they needed new tires only to be told their old tires still had tread to spare.

No one embodied that spirit better than Jake, one of our sales guys. One afternoon when Jake was new to the job, he noticed a customer was getting more upset with every delay. It couldn't be helped—mechanics kept finding problems and parts weren't in stock. Still, Jake sensed something more was going on. So he walked over to the woman and asked if he could help. Bursting into tears, she confided that she was a single mom and had just been transferred from a small town where all her family—and the only mechanic she trusted—lived. She was nervous about leaving work early to get her car worked on even though her boss—the only soul in town she knew—had recommended Tires Plus. Now, she was trapped in our lobby, worrying that her young daughters would be stranded at a bus stop after school, unsure where their new home was. Jake took out his car keys. "Come on," he said, "let's go get your girls." When the four returned to Tires Plus and her car still wasn't done, Jake handed the woman his keys. "Take my car," he said. "I'll call you when yours is done." Two words: lifetime customer. That grateful mom never missed an opportunity to bring brownies for the store crew every time her car needed an oil change or new tires.

Why gun for "legendary" customer service?

1 **It keeps 'em coming back.** Seat-of-the-pantsers spare no expense to get new customers in the door, yet often fail to provide a why-go-anywhere-else experience. Huge mistake. Customers are like spouses—take them for granted and they may go elsewhere to get their needs met. It's a vicious circle— businesses pour more and more resources into unearthing new customers to replace the ones lost to neglect. This ain't rocket science, folks. Showering attention on customers already in the fold keeps them in the fold, so your new customers become add-ons rather than replacements.

Take the time Pete Selleck, COO of Michelin Americas Small Tires, flew in to hammer out our partnership agreement. He asked for a store tour, so I showed him a few locations. At our Woodbury store, we introduced ourselves to a woman in the customer lounge and asked whether she had ever been to Tires Plus. "You bet," she said. "My husband and I actually fight over who gets to come here with the kids." Surprised, I asked why. "My goodness," she said. "I'm sitting here watching a movie, sipping your cappuccino, and my kids are playing with toys on a clean floor." Pete was blown away. Later, I learned he shared the story with every tire dealer he worked with.

That's why smart companies focus less on trying to make unhappy customers happy and more on converting satisfied customers into "top box" apostles. What does that mean? Enterprise Rent-A-Car, which raced past competitors thanks to remarkable employee and customer loyalty, asks customers to rate its performance on a scale of one to five. The company grades itself solely by the number of customers who check the top box—"completely satisfied"—on the service questionnaire. Industry standards back up Enterprise's belief that "satisfied" just doesn't cut it. About 35 percent of "satisfied" customers will come back or recommend your business to others. Not bad. But a full 80 percent of customers who check "completely satisfied" will come back and tell their friends.

2 **It pulls in new customers.** Don't just satisfy customers. Astound them. Lay out the red carpet, and guests will rave to friends and family. That sends new customers to your doors and website—at no additional cost. (Expect a dazzled customer to recommend you to two to three others.) On the other hand, one rude encounter with an employee can torpedo every future purchase from that customer, his family and friends—and *their* family and friends. (Expect a peeved customer to complain to three to eight others.) Precious word-of-mouth buzz—two words: free advertising!—is squandered whenever a customer has a less-than-excellent experience.

3 **It's the right thing to do.** Back in 1986, David Wagner, owner of Twin Cities-based Juut Salonspa, was surprised when a regular showed up without an appointment just two weeks after her previous visit. She wanted her hair styled, not cut, so

David assumed she had an important social engagement. Luckily, he had an opening. "I was in a great mood and I was really on," he recalled. "I gave her a great scalp massage and shampoo, and then styled her hair. We laughed and joked and had a lot of fun. When she left, she gave me a big hug that lasted just a little longer than usual." Two days later, David got a letter from her. He started reading, and froze. She explained that she had planned to commit suicide that day, and had come to the salon to get her hair styled so it would look good for her funeral. She changed her mind during the appointment because David had helped her realize life was worth living. She went home, confessed her plans to her sister, and agreed to check into a hospital.

David was stunned. "If you had lined up a hundred of my clients and asked me to choose the one who was considering taking her own life, she would have been last," he said. "She was gregarious, outgoing, and successful. I had no idea she was in such a dark place." David was grateful he had made a difference, and humbled by the experience. "I wondered what would have happened had I been upset or distracted when she came in and had just gone through the motions," he said. Something powerful shifted that day. David began feeling an enormous sense of responsibility. He wondered how many of his fifteen-odd clients each day were in crisis, and desperate for extra kindness and special attention. "I resolved then and there to treat every customer like I had treated my suicidal client," he said. David kept his promise, and wrote a best-selling book, *Life as a Daymaker: How to Change the World Simply by Making Someone's Day*. He defines daymaking this way: *To go about your life in a heart-centered, caring, and compassionate manner with a genuine intent to uplift others*. He also decreed daymaking as the official "noble purpose" of Juut Salonspa's four hundred employees.

Six ways to win legendary customer loyalty:

1 **Hire the right people and train them well.** We showed everyone involved in hiring how to spot applicants who loved helping people and making their day. But that was only the beginning.

Good employees also need training and inspiration. We enrolled new hires in a weeklong orientation where, among other things, I spelled out our mission—*"Deliver caring, world-class service to our guests, our community, and to each other."* The focus of countless meetings, talks, and training sessions, as well as big chunks of our employee playbook, dealt with how to treat our guests (we called them "guests" to inspire the kind of service you'd find at a fine hotel). You can't inspire daymaking service through occasional pep talks, memos, and meetings. It's gotta be walked, talked, and lived—day in and day out.

2 **Treat employees right.** If you leapfrog your people and focus chiefly on pleasing customers, you'll wind up with unhappy customers. Connect the dots, folks. Do you really expect employees who feel unappreciated to welcome customers with a big smile and a genuine desire to give them a positive impression of your company? Honor your people, concern yourself with their well-being, and respond to their grievances like they were customers. You'll be rewarded with invigorated, loyal employees who set new standards for performance and customer care.

3 **Establish clear policies.** No matter how attentive, bright, and spontaneous your people are, customer service should be as scripted as a political stump speech. Improvisation leaves too much to chance—even virtuosos rely on sheet music. In our business, guidelines were essential at three customer-care stages:

Initial contact. Guests were greeted with WHENS—Welcome, Handshake, Eye contact, Name, Smile. We then asked a series of questions to identify their needs. If appropriate, the salesperson walked outside with the customer to examine tire tread. He'd offer a solution, write up a work order, and invite the customer to relax in our lounge until her car was ready. Staffers also fielded phone calls according to a protocol I established in the early '80s: "It's a great day at Tires Plus. This is Jim. How can I help you?"

Warranty service. Salespeople were trained to welcome returning, non-revenue-producing guests like they were new customers. The reason should be obvious—customers prefer to go steady rather than have a one-night stand. That means coddling. We had scripts prepared for every eventuality—fixing faulty repairs, replacing defective warrantied parts, servicing prepaid maintenance programs.

Customer complaints. We welcomed them. No, seriously. They were opportunities to demonstrate we cared about our customers. We even deep-sixed the word "complaint" and replaced it with "guest opportunity." It's said that the value of a person's character is measured by how one deals with adversity. That's also true of the value of a company's character. Employees at every level need the authority to do whatever it takes to satisfy unhappy customers. Give guests the benefit of the doubt if there's so much as a sliver of gray. Does it work? You bet. Just as a broken bone comes back even stronger, we often scored more points by appeasing an upset customer than if the issue had been handled cleanly in the first place.

How do seat-of-the-pantsers handle complaints? My sister-in-law Pam had patronized a dry cleaner in Lexington, Kentucky, for fifteen years. One day I tagged along as Pam returned a pair of pants the cleaners had shrunk. The owner protested that it wasn't her fault, and implied that another cleaner had done the damage. She refused to make it right. Insulted, Pam never returned. Rather than spend thirty bucks to fix the problem, the dry cleaner lost a hundred times that in lifetime sales.

Enlightened organizations go from zero to hero by making these four complaint components customer-friendly:

- ✔ **The duration.** The longer it takes to fix a problem, the more frustrated the customer.

- ✔ **The layers.** When a customer calls to lodge a complaint, will she reach a real person or a machine? Automated receptionists are convenient and save money, but they also elevate customers' blood pressure. When she is connected to a human being, will that person help her?

Or, will she be ushered into a maddening maze of telephone tag?

✔ **The apology.** Two words solve most customer conflicts: I'm sorry. A wronged customer may give you an earful of details, but what she's really angry about is that no one seems to care. Regardless of the actual resolution, a lot of customers will leave satisfied if somebody simply listens earnestly to them. An assembly-line apology only makes things worse. If it isn't heartfelt, she'll take her business elsewhere—and bad-mouth you while she's at it. We used role-playing to get this across to our people. They practiced apologizing until their partner felt it was genuine. (Bonus: employees told me this exercise also helped when they owed an apology to an angry spouse.)

✔ **The action.** After gaining clarity, recapping the issue, and apologizing, we offered a tailor-made solution. If that was still unacceptable, we asked the customer what was fair. We granted all but the wildest requests. It's just smart business when you consider the value of a lifetime customer. As our playbook said, it's better to err a hundred times on behalf of an undeserving guest than miss satisfying a deserving one.

4 **Solicit and act on feedback.** Create as many comment channels as possible. You can't get better without knowing what your customers think. For one firm, that may mean comment cards and follow-up phone calls. For another, it may be web blogs. Dedicated complaint hotlines appeal to certain demographics. Some companies retain an outside service to conduct customer surveys, something Tires Plus did regularly. We also contracted a "mystery shopper" service—for both in-store and phone interactions—to get an objective, in-depth look at quality control.

Gathering information is pointless, of course, unless you act on it. We tweaked our store protocols all the time based on customer feedback. Every negative comment about an employee was routed to his manager's in-box (and cc'd to his district manager) so the offender could be coached back on track. When possible, we told customers about the fixes they inspired—and asked what we could do to win them back. If they said there was nothing we could do, we told them we understood because we had broken our promise. We also told them we hoped they were treated well by their new merchant because that's what they deserved. Our goodwill shocked some people and often turned them around. But that's not why we did it. It was a simple matter of decency.

5 **Measure and reward performance.** We had a customer satisfaction metric called GEI (guest enthusiasm index). Applied to individual stores and the company as a whole, it quantified the percentage of customers who would recommend us to friends. Below-average stores were targeted for extra coaching. It took a lot of sweat to push up our GEI one percentage point. Darrel Blomberg, our full-time director of guest enthusiasm (that's not a joke title), labored two-and-a-half years to move it from 92.0 to 98.2. Personnel knew every smile counted—their compensation was partially based on a mix of store, district, region, and company-wide GEI.

Don't forget non-financial rewards like public ego stroking. Throughout the year, we'd receive a number of unsolicited customer letters praising employees who had been especially helpful. We printed those employees' names in our year-end holiday party program, and prominently displayed the letters. During the party, these customer service all-stars basked in a well-deserved round of applause.

6 **Walk your talk.** Leaders give a lot of lip service to their commitment to customer service. Are you among the few who follow through? When you hear of a complaint, do you shake your head and joke about the customer being an odd duck? Or, do you urge your people to look at the situation through the customer's eyes and do what it takes to make her happy? Do you shout, "You gave away WHAT?" Or, do you say, "Good for you, you remembered our values and did the right thing." Great customer service will wither on the vine without the support of upper management. "One of the things that always made me feel good about working for Tires Plus," said regional manager Brad Burley, "is the comments I got from friends and neighbors about how well they were taken care of in our stores. That all-consuming focus on customer service started with Tom. If he hadn't been so passionate about it, we wouldn't have carried that message first to our people and then on to our customers."

FIFTY-SEVEN

FINANCE, ACCOUNTING, AND IT

Beyond Bean Counting

We were sitting on hundreds of thousands of dollars' worth of unpaid bills when Jim Bemis joined us as chief financial officer in 1993. We couldn't mail the checks because we didn't have the cash to clear them. In the previous twelve months we had added two locations in the Twin Cities and five in Des Moines, a new market. Two of the new stores were seriously underperforming; Jim advocated pulling the plug. He was right. We shut down the stragglers and regrouped. In the short term, we decided to only open stores in the Twin Cities, where our brand was more firmly established. Sure enough, every new homegrown store soon turned profitable. Eight months after Jim joined us, the checks were really in the mail.

Jim's financial leadership was pivotal. I was elated when he cleaned up our books and began delivering the P&L shortly after month-end. Even better, our auditors gave us high marks for the first time. Regrettably, many business leaders view "bean counters" as math geeks who were put here to clean up their messes, not lead the way. It's not a surprise, given that most entrepreneurs come from marketing or product development backgrounds, not financial ones (present company included). Had I read this chapter at the start of my career, my seat-of-the-pants days would have been a little less rocky.

CFOs and the Finance Function

Finance and accounting people are gatekeepers. They safeguard assets and make sure information is accurately captured, analyzed, and conveyed. Absent these controls, you open yourself to flawed decisions, theft, and embezzlement. That said, hire more than a checkbook holder or recorder of history. The CFO belongs on the executive team. The best ones are information hubs, providing the rest of the team with financial tools for running their departments. Without this mindset, a CFO's value to the enterprise is limited.

Good CFOs provide monthly analysis and presentations to the executive team—that includes profit-and-loss statements within five to ten days after month-end. They challenge other department reps—querying marketing on overspending, hitting up retail over slow-turning inventory. Still not convinced of the CFO's value? I yield to Dave Cleveland, a forty-year banking vet and founder of entrepreneur-friendly Riverside Bank in Minneapolis: "If I could ever find a company where the owner paid the CFO more than he paid himself, I'd make that loan automatically."

No matter your take on the finance function, be careful not to hand over responsibility and power. After an early CFO repeatedly failed to produce accurate, timely reports—and resigned as a result—I challenged our CPA firm for not alerting me to my CFO's shortcomings. That's when I realized that the CPA firm's loyalty to the CFO may have colored its objectivity (he had selected them, after all). That was the end of that relationship, and I actively helped choose our new CPA firm. From the outset, I made it clear that its responsibility was to me as chairman and CEO. I also scheduled periodic one-on-ones with the firm's partner-in-charge. The point is, get in the loop and stay there.

A publicly held company needs a superstar CFO. He's part workhorse, part show horse—someone who can hit the road and tell your company's story to investors, brokers, analysts, and money managers. To manage expectations, he needs to speak the language of both the buy side (mutual funds and other money managers) and the sell side (Wall Street). He needs to explain and justify the numbers, professionally and positively, although not so optimistically that he becomes suspect. In a word, your CFO has to be "streetable," a representative you can dispatch to Wall Street and do your company proud.

Every CFO's raison d'etre is cost containment. No matter what pricing position your company stakes out, cost-cutting is an ongoing exercise. Ryanair, the Ireland-based no-frills airline that's revolutionized European travel, is an extreme—and extremely successful—example of how driving down costs drives up profits. Michael O'Leary, who heads up Ryanair, got religion on cost containment after visiting Southwest Airlines' Dallas headquarters in 1991. His motto now: a penny shaved is a penny earned. Like Southwest, Ryanair flies point-to-point to smaller airports and limits maintenance costs by using just one airplane model.

O'Leary also did away with pre-assigned seats, travel agent commissions, and frequent-flier miles. He even eliminated seatback pockets to speed up cleaning. The strategy worked. Ryanair's average ticket price is more than 50 percent cheaper than its closest competitor. O'Leary wants to drop prices even lower, all the way to the ground. He hopes to someday give—yes, give—most tickets away and pull revenues from food, beverages, and other extras. By keeping costs low, Michael O'Leary is flying high—and definitely not by the seat of his pants.

You can always find more fat to trim, no matter how lean you are. Sit down with your management team and slog through the expense portion of your profit-and-loss statement. Line by line, ask two questions: *Does this add value to the customer experience? If so, can it be recovered through product or service pricing?* If the answers aren't yes, eighty-six it.

Some more waist-slimmers:

- ✔ Assume you're paying too much for absolutely everything, from your CPA firm to advertising to ballpoint pens (see chapter 53 for purchasing tips).

- ✔ Turn to your people for ideas to eliminate wasteful spending (our Profit Improvement Team included employees at all levels across all departments).

- ✔ Weed out underperformers.

- ✔ Measure costs by department.

- ✔ Boost inventory and manufacturing efficiencies.

- ✔ Recalibrate compensation levels to reflect market conditions and organizational value.

BUILDING YOUR BUDGET

A consultant once told me about an anonymous client whose monthly reports showed he was meeting budget. It left my friend scratching his head because the company was stuck in no-growth gear. He finally figured out his client was changing the budget whenever business conditions changed. The consultant's advice: commit to an annual budget and live with it till death do you part (absent any major errors, of course). Relentlessly and cold-bloodedly measure your performance against your budget. Mess with the numbers and you'll have no idea whether you're achieving the goals you established at the beginning of the year. (Forecasts, on the other hand, should be updated regularly—and spending adjusted accordingly—to reflect actual results.) Your budget's influence seeps into every aspect of your culture. Hit the numbers and esprit de corps soars. Miss 'em through flawed understandings or bad budgeting, and morale tanks.

A budget is your strategic plan translated into numbers. Begin the budgeting process by viewing your strategic plan through the lens of financial considerations. Plan conservatively but think optimistically by sketching three scenarios—upside, base, downside. Why? Let's say you start the year by shoveling piles of cash into an ambitious new product launch. Six months later the money's spent and sales are drying up. Panic Time. You scramble to salvage your business, not just for the fiscal year but forever. Had you laid out a worst case scenario—and run the numbers—during the financial planning process, you would have made more conservative management decisions. Budgeting forces you to ask the hard questions: *How much working capital will I need? How much labor will I need? What happens if I ramp up but revenue flatlines?* In 1519, Cortez, the Spanish explorer, arrived to conquer Mexico. Once ashore, he ordered his men to burn the ships that had carried them to the new land. It was a bold message—win or die. Cortez would have made a lousy businessman. Sometimes, retreat is the wisest call.

Some budget-building tips:

- ✔ Lay the groundwork for buy-in by involving all levels of management in the strategic planning process (chapter 20).

- ✔ Involve all managers—not just accountants—in the budgeting process. Getting everyone on the same expectations page is a must. Those who will execute the plan need to have helped build the plan.

- ✔ Begin the budgeting process in early November (or eight weeks before fiscal year end). At this point, your strategic plan objectives have been set and you've completed your prep work, such as building financial models and loading last year's numbers into them.

- ✔ Start fresh with a "zero-based" approach. Begin with last year's numbers—but don't assume they'll remain constant. Analyze where last year's business came from and what might change. Then build this year's numbers from the bottom up. Result? More accurate revenue forecasts and tighter expense control.

✔ Budget the "details." It's hard work but if you don't do it, you'll miss a key assumption or expense and miss your numbers every time.

✔ Exercise caution. Estimate revenues on the low side and expenses on the high side (but not too high, because people generally spend what's budgeted).

✔ It's okay to submit a more conservative plan with lower expectations to your bank. For instance, if your budget assumes 8 percent sales growth, the bank plan may assume 2 percent growth. Then, if you fall short of your internal plan, you still have a good chance of hitting the bank plan numbers and, more importantly, of meeting the covenants the bank created from the plan you gave it. Public companies may also benefit from preparing a more conservative plan for Wall Street and research analysts. In fact, no matter who your constituencies are (bank, analysts, board of directors), you can't go wrong with a strategy of UPOD—under-promise, over-deliver.

✔ Revise the budget quickly if you find a significant error—and communicate all revisions to your bank immediately. It's better to revise and report the revision than to miss a future projection.

Master the Metric System

You're in the driver's seat, so keep an eye on the dashboard. Every business should track daily, weekly, and monthly metrics—receivables, payables, gross and net profit margins, sales, average sale, inventory. Enlightened executives also insist on real-time measurements unique to their industry. For instance, three key manufacturing metrics may be:

Scrap rate. Let's say you make die-cut labels. On any given day the scrap rate is a hundred sheets. Suddenly, it shoots up to a thousand sheets. All that wasted material tells you someone's order is going to be late. See that someone hits the floor to find out why. Maybe a machine broke down. Maybe somebody ran the job on the wrong paper. Whatever the case, if you ignore the scrap rate, a quality problem could slip by undetected—until you get a call from an unhappy customer.

Backlog. Keeping orders flowing through the pipeline is vital. Too much downtime is murder on margins. (Have your CFO determine how to measure this metric.) Sales and manufacturing need to sync up to stagger orders and keep production rolling along—if every customer is promised next-day delivery, your plant better be stocked with defibrillator paddles.

Equipment utilization percentage. No metric screams "red flag" louder than this one. Too many entrepreneurs fall in love with equipment. One business owner I know had to have the latest toy but only ran it 20 percent a day. Idle employees passed the time watching wasted dollars—capital expense, depreciation, insurance, labor—swirl down the drain.

Numbers tell the story, but don't obsess too much about 'em. Leaders at smaller companies often succumb to analysis paralysis by studying too much—or the wrong—information. They whip out all sorts of spreadsheets but can't tell you their margins by customer and product. Ask yourself, *If I could only have eight pieces of company information every day, what would they be and why?*

Seat-of-the-pantsers often overlook the most obvious and important metric—cash. I found out how a cash crisis can sneak up on you when my CFO told me in '89 that we were $1 million in the hole and tapped out on credit. Your financial statements may have you believe you're raking it in, but next thing you know you can't meet payroll. The three biggest culprits are overdue receivables, slow-turning inventory, and growing too fast. All companies, particularly young ones, should keep close tabs on cash by forecasting their balances daily, weekly, and monthly—and then following up when they fall short.

MANAGING RECEIVABLES

My philosophy is simple. Not only do you have to get paid, you have to get paid on time. To optimize management of your receivables:

Get it in writing. Use a credit application to document mutually agreeable payment terms—date due, finance charges. Dot the i's and cross the t's—so you don't have to cross your fingers come collection time.

Know your customer. Don't rely solely on credit reports for information on commercial accounts—such info is often two years old. Call and get references to check current pay histories.

Establish a personal relationship. It's not always practical, of course, but it can tilt the payment odds in your favor.

Walk away from large, suspect sales. If you're not completely confident an account can or will pay you on time—and the sale is large enough that not collecting the cash can hurt you—don't take the sale.

Use liens when appropriate. If you're selling certain property or services, be sure to document your lien rights. If you're selling inventory, for instance, your bank can help you file a lien on the property sold. A lien can be your best friend (why do you think banks always get paid first?).

Get strict with past-due accounts. Contact the customer as soon as your protocol permits (in our company it was seven to ten days after a missed due date). Wait until an account is ninety days past due and you may be too late. Do all future business C.O.D. (cash on delivery) until the customer is current again. No exceptions, no matter who the customer is or how long you've had a relationship. Get lax and the account may snowball out of control. Then there will be two companies in trouble.

Establish phone protocol. The first call to a past-due account is always a relationship-building call: "I'm just calling to make sure you received the invoice." The second is a problem-solving call: "I'm just checking in to see if there's a reason why we haven't received your payment." If there's a pause, don't fill it; wait for the customer's response. Subsequent calls should always be firm, fair, and professional.

Tutor customer relationship "owners." School them (often your salespeople) in accounts receivable policies and procedures. Feed them clear, easy-to-interpret aging reports. Account relationship decisions should be led by those who own the customer relationship. After all, they have a vested interest in the outcome. That said, final decisions regarding ongoing credit are the credit manager's call.

Meet regularly with your credit staff. At least once a month, review all accounts. Ensure action steps are being taken—phone calls, past-due letters, final demand letter, collection agency, legal action—to resolve past-due accounts.

Dealing with overseas customers? Be prepared to be resourceful, especially if you've never met the customer and credit references are impossible to come by. Skip Thaler, an old friend and importer-exporter, once sent a shipment of tires to Italy. The customer never picked up the order. As far as Skip knew, a UFO had scooped her up. Because freight and duty fees were too high to retrieve the shipment, Skip got on the horn, dropped his price, and found another Italian buyer. When determining a payment protocol for foreign customers, factor in these three primary risks:

1 **Country risk.** Before you pursue an overseas deal, consult country risk ratings published by folks like Dun & Bradstreet, Veritas, and World Bank. Already shipped product to, say, Venezuela? Good luck collecting payment. Domestic problems weaken a country's currency, so governments often restrict hard currency from leaving their borders, which would raise inflation, interest rates, and exchange rates vis-à-vis the U.S. dollar. That's not to say you can't pry dollars out. You'll just need a really big lever.

2 **Currency risk.** If, on the other hand, you agree to take payment in foreign currency, protect yourself against fluctuations by contractually specifying a minimum conversion rate. (Don't forget to include conversion fees.) It's not unheard of for currency rates to plummet 50 percent from the time you seal a deal to collection day.

3 **Payment risk.** What's the cardinal rule of international trade? Know your buyer. Begin every business relationship by pricing your product in U.S. dollars and asking for advance payment. (Make sure your bank processes international wires.) Sure, it's a stern approach, and revenues may suffer in the short-term. But it's better to lose one-time buyers than it is to expose yourself to ruinous risk. Upfront, tell your trading partner that as your relationship matures you can explore more equitable ways to share risk. In time, move from advance payment to letters of credit to documentary collections (they're less onerous than letters of credit). After building a solid history, settle into open payment terms.

BOND WITH YOUR BANKER

Your bank is a partner, not an adversary. Get your banker on board by communicating early and often. Get in the habit of reviewing your monthly financials together—bankers love it when you consider them an extension of your management team. Be especially forthcoming when you've got bad news. It's human nature—who likes to tell the banker when there's a significant negative variance between projected and actual income? Some execs roll up their sleeves and quietly try to turn it around. A month goes by. Two months. Things get worse and one or more of the loan covenants are blown. Sheepishly, they call their banker, who's none too happy to be the last to know. You're better off coming clean with your banker right upfront: "I thought I'd give you advance notice. We just calculated that, due to weather, we're not going to hit our November numbers." Chances are he'll waive the company's covenant before D-Day. He's human, too—the last thing he wants to do is go to the loan committee with bad news after the fact. Avoid that scenario by committing only to loan covenants—current ratio, leverage ratio, debt/equity ratio, interest coverage—you know you can meet. (FYI, aggressively negotiating those covenants earns your banker's respect.)

One of the smartest things you can do is take a lender to lunch. Lay the groundwork by getting to know three key people in your bank—your relationship manager (typically an up-and-comer), her boss or her boss' boss (the closest thing nowadays to the traditional gray-haired banker), and, most importantly, the person who chairs the credit committee. It works like this. Your relationship manager goes to her boss. They decide whether to, say, extend your credit or amend your covenant. After a credit analyst reviews the request and writes up a report, it's taken to the credit committee where your fate is decided. The credit chair's job is often drudgery—he's chained to his desk analyzing financial information all day. The big secret is he never gets invited to lunch. He has no idea who the companies are behind the loan requests. So, when your relationship manager introduces you to her boss, invite the boss—and the credit chief—to tour your company and have lunch. The credit guy will love taking a break from the dungeon. And it's a coup for you. The credit chair will have a better grasp of your business *and* you're no longer just another name on a loan request. Those two factors alone could make a big difference when your loan comes up for review or you need a covenant waiver. But it'll be too late if you wait for stormy weather. Do the meet-and-greet now, while the sun is shining and there's not a cloud in the sky.

MANAGING IT (INFORMATION TECHNOLOGY)

Purchasing, finance, and IT people rarely speak the same language. Techies get excited about new toys that bean counters don't have the chops to critique, and jargon-challenged purchasers are often at the mercy of tech-savvy vendors. That skills gap is difficult to bridge, leaving a big hole for IT investments to plunge through. Building that bridge requires three main pillars:

1. The integration of IT into the strategic planning process

2. The unqualified support and leadership of upper management (which should include the IT director)

3. The realization that IT investment is ongoing

Building IT into strategic planning is the best way to align IT strategy with business strategy. Plus, getting buy-in from all departments from day one is critical. Why? Because IT failures are generally rooted in business, not technical, breakdowns. It all comes down to change management. Implementing an IT initiative starts a domino effect—every business process also changes. That's why upper management must own and manage an "IT project." Most people resist change—especially technological ones. Your IT staff can manage the technical side, but they can't mandate that users accept the change. If key users haven't had a seat at the designing-testing-training table, and don't view the new process as markedly better than the old, a project is doomed before it begins. Senior execs have to hammer home the point that promised returns will materialize only if everyone gets on board and adjusts the way they operate.

A big IT fallacy is that ROI will magically start growing like a weed. Don't count on it. Maximizing ROI demands that you keep investing in the solution. That means training both IT and users on technology, applications, and enhancements. It means budgeting money for support (think "help desk"), process redesign, and upgrades. (The upgrade cycle of enterprise software is generally one to three years; each event can require one to four months.) Failing to fully invest in IT solutions is why many companies are using only 20 percent of the functionality they buy. How can that happen? Easily. A hot project plops in the lap of top management. They dutifully approve an IT spend in accordance with the company's capabilities and growth projections. The bare bones functionality of the IT solution is implemented. The hot project is completed and everyone moves on.

That waste can be minimized—at least for non-strategic IT solutions—by partnering with an MSP (managed service provider, a.k.a. outsourced service provider or utility computing service provider). Thanks to MSPs, which deliver computing resources over the Internet like a power utility delivers electricity, management can now focus on IT's use and not its generation. And, like other commodities, users are billed only for the services they use. Bottom line: most organizations' core competency isn't, and shouldn't be, IT systems deployment and management. Today's IT focus is on access, not assets. Asset-based IT—owning hardware and software—is going the way of the passenger pigeon. According to Gartner, Inc., the leading provider of research and analysis on the global IT industry, 80 percent of large-company IT investments now go to MSPs. Why the migration? Lots of reasons. Partnering with MSPs

- reduces your IT infrastructure and deployment risks;
- allows you to quickly scale your IT infrastructure up or down;
- lowers upfront costs as well as costs associated with excess IT capacity;
- eliminates the need to staff up for peak demand periods;
- allows your IT group to concentrate fully on strategic issues;
- can begin with well-defined and fairly generic applications—e-mail, messaging, connectivity, hosting, security, redundancy, storage, disaster recovery, standalone applications (like sales automation).

More IT success strategies:

Cycle IT leaders throughout the company. Don't confine your senior IT people. Give them operational experience in other departments so they understand the business better and know what the company needs to succeed. Our Adopt-A-Store program required IT staff to spend time at a particular store each month learning different skills—store opening and closing procedures, receiving freight, doing inventory. We wanted them to understand the capabilities and needs of the people who used the systems they designed. Computer programmers are a different breed. They may be able to operate a system in their sleep but that doesn't mean the average user can. Keeping the people who design your systems connected to other parts of the company ultimately helps both your internal and external customers.

Hold your IT chief accountable. It's every leader's nightmare— the break-the-bank software purchased two short years ago is obsolete. Make sure your IT head invests in flexible open architectures that allow your company to change with the market. Growth potential also needs to be taken into account—big investments should include volume price breaks for future users, computers, or servers. (An outsourced MSP solution might be your best bet.)

Embrace industry standards. That means not building proprietary solutions. Why? Highly customized software is like a drug. You get hooked and can't get off it. It begins to cost more and more. Before you know it, you can't switch dealers—er, vendors—because your cost to move off their solution is higher than the incremental cost of your next fix—er, upgrade. Mandate that IT solutions be compatible with other primary systems within the organization.

Don't create more problems than you solve. In the late 1990s, CRM (customer relationship management) solutions were all the rage. A lot of organizations coughed up big bucks for CRM software without specific plans on how to use it. The result? ROI was DOA. Software is a tactic, not a strategy. Develop a strategy first, then secure the tactics to support it.

Demand ROI from most IT investments. When a business unit proposes an IT solution, challenge them to prove that it will directly benefit the company in measurable ways. Require that they, and IT, budget it. Then hold IT accountable for the technology and the business unit responsible for results. Make sure your financial reporting is clear and transparent so results can be traced to specific investments. Caveat: there are exceptions. Up to 20 percent of your IT spend should be R&D-related. Your IT staff needs to stay on top of advancements that can translate to competitive advantages. Without an R&D budget, all your staff can hope for is to stay afloat.

Be wary of big promises. Benchmark industry IT investment as a percent to revenue. You'll need it as a shield against slick-talking sales folks. Skilled IT vendors can construct an ROI model showing you can invest as much as your total revenue and still get a rosy ROI. Hello? If Wal-Mart—perhaps the smartest technology user in the game—isn't able to squeeze more ROI past a certain percent-to-revenue threshold, what makes you think you can?

Managing and Funding Growth

Businesses are like sharks. For survival they depend on forward progress. Sometimes that means adding new stores, plants, or regional offices. In many businesses, it means selling more units to existing customers, creating new products, or upping same-store sales. Even if you're content to stay comfortably small, standing still is not an option. Costs rise, competition lurks. Unless you grow—and allocate escalating costs over an expanding base— you'll gradually take on water. But watch out. Growth has a voracious appetite and sharp teeth—not just for capital but also for people and systems. Focusing on growth, growth, growth rather than day-to-day necessities may starve the operation's core, where life-giving income is generated.

Entrepreneurs are typically more "growth aggressive." Founders of companies tend to be builders of things. They love to build product and expand capacity. It's in their DNA. They're confident they'll get the business to justify the expenditures. Each new success emboldens an entrepreneur to take even greater risks. Trouble is, as a company gets larger, new layers of complexities arise and its risk profile changes dramatically. The enlightened executive upgrades his skills to meet these challenges head-on. He knows an adrenaline-fueled, "let it ride," Vegas-craps mentality can leave a company in ruins. Here's where a board of advisors (chapter 59) is worth its weight in stock options.

Retained earnings are clearly the Wheaties of business growth. However, absent sufficient earnings and unable to borrow, raising capital may be an option. The risk here is that selling stock is how many entrepreneurs lose control of their company. One CEO I know owned well over half his company. When his ambitious plans outstripped resources, he was forced to raise money by selling shares on the cheap. Ultimately, his stake was whittled down to a nominal 5 percent.

Avoid the growth-gone-bad nightmare—do your due diligence. Before adding all the ingredients—people, equipment, inventory, real estate—prepare revenue and expense projections to determine whether your plans are affordable. Sophisticated businesses and private equity pros run the numbers through capital investment formulas based on discounted cash flow (DCF) models and targeted internal rates of return (IRR). These calculations answer two basic questions:

1. How soon will the investment break even so you can pay shareholders?

2. What will be the return on investment?

Nailing down these numbers eliminates mystery from the investment's "go/no go" call. To ignore number crunching in favor of going with your gut is to court disaster. The gut-instinct system can't appreciate that "units"—equipment, storefront, salespeople—have to quickly support themselves (payback) and contribute profitability (ROI). And that it has to be done according to precisely targeted financial goals.

The best acid test for profitability is a "capex" (capital expenditures) calculation. Here's how you do it. (Scholars may laugh at my simplification, but all I care about is helping ethical, hard-working folks make money.) Divide your expected cash flow from the new unit (a store, say) by its cost (initial capital outlays, inventory, one-time pre-opening expenses, and so on), then divide the result by number of years invested. Carry over the sums on a cumulative basis—if you add more capital equipment, for instance, increase the denominator accordingly.

For example, say the cost to open a store is $1 million, and its first-year EBITDA (earnings before interest, taxes, depreciation, and amortization) is $100,000 in the hole. Your capex calculation is:

$$-\$100,000/\$1,000,000 = .10/1 \; year =$$
$$-.10 \; (ROI \; is \; under \; water \; by \; 10 \; percent)$$

Now, assume the second-year EBITDA is $600,000. The cumulative EBITDA becomes $500,000 (-$100,000 + $600,000). The new capex calculation is:

$$\$500,000/\$1,000,000 = .50/2 \; years =$$
$$.25 \; (ROI \; is \; 25 \; percent)$$

The Really Big Question: when do you reconsider the investment? The Simple Answer: if you can't put money back into shareholders' pockets at the end of three years (ROI of 33 percent) or four, tops (ROI of 25 percent). A piece of equipment can often pay for itself in less than a year—an ROI of more than 100 percent. I watched a national fitness chain fail at the basics as it rolled out dozens of new fitness centers. While each one was profitable, it took more than seven years for the company to recoup its initial investment via earnings. Yet, because the heavily trafficked centers required upgrades every seven years, the owners had to double down their capital expenses before they could turn a profit. It's like Sisyphus and his rock. Each time he pushed it up the mountain, it rolled back down again.

Where you grow is just as crucial as what, when, and how. Location is the X-factor in any ROI calculation. If customers are coming to your offices or stores, you're typically better off selecting an A site (the premium choice in the commercial real estate world). Don't be swayed by promises of lower occupancy costs at a B, C, or even D location. Do the math. Let's say Site A cost $1,000 more per month than Site B. But you determine that Site A will bring in three more customers per day at an average sale of $100. That $9,000 in extra monthly revenue nets you $3,000 after product acquisition and variable operating costs. Result? An extra $1,000 a month in your coffers. Not sure how many more customers you'd get at a premium site? Calculate how many more you'd need just to break even—it's probably fewer than you think. If you're looking at office space, the benefits are less tangible but just as important (unless clients never visit). In business, perception becomes reality. Bottom line: don't let higher occupancy costs scare you. What Goliaths understand, and most Davids don't, is that it's not what you pay, it's how much net profit you generate for what you pay.

Growth through acquisition presents another set of challenges. Tires Plus marched into Kansas City and bought six stores that we immediately remodeled. Sixty days later, our signs were up and the stores were open. The transition was seamless because customers viewed the old locations as brand-new stores. Later that year, we acquired a dozen stores in Omaha. I'm still scratching my head over why we didn't follow the Kansas City script. Instead, we kept the stores open under the old name. We waited months to re-brand them, and remodeling took an entire year. We also took our time replacing employees who didn't fit our culture. It wasn't exactly a shocker when we fell a country mile short of our sales goals.

If you plan on acquiring other companies:

Expect culture clashes. Buyouts push employees out of their comfort zone, triggering an avalanche of emotions. They fear their jobs are in danger and the new owners could ruin everything. Remedy: communicate early, often, and with empathy.

Weigh the pros and cons of organic growth. Taking over an existing outfit inserts you instantly into the marketplace. But a lot of companies—especially big boys like Best Buy and Wal-Mart—like to start from scratch. Why? It's easier to retain complete control and ensure that reputation is built—and employees are trained—the right way.

FIFTY-EIGHT
LEGAL

Protecting Your Business Interests

Lawsuits are like accidents, they're impossible to predict. For instance, fifteen years after Jeff purchased a Tires Plus franchise in St. Paul, a better location developed near a major shopping mall. Jeff declined to relocate or open a second store, so we built a company store there. It was outside, barely, of Jeff's exclusivity radius, but Jeff sued us anyway. As it happened, our company-wide franchisee meeting fell during the dispute. At the meeting, I walked over to Jeff. "Wanna stand up for a minute?" I said, turning with him to face the other franchisees. "I wanted to let you all know," I said, "for those who hadn't heard, Jeff and I have different perspectives on an issue and we're letting the judicial system determine the outcome." I put my arm around him. "I just want everyone to know," I said, "that I still care a lot about Jeff. He believes he's right, we believe we're right. Regardless of how it's decided, we're going to remain friends." A few weeks later, Jeff settled for the rights to develop another franchise in a different area. (I took it as a compliment that the resolution was built around Jeff's desire to stay, even expand, with us.)

Avoid litigation if at all possible. The legal system wasn't designed by our forefathers to resolve business issues. Winning a case on the merits is beside the point. Add to your mounting legal fees the time spent by the executive team on pre-trial discovery, document review, general trial preparation, and the trial itself. Even when you win, you lose.

Steps to ward off legal woes:

Hire the best. Take the time, do the research. Solicit referrals from your network. Ask prospective attorneys for phone numbers of three clients who'd be willing to talk to you. Do what it takes to retain the best legal eagle you can afford, a skilled business analyst who delivers practical (not theoretical) solutions. Experience, efficiency, and quality of work count more than hourly rate. If Lawyer A takes three hours to prepare a contract, and Lawyer B takes one hour at twice A's hourly rate—*and* does it better—well, you do the math.

Read the fine print. Business leaders sign countless contracts. From equipment leases and supplier agreements to strategic partnerships and employment pacts, don't just flip to the last page and sign. It's your job to spot the fox in the henhouse. Certainly, legalese is sleep-inducing—kinda like flipping through a medical journal. Power through and read it anyway. Highlight what you don't understand. Ask your attorney to explain the mumbo jumbo, but only after you explain to him the business issues involved.

Be thorough. My longtime corporate attorney once reviewed an office lease that allocated $4,500 for tenant improvements. That was one crucial zero less than the $45,000 his client was promised. Fortunately, the client had thoroughly briefed his attorney on every detail before feeding him the contract—an ounce of prevention that saved him forty grand worth of pain. Also, make sure important contracts specify worst case scenarios—and comfortable solutions for when (not if) one of those cases occurs. What happens, for instance, to your volume discount if a supplier runs out of merchandise during your busiest month? Agreements are often stitched together at the eleventh hour but even then—in fact, especially then—take the time to do a first-class review. A few extra hours upfront can avoid contentious renegotiations or costly legal battles.

Protect your intellectual capital. In our early days, tire dealers in other states were using our brand name and plagiarizing our Yellow Pages ads. The dealers weren't direct competitors. But, given our expansion plans, they certainly would be soon enough. We didn't relish the idea of competing against our own brand name and ads, so we mailed cease-and-desist letters to the poachers. Problem solved. Don't wait to trademark your brand name, tag line, and logo, or to copyright your ads and marketing materials. Be sure to also protect any proprietary products or processes to preserve your competitive advantage. "Protection money" pays for itself many times over by increasing your brand equity. When we sold our 150 stores to Bridgestone/Firestone in 2000, they changed the name of their four hundred existing stores to Tires Plus in order to capitalize on the excellent name and our brand's added value.

Keep your coverage current. Sit down annually, especially if you're a small business, with your commercial insurance agent to make sure coverage in key areas (workers' comp, general liability, payroll insurance) is keeping pace with your growth.

Clarify ownership issues. Great partnerships can run smoothly for decades. Others sputter after a few weeks. A corporate lawyer's job is to assume the latter and think, *What agreements can we write to keep the business going when the starry-eyed shareholders are no longer on speaking terms?* It doesn't matter how long you've been up and running. If you haven't clarified these important issues, complications may arise as shareholder perspectives grow more divergent. Before it gets nasty, consult an attorney about:

✔ **Liability.** If you're like most business owners, your lender required personal guarantees to secure financing. A contribution agreement among guarantors ensures that the guarantee responsibility pie is divided up in the same proportion as the shareholder ownership. Otherwise, the bank could force the guarantor with the deepest pockets to cough up the entire amount. If only one shareholder guarantees the loan, he may ask for a guarantee fee from the company for assuming all the risk. Paying a fee ensures the guarantor that management will be more deeply invested in producing a positive outcome. The fee will be higher if the company couldn't survive without the guarantor's signature, and smaller if the company has a higher net worth and the guarantor faces less risk.

✔ **Role of equity.** How many classes of stock or membership interests do you have? Do voting rights differ for each? Which is best for you? It's an oversimplification, but let's say one class provides equity and financial rights only and another also has voting privileges. The former may be fine if you're willing to be a passive investor; the latter is better if you want to exert influence on strategic decisions.

✔ **Decision making.** Cofounder Don Gullett and I agreed that I would have majority ownership since the business concept was my idea. An employee stock ownership plan later diluted our fifty-five/forty-five split but I always retained 51 percent of the voting stock. My unequivocal advice here: do not slice up the ownership pie even-Steven. I served on the board of a fifty-fifty company in which the co-owners, after a brief honeymoon, refused to speak to one another. Intermediaries had to shuttle messages between them. Every company needs a clear, buck-stops-here leader. She's someone who strives for consensus but isn't afraid to stamp a veto when the organization's mission, vision, and values are threatened.

✔ **Value of contributions.** Make sure the executive compensation program is in writing, whether for common stock given for sweat equity, or for stock options granted to key employees.

✔ **Shareholder's buy/sell agreement.** This crucial document addresses how the company will be valued, how shareholders must first offer their stock to the company or other shareholders, and what happens upon the death of a shareholder (include life insurance planning in the mix so a buyout in the event of a principal shareholder's death doesn't break the company bank). Each shareholder should have their own attorney eyeballing these issues. Details of the agreement can vary depending on why a shareholder is cashing out. If somebody voluntarily gets off the bus before reaching the destination, buyout price and payment terms may be more draconian than if a shareholder dies or becomes disabled. To protect majority shareholders, include a "drag along" provision that contractually requires all shareholders to participate in a sale at the same price per share (many buyers are interested only in acquiring 100 percent ownership). To protect minority shareholders, include a "tag along" provision that guarantees that all shareholders can participate in a sale at the same price per share should the majority decide it's time to sell.

✔ **Exit strategy.** Make sure your strategic plan addresses how principals can cash in their chips. Under what circumstances can shareholders—including venture capitalists—force the company onto the block to recoup their investment?

✔ **Strategic planning.** Long-range objectives may be undermined if the buy/sell agreement, exit strategy, and other aspects of ownership are not seamlessly coordinated with estate planning and succession planning. Once or twice a year, convene a team meeting that includes your attorney, accountant, estate planner, insurance planner, and other service providers to make sure all angles are covered before important decisions are made. Relying on just one expert's opinion can be lethal; your attorney may have a brilliant legal mind but unless he's also tax savvy his advice may not consider important tax ramifications.

At the end of the day, litigation happens. When it does, show respect for the people on the other side of the courtroom. More often than not, an aggressive yet empathetic approach will save you money and produce a mutually beneficial outcome. A legal battle engaged with revenge on your mind is likely to end with a thud.

FIFTY-NINE

BOARDS

Getting Help, Not Headaches, from Outside Advisors

It was early 2000. The country's runaway stagecoach of an economy was lurching a bit but still rolling along. A packaging company purchased five months earlier by National City Equity Partners, Inc., a Cleveland-based private equity firm, was planning to build a fourth manufacturing plant. Yet, when Carl Baldassarre, new board member (and National City Equity Partners' general partner), looked down the road, he saw potholes opening up. "I didn't know if the wheels were going to fall off," said Carl. "But knowing that the packaging industry closely follows the economy, clearly it was time to pull back the reins."

But how hard? You can't just ride into town on a white horse, grab the longtime sheriff by his vest, and lay down the law. Carl had to persuade the packaging firm's successful CEO to abort his expansion plan without alienating him. (Taming hyenas is easier than "advising" a successful CEO.) The CEO acknowledged it could take two years to build enough volume for the new plant to be viable on its own. He reasoned that the other plants were humming along at full capacity and could offload business to the new facility. On behalf of the board, Carl asked the entrepreneur's team to calculate how various revenue-softening scenarios would impact efficiencies and profits at the existing plants. At the same time, added Carl, lay over the cash output for the new facility's lease, capital equipment, labor, and other one-time expenses.

Snapping the CEO out of his passion and into objective analysis had a sobering effect. He recognized that even a 10 percent drop in top-line revenues, combined with the new facility's start-up costs, would jeopardize the company's liquidity and bank covenants. At that point, abandoning facility construction would alarm customers, employees, and the marketplace. "Asking the CEO's team to run the numbers," said Carl, "moved them out of a defensive posture and helped achieve consensus. In the end, the CEO strongly recommended that we not pursue the expansion. Given the recession that followed soon after, it proved to be a wise choice."

If you're lucky, your board is filled with Carl Baldassarres. His firm manages a billion-dollar investment portfolio with stakes in over sixty companies, three-quarters of which generate $25 million to $150 million in revenue. Carl, who serves on seven boards (I've been fortunate to join him on one), is the perfect blend of caring and fairness. He's tough, but not rough, smart as a whip, and understands the value of relationship-building. Follow these board benchmarks to pull the most value out of your wise men and women.

THE DYNAMICS

Compensate fairly. Board members are making more and more. They're also taking on more and more risk. The 2002 Sarbanes-Oxley Act, the congressional response to two years' worth of high-profile corporate accounting scandals, instituted tough new requirements for public companies. Bottom line? Officers and directors are now held more accountable. The bar has been raised for privately held companies, too. Higher expectations, an increased work load, and a greater threat of litigation have turned board members into cold-eyed realists—*My time is valuable. I'm assuming more risk. Pay me what I'm worth.*

Still interested in tapping their wisdom? First, write a check for directors' and officers' (D&O) liability insurance. (Board candidates may still beg off, citing potential coverage holes.) Second, expect to shell out anywhere from $12,000 to $30,000 annually to each of your directors at small-to-midsized companies. The sky's the limit at larger firms. Third, equity is typically thrown into the mix (in the form of stock options and purchase programs). That's good. Give everybody their own oar and a stake in what's on shore, and they'll row more purposefully regardless of the tide. Caveat: if, as expected, the Financial Accounting Standards Board rules that stock options must be expensed in a company's P&L, fewer stock options may be granted.

Looking for a budget-conscious alternative? In contrast to a statutory "board of directors," there's no legal exposure for members who serve on a "board of advisors." In the former, executive management must implement the board's decisions; the latter is a less formal advisory relationship in which the CEO calls the shots. Private companies tend toward boards of advisors, especially if the CEO has a controlling interest. The advantages: avoiding D&O insurance expenses, less difficulty in finding board members, and the choice to accept or reject the board's advice. A board of directors typically sprouts when a company has multiple investors, none of whom has controlling ownership. It's the best way to maintain checks and balances on management.

Diversify. A board typically has five to nine members. Pick people from both inside and outside your industry who have knowledge and experience outside your wheelhouse. Complementary skill sets—finance, marketing, operations—among members is a plus. A lot of boards reserve a chair for a "gray hair," the retired sage. Certainly, there's a role for wisdom, but the greatest need is for contemporary knowledge. The most valuable directors have been through the wars of growing, building value, and exiting a company. They've already done what you want to do, and on a larger scale. Yet, they're still in touch with day-to-day operations.

Select straight shooters. A board needs members who say what needs to be said. I once challenged a minority-shareholder CEO when he said he deserved more company stock. I felt it sent the wrong message because the firm he founded had consistently fallen 80 percent short of revenue targets. We should either move the CEO to another important position and bring in a seasoned exec, I said, or keep him as CEO and grant performance-based stock options. That would be more in line with shareholders' interests, and ultimately with the CEO's as well. After an awkward silence, the matter was deferred. A few days later, the CEO offered a buyout of my stock and an invitation to leave the board. I accepted both. Leaders who hire yes-men and yes-women are boring holes in their own boat. Good board members advise on the forest that management sometimes can't see for the proverbial trees.

Structure strictly. Boards of privately held companies need to spell out how they do their work, lest conflicts of interest creep in. Then everybody should stay out of each other's way. An audit committee composed of outside board members should review financial statements and deal directly with the company's outside accountants. Executive compensation is determined by a committee composed of at least two outside board members—and the CEO if he or she is majority shareholder. Each committee elects a chair, who reports to the board of directors—not the CEO. Make sure each committee's protocol and responsibilities are clearly defined.

Disclose rules. In the interest of transparency, good boards post their principles on corporate websites (standards vary for publicly held and private companies). They may include how a board relates to management, how stakeholders access the board, and why the board does or does not separate the roles of chairman and CEO.

Process, process, process. Translate the board's principles into simple processes. They should dictate how to implement strategy, how to evaluate the executive officers, and how the board will keep up with the company's performance. Best-practice boards evaluate not only their own performance but also those of their committees and individual directors.

Get the soft stuff right. It used to be that board members were concerned only with strategic planning, financial health, and picking executive officers. That is so twentieth century. Boards now decide standards of ethics and help weave them into the cultural fabric. That requires aligning everyone's values—the board's, individual board members', and the organization's.

Manage the board. Like every collection of people, a board has its own agendas, egos, frailties, and conflicts. Be mindful of a board's needs and personalities. A good CEO works his board—which has nothing to do with manipulation. Build the board into your consciousness. Between meetings, do quick one-on-ones over coffee. Share information—e-brief members regularly to keep them current. Solicit input, not for consent or assent, but to stay connected and keep everyone in sync.

THE MEETING

Start spreadin' the news. Distribute the "board book" (agenda, financials, meeting minutes, updates on issues and external relationships) digitally or via hard copy three to five days before the big board meeting. Do it any earlier, and the info goes stale. Any later, and members lose precious processing time. Everyone should be up to speed by the opening bell.

Balance the tell/ask ratio. These meetings have two halves—management (typically the CEO, CFO, and v.p. of operations) presents information about various agenda items, then the board members earn their fee by providing feedback and counsel. I've watched too many executives spend more than two-thirds of the meeting presenting and less than a third soliciting feedback. Reverse that ratio. Some CEOs erroneously consider it a sign of weakness to ask for help; they view board meetings primarily as stages on which to trumpet their team's feats.

Good boards walk a tightrope between coaching and challenging. A board straddles two constituencies—shareholders (which it represents) and management (which represents the interests of the workers.) A good board advises your management team on strategic plans while simultaneously grilling your execs to make sure the strategies are credible, in everyone's best interests, and well executed.

Boards don't run companies, management does. Seasoned management needs space. That's why good board members generally don't overstep. They ask questions until the truth reveals itself. The gloves come off only if company execs are dishonest or in deep denial—a direct challenge is then in everyone's best interests. Board members can look over the CEO's shoulder by asking simple questions like, *Is the company meeting its goals and performing well compared to industry benchmarks?* If yes, the board should stick to strategy. A "no" is a green light to venture into operations.

Lead with the numbers. Companies on the move like to crow about the numbers early and often. In down times, the financials magically slide to the bottom of the agenda. Imagine which meeting is interminable. Avoid frustration—now and at future meetings—by getting to the financials early. It keeps the clock on your side, adds clarity and realism to the agenda, and presents tough, hidden issues when everyone is fresh.

Maintain an "action item" list. After digesting the financials, review the status of actionable, management-level items generated at the last meeting—what was to be done, by whom, and by when? Update the list as the meeting progresses. Absent this discipline, key initiatives can slip through the cracks of faulty memory and benign neglect.

Keep it short. The longest a meeting should run is four hours. Any longer, and it's not a board meeting so much as an unfocused-company-in-trouble meeting. Marathon meetings can devolve into dysfunction, with advisors—even when they're sated with a pricy dinner—becoming restless. Do not waste the board's time. Keep things moving with good preparation and agenda restrictions that limit the number of critical issues. Appoint a watchdog who (judiciously) brings issues to a head.

Make yourself scarce. Give directors management-free discussion time before or after regular meetings. This new practice is good corporate governance. If the CEO is the board's chair, the board appoints a "lead director" to conduct the session instead.

X.
BONUS SECTION: WEATHERING WORST CASE SCENARIOS

STRICTLY BUSINESS
- CALLING THE LOAN
- THE COMPETITION ATTACKS

EXIT STRATEGIES
- BOLTING KEY EMPLOYEE
- FORCED DOWNSIZING
- BOLTING MAJOR CLIENT

ENLIGHTENED EXECUTIVE

SUCKER PUNCHES
- NATURAL DISASTER
- PERSONAL CRISIS
- PUBLIC RELATIONS CRISIS

PART I

PANIC BUTTONS

When Bad Things Happen to Good Companies

FDR was wrong. Business leaders have plenty to fear but fear itself. At any moment, the unexpected can splinter your operations, rupture your strategic plans, and jeopardize your survival. I've spent many anxious days and sleepless nights worrying about nightmare scenarios. After fumbling a few pressure-packed incidents, I developed a crisis drill:

Ease physical tension. Jerked into panic mode, your muscles tighten and breathing grows shallow and fast. Take slow, deep breaths for a few minutes. Continue to breathe deeply while massaging your neck and shoulders.

Get a grip. "Worst case" is a relative term. No matter how stressful and expensive a business challenge is, it's not in the same league as a death in the family. Pull yourself into positive territory by looking for hidden opportunities and appreciating what you've got—family and friends, dedicated employees, a great product, loyal customers. Keep reminding yourself of what's truly important in life, especially when your mind races and queasiness bubbles in the pit of your stomach.

Create and execute action steps. Pick yourself up, dust yourself off, and start writing a bulleted survival strategy. Paralyzing anxiety dissipates the more you organize your thoughts and begin mapping your way out of the rubble. Then, start working the plan—every step moves you closer to regaining control. Here's a spur-of-the-moment action plan I wrote when a key employee resigned:

- ✔ Place an ad in the paper.
- ✔ Network with professional contacts.
- ✔ Consult list of potential candidates.
- ✔ Consider promoting Cathy and compressing her development schedule.

Worst case scenarios drop from the sky, sometimes right into your lap. Take the April day I opened a letter from my executive committee. "Dear Tom," it began, "we want to inform you that we, your entire management team, are resigning to form a competitive tire company. Hopefully, we'll be friendly competitors. Thanks for everything and we wish you well." It was signed by everyone who reported to me. For a moment I panicked—a mass exodus was my greatest fear—until I spotted the postscript at the bottom: "p.s., April Fool's!" I looked up to catch everyone marching into my office and enjoying a big laugh.

Worst case scenarios don't have to end up with worst case results. Handled correctly, they can turn out to be blessings in disguise. When your feet are to the fire and you come out on top, you're stronger and more confident for the experience. One thing's for sure—you find out what you're made of. You also deepen your business knowledge, which makes you a better leader in the long run. So follow the advice of Winston Churchill: "If you're going through hell, keep going." The stories that follow can get you headed in the right direction—turning worst case scenarios into catalysts for growth.

SIXTY
EXIT STRATEGIES

EXIT STRATEGIES SCENARIO #1:
BOLTING KEY EMPLOYEE

Option #1: Let 'Em Go

It was an ordinary afternoon—until my CFO and HR chief interrupted a meeting in my office. "We have to talk ASAP," one said solemnly. My heart sank. I motioned them in and instinctively asked the dreaded two words: "Who's leaving?" Our head of IT (Information Technology) had resigned after a non-competitor lassoed him with an above-market offer. I convened an emergency session of our core executive team to consider our options. We brainstormed awhile but decided to sleep on it. It was a long night. A disruption in any of the mission-critical initiatives IT was spearheading could prove costly. I practiced some deep breathing, focused on all the things that were going right, and began mapping out an action plan. By morning, I had regained perspective. My philosophy was, *We don't lose anyone we don't want to lose.* But we decided to make an exception, concluding that matching the offer would throw our salary structure out of whack. We named an interim head from within the department and, six weeks later, found a knock-your-socks-off replacement.

Option #2: Try to Keep 'Em

I was never resigned to losing a valuable employee. As long as she hadn't turned in her ID badge I figured I had a shot at keeping her. First, I shifted my mindset from *How will this person's absence make things more difficult for me?* to *What's best for this person?* I'd sit down with her and say, "I have mixed emotions, Jane. On one hand, I hate to see you go. On the other, if you think this is an opportunity you can't pass up, then good for you. You deserve the best. I'm not going to try to talk you out of it. I just wanted to thank you for your contributions. And, if you're open to it, we could brainstorm a bit to make sure you're making the right decision."

If she agreed, I'd sketch out a Ben Franklin balance sheet by drawing a line down the center of a whiteboard. In the left column, I'd list the pluses of the new company. In the right column, I'd list the pluses of staying with us. As the list grew, I duly recognized the positives of the new job. But I also objectively, with her best interests in mind, pointed out the drawbacks. For instance: "You'll have to work fifty-five hours a week? We can arrange for you to max out at forty-seven. A thousand dollars is all that separates us? You're scheduled for a raise of at least twice that at your next review." Depending on circumstances, I'd occasionally use a more sophisticated decision-making model called the "Weight & Rate" (opposite page). Its beauty is that it considers both the relative value of each decision point and the likelihood that either job will deliver it.

These exercises shed light, yet logic only takes a person so far. After reviewing the pros and cons and adding up the numbers, the wild card is the employee's gut feeling—and if your caring attitude hasn't turned the tide, all you can do is respect where she's coming from. My impromptu brainstorming sessions worked about half the time. The other half, I usually ended up agreeing that, yes, our analysis showed she was better off accepting the new position.

Burned Bridges

All bets are off if the departing employee poaches a key client on his way out. This threat causes more heartburn than a triple-decker meatball sandwich. It's particularly acidic for leaders of financial service companies, sales-driven outfits, law firms, and

WEIGHT & RATE DECISION-MAKING MODEL

In four steps, you can help an employee achieve clarity about her choices.
In this example, one job promises an unbeatable schedule while the
other offers a much higher salary.

1 Write in the leftmost column the factors influencing the employee's decision. The list can be as long as she likes.

2 Ask her to weigh each factor's importance (column A in the example) by assigning it a number from one to ten, with ten being the most important. The same number can be used more than once. In the example shown, a chance for further education and a supportive corporate culture are both rated a six.

3 Now, ask her to take her best guess at rating the likelihood that each job will offer what she wants (column B in the example). Again, use one through ten, with ten being the most likely.

4 Multiply column A by column B to get a subtotal for each factor, then add up the subtotals for your final result.

THINGS I WANT FROM A JOB	JOB OPTION 1			JOB OPTION 2		
	A Importance of this factor to me	**B** Likelihood this job will give this	SUBTOTAL	**A** Importance of this factor to me	**B** Likelihood this job will give this	SUBTOTAL
Flexible working hours	10	x 10	= 100	10	x 5	= 50
Sufficient money	9	x 4	= 36	9	x 10	= 90
Good benefits package	8	x 6	= 48	8	x 7	= 56
Chance to further my education	6	x 8	= 48	6	x 5	= 30
Supportive corporate culture	6	x 9	= 54	6	x 3	= 18
	TOTAL POINTS = **286**			TOTAL POINTS = **244**		

other organizations where clients value account-manager relationships over the business itself. The best strategy is to wake up before this nightmare begins. Odds are low that employees will skip out with clients (or colleagues) if you've won them over with a healthy culture that makes them feel trusted and valued.

Start knitting a safety net anyway. Make sure top execs—including you—and support staff go out of their way to build relationships with big clients. Any good CYA (cover your, um, behind) plan includes signing linchpin people to fair non-compete agreements. That said, do what you can to resolve the matter without lawyers. Try a little soft reasoning with departing staffers: "I know you need to do what you need to do. But how do you feel about having a mediator determine who's right here?" If you're turned down, your attorney counsels action, and the bolting employee endangers your team, tell him you have no choice but to take him to court. (That also sends a message to the rest of the company that your contracts have teeth.) Then focus on replacing both him and the lost sales.

Additional proactive strategy: Succession planning (chapter 44).

EXIT STRATEGIES SCENARIO #2: FORCED DOWNSIZING

Layoffs are as reliable as seasons. When we sold the company, 6 percent of our workforce lost their jobs. We did everything we could to soften the blow. We tried to find them jobs elsewhere in the company (most had turned down positions at the new Florida headquarters). We offered generous severance packages (many also had stock options). We also provided career counseling and sponsored job fairs.

Most importantly, we pulled teammates together for a few meetings so they could ask questions and vent frustrations. Some comments were blistering. They wanted me to explain what happened, and apologize for disrupting their lives. They weren't happy, but they seemed to find some measure of satisfaction in expressing their grievances and hearing honest, respectful responses. Downsizing in a seat-of-the-pants environment usually leads to lower productivity and morale among survivors. Start building an enlightened organization now. Otherwise, you may as well go ahead and hang that famous sign: *Beatings will continue until morale improves*.

Proactive strategy: Grow a healthy culture (chapters 10–14).

EXIT STRATEGIES SCENARIO #3: BOLTING MAJOR CLIENT

The phone call couldn't have come at a worse time for Alexis Bloomstrand. The sole owner of New Morning Windows, she had just had surgery to fuse four vertebrae, and faced months of recuperation. She was also in the midst of building a new house on the heels of divorce. And she was negotiating with her ex to buy the Minneapolis building that housed the business they had launched twenty-two years earlier. On top of all that, it was just a month after the 9/11 terror attacks. She had an inkling bad business news was brewing. Two weeks before going under the knife, she asked her flagship client, one of North America's largest window manufacturers, whether the rumors were true about its impending purchase of her competitor, a Canadian custom-window manufacturer nearly three times New Morning's size. No deal was in the works, her client assured her.

Four days after her surgery, the phone rang. The client had indeed purchased Alexis' competitor and was giving sixty days' notice that its strategic alliance with New Morning would be terminated. Overnight, revenues plunged from $8 million to under $3 million. Alexis managed to keep all seventy-five employees on through the winter holidays but eventually cut the staff to thirty. The new year brought more bad news. A major lender acquired Alexis' bank and issued her a default notice. A few months later, referred by both her attorney and a trusted consultant, she looked to the Platinum Group, a Twin Cities-based turnaround firm. "I couldn't have gotten financing without them," said Alexis. Platinum tutored her in cash-flow models, inventory management, new production efficiencies, and cost-cutting strategies. Eighteen months later, New Morning's revenues rebounded, and then some. "In three years of hell," said Alexis, "I learned more about running a business than I had in the last twenty."

Losing your biggest client is traumatic. When revenues nose-dive, these proactive strategies can help soften the landing.

Build a stable of advisers. Panicked business leaders don't make good decisions. When one of New Morning's suppliers later hit a rough patch, Alexis suggested he pony up for expert advice like she had. It was an expense he said he couldn't afford. "I told him he couldn't afford not to," said Alexis. "Our legal and consulting fees were $200,000 one year. That makes me sick. But if we hadn't spent it, we wouldn't be here today."

Upgrade financial fluency. Working with consultants helped Alexis learn the nuts and bolts of cash flow and cash management. "I knew the basics," she said. "But they showed me the importance of mastering the financial end." She now knows how to build a financial planning model to prove the company's long-term viability and attract new financing.

Raise the performance bar. Forced to scour her labor costs, Alexis didn't like what she saw. Some veteran employees were coasting on inflated salaries built by automatic annual raises. She tackled productivity issues head-on by implementing education and training programs. She upped the ante on task-heavy job descriptions by spelling out challenging, but reachable, goals. Most importantly, she tied a large portion of salary to performance. For icing, she pledged to the staff an equal distribution of 15 percent of after-tax profits. Today, after three rounds of layoffs in three years—and with thirty-nine employees instead of seventy-five—morale has never been higher.

Contain costs—at any cost. Getting lean and mean is an ongoing discipline. It's what the big boys do best. Check out the cost-containment strategies in chapters 53 and 57.

Expand your customer base. Alexis recruited new sales reps to pursue new markets, an important part of her strategic plan. But don't overlook existing markets when you need to replace lost sales. When a wholesale customer dropped us, for instance, we called his strongest competitor and delivered a message that was hard to refuse. We could increase sales, we told him, because we understand the local market and carried brands with established name recognition—built courtesy of his competitor.

Think big. The more your business is fueled by synergy, the quicker the pieces will click into place. Alexis stepped up training and mentoring for employees at every level. She cleared communication channels and established a bonus plan to invigorate the culture and drive innovation. She streamlined operations and reorganized workflow to do more with less. Bottom line: think macro, act micro.

Have a plan in place to change the client's mind. I'd pull out all the stops to win a customer back. I'd appeal to decision makers to—please, please—in recognition of our longstanding relationship, at least sit down and talk things through. (In a case like Alexis', obviously, that isn't an option.) Together, we'd explore what our rival offered versus what we had. If we were outgunned, I'd be the first to admit it. More often than not, a few tweaks here and a few concessions there were enough to save the relationship.

Additional proactive strategy: Customer service (chapter 56).

SIXTY-ONE
SUCKER PUNCHES

SUCKER PUNCHES SCENARIO #1:
NATURAL DISASTER

When a 1981 tornado took out his biggest cash cow—the most profitable of his nine Sound of Music stores—Dick Schulze focused on possibilities, not pain. The storeroom, remarkably, was spared. So Dick held a Tornado Sale in the parking lot. Lured by steeply discounted stereo gear, thousands of Minnesotans swarmed the place. Police had to shut down traffic, so great was the frenzy stirred by the overnight best buy in town. Realizing he had stumbled onto something, Dick phoned his other eight stores: *Bring over more hi-fi components and car stereos!* Within two years, he had completely transitioned from average prices/average volume to deep discounts/high volume. It worked. Oh, he also slapped on a new name—Best Buy.

Message: when disaster strikes, force yourself to ask quality questions. Don't moan, "Why me?" Instead, think, *What can I do right now that will make things better?* or *How can I turn this setback into an advantage?* Asking positive questions shifts your mind into creative gear. Suddenly, you see ways to capitalize on whatever Mother Nature (or market forces) throws at you. During 1997's Flood of the Century in Grand Forks, North Dakota, our employees asked themselves, *How can I help?* Flooding had begun seventy-five miles south in the Fargo-Moorhead area. Regional manager Mark Lessin rounded up his Tires Plus teammates and hit the streets.

"The house of one of our Moorhead mechanics was about to get swallowed up," said Mark. "So we camped out in his driveway for four days and filled sandbags."

By the time the Red River's surge reached Grand Forks, it had risen out of control, threatening dikes and levees. More than fifteen Tires Plus employees—and their families—from Fargo, Moorhead, and Grand Forks reported for duty. They worked a shift at the store, then rushed to the dike to fill sandbags for another six hours. "It was a lot of long days and late nights, but we saved several communities," said Mark. We also stationed water trucks at our stores to supply residents with fresh drinking water. The overtime pay—everyone was on the clock throughout the ordeal—took a bite out of monthly profits. But our roots in the communities grew deeper, our bonds with employees grew stronger, and sales quickly trended upward. In the long run, we came out ahead. Bottom line: we did the right thing.

Proactive strategy: Pray a lot.

SUCKER PUNCHES SCENARIO #2: PERSONAL CRISIS

It was an ordinary Monday night for Larry Dennison—except for the killer headache. Everyone else in his Farmers Insurance Group office had gone home, so Larry dialed 911. The one-time district manager of the year was lucky. Most aneurism victims don't make it to the phone. One month in an intensive care unit and two surgeries later, Larry was left with unintelligible speech and double vision, and confined to a wheelchair. A doctor told Larry's wife, Gay, that her husband was months away from rehab. A nursing home, the doc said, was the best option. She shot back four words: "Over my dead body." Gay saw to it that Larry stayed put.

Larry filled the Farmers' leadership void by handing over temporary control to his daughter, Hayley, the agency's head of recruiting and training. Like an air-traffic controller guiding in an accidental pilot, Larry advised his daughter from his hospital bed (Hayley was one of the few who could decipher Larry's speech). Hayley wasn't about to let her dad down; she worked around the clock to meet the district's goals. Farmers was so impressed they featured Hayley in a company video.

Larry beat the odds. In October 2001, nine months after his aneurism, he returned to work. His balance, speech, and vision were still severely impaired. His patient staff helped him operate his keyboard, and they weren't shy about asking Larry to repeat himself. He used a walker to navigate corridors. Month by month, Larry grew stronger. Today, I can understand almost everything my friend says. His handshake is firm and he walks without a cane. And once again his district is one of the country's top producers. He even went on to win two more President's Council awards. Larry's recipe for recovery? He surrounded himself with good people. He expected the best and prepared for the worst. He picked himself up every time he fell. And he never lost his sense of humor.

I faced my own personal challenge when, at age forty-two, a triple trauma of divorce, cancer, and cash-flow crises left me in no condition to run a company. I needed a few months to recover. But before I dropped out of circulation, I had to take care of business. I shelved the want-to's, divvied up the have-to's, and communicated, communicated, communicated. I drafted a letter to employees that offered some explanation. I asked for their patience and thanked them for keeping us afloat during my leave. Then, one by one, I told my key people exactly what I needed. Finally, I briefed our bank and vendors that I was temporarily releasing the reins. Over the next six months, I communicated sporadically with the office. If I did drag myself into work, I just lay on the couch in my office. After three months of vegging out and another three months of healing strategies—therapy, yoga, meditation, nutrition, self-help books, retreats—I returned to work rejuvenated.

Fortunately, Mark Sathe's 2000 odyssey also had a happy ending. Given the sentence of a year to live following a malignant melanoma diagnosis, Mark, fifty-two, turned over control of his

Minneapolis headhunter firm to a young exec. He crafted a stock plan that gave each of his six employees 1 percent of the company, plus incentives for more. Mark's plan, which included diet and lifestyle changes, worked. No one jumped ship, revenues held, he never stopped working—and he's now cancer-free.

Not everyone gets advance notice from the grim reaper. That explains the growth of "key-man insurance"—a life insurance policy that names the company as beneficiary. The payout helps it survive the blow of losing the person who made it work. These stories also underscore the importance of periodically consulting experienced tax and estate planning attorneys.

Proactive strategies: Minimize potential health crises (chapter 51). Succession planning (Chapter 44). Estate planning (chapter 58).

Sucker Punches Scenario #3: Public Relations Crisis

A salmonella outbreak had sickened tens of thousands of Minnesotans. The culprit? Schwan's ice cream, state officials told the manufacturer's senior management during a conference call. Before hanging up, Alfred Schwan ordered his people to stop making and selling the company's flagship product. He cut his business trip short and caught the first flight home. The next morning, the media descended on Schwan's rural headquarters. Alfred was ready. When a reporter asked what he was going to tell customers, Alfred's reply revealed the depth of his character: "Don't eat Schwan's ice cream." The outbreak, he said, was unacceptable. He apologized to his customers and announced a recall of every last scoop. A week later, authorities nabbed the perpetrator. The salmonella was traced to a subcontracted trucking company that had carried Schwan's ice cream ingredients in the same tankers it used to transport raw eggs.

It was a flashback to the 1982 Tylenol scare twelve years before. Once again, aggressive crisis management prevented a sterling brand from being tarnished. Schwan's actually walked away with its reputation enhanced. "With the trust Schwan's had built through the years," recalled former Schwan's president Ken Noyes, "our customers forgave us a lot quicker than we forgave ourselves." He wasn't exaggerating. Some customers even refused to hand over half-empty cartons of ice cream when Schwan's trademark home-delivery trucks rolled up. "We said we had to ask for their ice cream as a precautionary measure and promised to give them free replacements when we got things resolved," said Ken. "They said, 'No, I like my Schwan's ice cream. I'm not giving it up.'"

Schwan's handling of its salmonella crisis should be on page one of every public relations textbook. Every p.r. predicament, of course, has its own challenges. Perhaps you're closing a plant and offshoring production. Or, maybe one of your executives was arrested under embarrassing circumstances. When the media show up and thrust a microphone in your face, the experience will be less damaging if:

You're prepared. Start now by identifying who would serve as front-line contacts should "the worst" happen. Crises rarely strike during working hours, so ensure that everyone has a contact list. Agree upfront on the values and commitments that will drive the message of any crisis response—responsibility to the community trumps profit concerns, for instance. Planning beyond that may not be helpful. Most execs overestimate the value of a "crisis plan." They commission their team to spend all kinds of time putting together a three-ring binder that gathers dust and can't possibly foresee the situation that actually unfolds. When an incident does occur, its unique nature will shape the response. That said, your team should always include an attorney, and a p.r. professional who can school your spokespeople in media relations. Also, identify your "publics" (employees, employees' emergency contacts, customers, investors, suppliers, bankers, retirees, neighbors) and know how to reach them. Quickly. News that used to take days to travel now ricochets through cyberspace in nanoseconds.

You've got the facts. Gather every shred of information from as many sources as possible. Then determine how much to release.

You apologize. No. 1, be contrite. No. 2, be contrite. No. 3, be contrite. This is more difficult than it might appear. Look at the rogues' gallery of disgraced politicians, sports stars, and domestic divas who made matters worse by getting their back up. There's no better lifeline for a spiraling reputation than genuinely expressing regret, taking responsibility where you should, and patiently explaining what steps are being taken to ensure the incident won't happen again.

You're sincere. Step out of your insular universe and imagine what the situation looks like to the public. Empathize with their concerns. You'll come off as a stooge if you or your people simply parrot a duplicitous party line.

You're honest. Never, under any circumstances, lie. Lying to the public will irreparably damage your corporate image, to say nothing of your personal credibility. It takes only one hit to knock off the crown of a good name. If you don't know an answer, say that you don't know, and that you'll get that information if possible. If a question is best left unanswered, pledge to address it when the full picture comes into focus.

Proactive strategies: Uphold the highest ethical standards (chapters 17–18). Peak personal performance expands your capacity to lead during a crisis (chapters 45–52).

SIXTY-TWO
STRICTLY BUSINESS

STRICTLY BUSINESS SCENARIO #1:
CALLING THE LOAN

I had the seven-year itch. After six years in business, it was time to expand our retail operation. Research had convinced me the future of the tire business was in retailing. Before long, wholesalers like me would be strangled by squeezed margins. So, I went for broke. In one year we doubled our store count, from three to six, and poured money into marketing, equipment, and personnel. The rub? That little matter of being woefully underfunded. Because our marginally profitable wholesale division couldn't support us, we were quickly up to our windshields in retail red ink.

One day over lunch, my banker and friend Jeff Mack dropped the hammer. "I'm sorry, Tom," he said. "Our auditors reviewed your financial statements, and they're telling me we should call your loan. You had a successful wholesale business and you blew it by expanding into retail." If I couldn't pay off the note, he added, the bank was prepared to collect its collateral—our company. Panic Time.

Clearing my heart from my throat, I said, "Jeff, hold on a minute. Let me show you what we're doing." I pulled out our projections and explained how profitable the new stores would be once they matured. I showed him our new business plan. "Please," I said, "give us two months and I promise you'll see a turnaround." Jeff took our plans back to the bank, met with the audit committee, and called the next day. "Okay," he said. "You've got sixty days.

That's it." Flush with adrenaline, I challenged my team to execute our plan and do whatever it took (while still observing the law!) to maximize profits for two months. It worked. We got back in the black just in time to hold off the liquidators.

Consider bank skirmishes the cost of doing business. Eight years later, in 1991, I was fighting off yet another bank. Our local lender had been acquired by a faceless national bank. Soon after, one of the mega-bank's low-level henchmen called to inform us our business model didn't mesh with the bank's philosophy. "We're giving you sixty days' notice that your line of credit is being eliminated," he said. We had two months to come up with $2 million. Panic Time, the sequel. We approached every bank in town, including Riverside Bank in Minneapolis, the reputed last stop for desperate entrepreneurs. If I had to pick a low point in my professional career, being turned down by Dave Cleveland, Riverside's president, would be it. Word was if Dave wouldn't loan you money, nobody would. It was true—he didn't, and they didn't.

Once again, we scrambled to free up every dollar that wasn't nailed down. We met with suppliers and reminded them of their vested interest in our success. We told them if they wanted our business they had to help us out by taking temporary promissory notes instead of payment on inventory. Two suppliers agreed. Boom—there's $1 million. We cobbled together another million by extending other payables, reducing inventory, and offering discounts to wholesale clients for paying us ahead of schedule. By day sixty, the bank had its money. And we had a new bank. (To my sweet satisfaction, Dave Cleveland was in the audience four years later when *Inc.* magazine awarded me the 1995 Midwest Entrepreneur of the Year Award. He told me turning us down was the biggest error of his career.)

Six months after that '91 bank crisis, I was in the Cayman Islands with my sons. As we were getting ready for dinner, the phone rang. It was John Berg, our new CPA at Coopers & Lybrand (now PricewaterhouseCoopers). He was finishing his first audit of

Tires Plus and had serious concerns. We had turned a profit but our rapid growth had backed us into a highly leveraged corner. We were pouring money into new stores faster than we were draining it from existing ones. John said approving our audited statement would, under auditing standards, be stating that we would be able to continue as a financially viable entity. He was having difficulty drawing that conclusion.

For the next hour I tried to persuade John to sign that statement. I patiently explained our strategic supplier relationships and budget projections. "John," I said, "you know the stores that have been open awhile are doing well and that the new stores will mature. We have a solid history." Then I locked in on two important points: our track record of conservative accounting practices and our heavy—and wise—investments in systems and people. Finally, he saw the light and signed off. A bit wobbly, I hung up and collapsed backward on the bed. I asked my boys to give me a minute. Then I put on a fresh shirt and we went to dinner.

When faced with a cash crunch:

Lower labor costs. Where appropriate, hire part-timers or try outsourcing. For sales, offer new hires straight commission or, if necessary, a modest draw. A differentiating product or service and sizable market will attract the right salespeople.

Get concessions from suppliers. Share your strategic plan and growth projections. Smart suppliers will see where you're going and how long it'll take. They'll get darned excited—and loosey-goosey with terms—if you can convince them your business will triple in five years.

Ask suppliers for promissory notes. You sign a note for, say, $1 million. The supplier credits your account for that amount and "sells" you $1 million in inventory. If you hit your numbers and continue to grow, you never accrue interest. The note's just deferred year after year, like a self-renewing, interest-free loan. As long as everything follows plan, the extra inventory finances the growth necessary to generate the income to pay off the note. This strategy can save your bacon. But use it cautiously. It comes with two downsides: One, it uses up a chit—there's a limit to a supplier's goodwill. Two, you may be facing an uphill struggle in future negotiations. In other words, if the supplier's unhappy, they can "call the loan."

Speed up receivables. Do the math. If your credit line is maxed out, offer customers a 1-percent-per-month "anticipation discount" for paying cash immediately instead of waiting thirty days. In effect, you're borrowing at 12 percent annually (sky-high, but remember, we're in the crisis section) while benefiting in three ways. One, you avert a cash-flow crisis. Two, you fund growth without giving up equity (venture capitalists expect returns a lot better than 12 percent). And three, your invoice shoots to the top of your customers' "pay list," which shrinks your bad-debt ratio.

Extend payables. Ask suppliers if you can pay in sixty days instead of thirty. Then pay on the very last day. It's interest-free money. The bigger you get, the more likely you'll get favorable terms.

Manage inventory. Thanks to technology, inventory management has never been easier. Good news, because just-in-time inventory is a competitive necessity. Turning stock every thirty days instead of every sixty days frees up boatloads of cash. Better still, with thirty-day turns and thirty-day terms, your cost of inventory is $0. Sixty-day terms are even better—collect in thirty, pay in sixty, and you get the use of your supplier's money for thirty days.

Proactive strategies: Supply management (chapter 53). Finance and accounting (chapter 57).

STRICTLY BUSINESS SCENARIO #2: THE COMPETITION ATTACKS

The day that an arm of one of the country's largest companies announced its intent to crush us was like my own professional Pearl Harbor. They had boasted in a video at a national media fest that they were going to enter certain new markets and turn regional competitors like Tires Plus into roadkill. (Our Twin Cities base was their No. 1 target market.) Overnight, we shifted into warrior mode to defend the interests of our employees, customers, suppliers, and shareholders. Like a football coach who posts an opponent's insults in the locker room, we used their braggadocio to whip our people into a competitive frenzy.

We had eighteen months to plan our counterassault. First, we chartered a plane for our top managers to scout the competition's closest market. The battle plan: neutralize their every strength, exploit their every weakness. (It wasn't quite *The Dirty Dozen*, but we *were* on a mission.) At some of their stores, we posed as customers. At others, we made like fawning tire dealers from far-away markets dying for a tour of their finely tuned machine. We snapped rolls of photos and took pages of notes. Once home, we benchmarked their prices from dozens of newspaper ads and conducted thorough price surveys. In no time at all we had reams of data.

Next, our top people hopped a bus for a fourteen-hour tour of the five areas in our market our opponent was targeting. We wanted to see, through our customers' eyes, how we stacked up. With diverse backgrounds and representation from every department, we recorded what each store felt like and what was needed to stave off the big boys.

Finally, we brainstormed around the clock. Within weeks, we had a fifteen-page action plan. A full six months before the invasion, we were on war footing. We remodeled stores at each front, staffed them with our best people, lowered prices, and bumped up stocking levels. On the wholesale side, we blitzed commercial and fleet accounts in a five-mile radius of each threatened store. We even launched a mini-preemptive strike, snatching a prime location our competitor was bidding on.

It was a healthy, spirited competition. We had great respect for the other side, even as we ferociously prepared for combat. But all the (above-board) traps we had set turned our adversary's gung-ho into a frustrated oh-no. They tried to build mega-stores right next to our locations, so close to the road they would've obscured our signs and buildings—a direct violation of the zoning laws we had scrupulously obeyed. They hired the best real estate attorneys. They retained former city officials who knew how to circumvent ordinances. When our competitor won preliminary approval in one city, I directed our attorney to mount a legal challenge. I also lobbied at city council meetings. We didn't ease up until we had secured a level playing field.

For months after opening, they slashed many prices to well below cost. We matched 'em dollar for dollar—one tire free-fell from twenty dollars down to five bucks. I remember one teammate asking, "How can we keep doing this? It's brutal." "Hey," I told him, "we've worked our tails off for too long to let somebody waltz in and steal our market." We vowed not to rest until they hoisted the white flag. Less than three years later, they shuttered their stores and got out of Dodge.

Other competitors were smarter. They did their due diligence, saw we weren't vulnerable, and backed off. Home Depot, for one, tested tire retailing in our region. We girded for battle, they took notice. Six months later, they quietly abandoned the idea. Another time, a friend—the CEO of a national tire giant—asked for a store tour. He and his attorney flew in on his Lear jet. The first thing he asked was how big he should make the check. I said we weren't for sale. Before the tour, my friend excused himself during lunch. In his absence, his attorney leaned in and said, "You might want to change your mind about selling because we're coming in anyway." I just smiled. Later, after touring our stores and taking in our locations and friendly personnel, I drove them back to the airfield. As my friend showed me his jet, he said, "You should be very proud of what you've built, Tom. We won't be coming in here anytime soon."

Additional proactive strategies: Strategic planning (chapter 20). Marketing (chapter 54). Continuous process improvement (chapter 19). Action plans (chapter 48).

SUMMARY

PERPETUAL PROGRESS

The Synergy Circle System

The Synergy Circle illustrates how a unique blend of organizational ingredients produces peak profitability. Start with a meaningful mission that guides savvy people in a caring, accountable culture, one supported by efficient processes and clear communication. Add just the right mix of inspiration and incentives, educational enrichment, and encouragement to grow through self-mastery strategies. Top it off with success secrets from seven key departments, and you've got a complete, no-nonsense business management guide.

Throughout sixty-two chapters, we established that sustainable success starts with a management system that draws together every corner of the company. Neglect even one area and you can wind up courting disaster. A business can run only as efficiently as its least efficient component. My Synergy Circle system is practical for organizations of any size and at any stage of development. Fuel your rocket ride to the top by combining hard-nosed accountability and efficiency (profits first) with a warm-hearted, enlightened approach (people first).

I wish I'd had a reference guide like this on my desk. (The years of anguish I would've avoided!) No matter the challenge that presents itself, you'll find guidance by thumbing through the table of contents. Morale is plunging? Start with the culture section, then turn to the motivation chapters. An employee is fumbling a project? Flip to chapter 31 for tips on clarifying and tracking assignments; then scan chapter 21 for a refresher on execution protocol. Whether it's muddled meetings (chapter 22), closing more sales (chapter 55), retaining your customer base (chapter 56), or attracting more customers (chapter 54), the fix is here. You'll also find real-world tips for turning worst case scenarios into catalysts for growth. Each chapter flows into the next until everything circles back to give you 360-degree understanding.

The speed of business is forever accelerating. It's the enlightened executive who rides efficient protocols, people skills, and the latest technological advantages into the lead. These pages contain the knowledge and wisdom that can help you shed your seat-of-the-pants ways and navigate the swerving path to enlightened leadership. May your journey be a fruitful one.

ABOUT THE AUTHOR

Tom Gegax served as chairman and CEO (head coach) of Tires Plus Stores for twenty-four years. By the time Tom sold the company to Bridgestone/Firestone in July 2000, it had mushroomed from a concept sketched on a restaurant napkin to a market leader with 150 upscale stores in ten states and $200 million in revenue. The company was so well managed and profitable that Tom was able to bypass outside investors and retain ownership control.

Tom was a pioneer of the tough-minded, warm-hearted coaching style of management. Tires Plus' healthy corporate culture was legendary for its focus on the well-being of its employees and customers (or, as Tom preferred to call them, teammates and guests). The unique pairing of hard-nosed efficiency and a caring environment was a core ingredient in the company's secret sauce. Tom's comprehensive, no-nonsense management system catapulted Tires Plus to the top in a competitive industry populated by some of the largest companies in the world.

Tom's groundbreaking management methods have been featured in the *New York Times* and *Fast Company* magazine, and on CNN, CNBC, and PBS. He was named a 1995 Midwest Entrepreneur of the Year by *Inc.* magazine and Ernst & Young, and is the youngest person to be inducted into the Minnesota Business Hall of Fame™. Tom has served on numerous corporate and nonprofit boards, including the Center for Ethical Business Cultures.

Tom's first book, *Winning in the Game of Life: Self-Coaching Secrets for Success*, is a blueprint for creating a productive, well-balanced life. It received critical acclaim from publishing industry bellwethers Publishers Weekly and Booklist, and from national business leaders like Ken Blanchard (*The One-Minute Manager*), Harvey Mackay (*Swim with the Sharks Without Being Eaten Alive*), and Richard Schulze, founder and chairman of Best Buy.

Tom founded Gegax Management Systems in 2000 to deliver his Synergy Circle business management system to growing companies. He has offices in Minneapolis and San Diego. To learn how Tom can help solve your business challenges, visit gegax.com, or e-mail him at tom.gegax@gegax.com.

Phil Bolsta can be reached at pbolsta@yahoo.com.